THE INDIAN SUMMER OF ENGLISH CHIVALRY

To Jane

THE INDIAN SUMMER
OF ENGLISH CHIVALRY

STUDIES IN THE DECLINE AND TRANS-
FORMATION OF CHIVALRIC IDEALISM

ARTHUR B. FERGUSON

Department of History
Duke University

DUKE UNIVERSITY PRESS · DURHAM, NORTH CAROLINA · 1960

© 1960, DUKE UNIVERSITY PRESS

Library of Congress Catalogue Card number 60-8743

CAMBRIDGE UNIVERSITY PRESS, LONDON, N.W.1, ENGLAND

PRINTED IN THE UNITED STATES OF AMERICA
BY THE SEEMAN PRINTERY, DURHAM, NORTH CAROLINA

Preface

The studies contained in this book are, in a sense, a by-product. In the course of a somewhat broader investigation of social and political attitudes in late medieval and early Renaissance England, I became more and more aware that, in the picture we have of the English mind during that transitional era, indistinct enough at best, there was one fairly large area in which the outlines were especially shadowy. It affected the thought of the governing class, from the king to the lowest armiger, then in the process of adjusting itself to broadening responsibilities in an increasingly complex society. Those adjustments involved the scheme of values which, though never in serious conflict with the teachings of the church and, in fact, generally sanctioned by them, reached nevertheless well beyond them to serve as a guide to the secular life of the knight or gentleman and even at times to the policies of government. It all somehow turned on the problem of chivalry. Yet in what ways, and to what extent? What, indeed, constituted the chivalric way of looking at things? These were questions for which there seemed to be no ready-made answer. And so I decided to re-examine the scattered and often scanty materials relating to the subject in the hope of filling in, if only sketchily, the missing part of the picture. If the results of my investigation will be of help to others in answering similar questions I shall feel that my efforts are justified. Meanwhile the quest has been exciting.

For providing valuable time in which to pursue this research I am indebted to the Ford Foundation's Fund for the Advancement of Education. I am also indebted to the Research Council of Duke University for financial assistance in preparing the manuscript and more especially, in defraying the

cost of publication. I must express my special gratitude to my brother, Professor Wallace K. Ferguson and to Margaret Wing Ferguson for invaluable counsel and criticism at various stages in the process of research and writing and for unclassified aids beyond the call of duty. My thanks also to Professor John Fisher of Duke University for his thoughtful and critical reading of the manuscript. I should like also to acknowledge the courtesies extended to me by the Widener Library and the Folger Library, and the patient assistance I have received from the staff of the Duke Press. My wife's devoted assistance on proofs and index have saved me from many errors. For those that remain I am alone responsible.

In the interests of the reader whose concern, like my own, is not primarily philological, I have modernized the spelling of quotations from English sources and translated all others. Occasionally I have added punctuation necessary for clarity. I have, however, kept as close as possible to the original texts.

Arthur B. Ferguson

14 March, 1960

Contents

Introduction

To the medieval mind chivalry had a practical significance, an immediate relevance, an appearance that reflected not too inaccurately the reality of medieval life. Chivalric ideals served as a guide for the secular activity of the governing class and were supposed to be for that purpose sufficient. By Elizabeth's day, however, chivalry had become a memory, consciously cherished, highly evocative, vivid enough to inspire Spenser's epic and the exploits of that latter-day knight Sir Philip Sidney, but a memory nonetheless and, in the sense that it remained associated with a society long since transformed, insubstantial. This transition from the reality to the memory, from the immediately relevant to the romantically inspiring, from the living ideal to the stuff of which symbolism is made, is an important strand in that tissue of changes which brought about the English Renaissance—which *was,* in a sense, the English Renaissance. Part of its story has been told in the course of recent inquiries into the nature and nurture of the Renaissance gentlemen.[1] In them we are permitted to observe in some detail the development of the new ideal of the gentleman-governor that absorbed and in the long run replaced the chivalric ideal. We also know a good deal about the chivalric ideal in its heyday (whenever that was—like most Golden Ages it tends to recede as investigation proceeds).[2] But we

[1] See, in particular, Fritz Caspari, *Humanism and the Social Order in Tudor England* (Chicago, 1954); Ruth Kelso, *The Doctrine of the English Gentleman in the Sixteenth Century* (Urbana, 1929); J. E. Mason, *Gentlefolk in the Making* (Philadelphia, 1935). For comparative purposes, see W. L. Wiley, *The Gentleman of Renaissance France* (Cambridge, Mass., 1954).

[2] Although English chivalry has suffered from the competition of the more established and sophisticated version developed in France, some very useful work has been done on the chivalric ideal in England, especially in the thirteenth and fourteenth centuries. See especially Bruce McCully, "Chivalry and Romance in Fourteenth Century England" (Harvard diss., 1910); W. H. Schofield, *Chivalry in English Literature* (Cambridge, Mass., 1925); Kurt Lippmann, "Das ritterliche Persönlichkeitsideal in der englischen Literatur des 13. und 14. Jahrhunderts" (Leipziger diss.,

still know very little about the passing of the old ideal, or about the beginnings of those new attitudes out of which the Renaissance ideal in its fully articulated form emerged. Especially obscure remains that period—roughly from the close of the Hundred Years' War to the beginning of the Protestant Reformation—when the old ideas still seemed valid to the popular mind despite the fact, more apparent to the historian than to men of the day, that the social foundations supporting the old order had to a large extent disintegrated, and when thought was already in the process of adjusting itself in a hundred subtle ways to the condition of a new society.

Many things have helped to make this a peculiarly opaque era in the history of English culture, disclaimed by students of the English Renaissance, too often ignored by the medievalists. The materials—those at least that reflect at all directly the mind of the period—are frequently too sparse for the historian, accustomed as he is to copious documentation, and too nearly devoid of aesthetic merit to interest the literary scholar. A major portion of the work on late English chivalry has been done, and done admirably, by the latter; but they have naturally restricted themselves to the questions pertinent to the appreciation of *belles lettres,* which do not always include the questions the historian would like to have answered. The two find themselves with fortunate frequency laboring in the same vineyard. But the fact remains that most of the work on English chivalry has been done by scholars who are concerned primarily with the courtly love tradition or by those who have devoted themselves to a critical elucidation of Arthurian romance. The historian of ideas wants also to know what bearing the traditions of chivalry have on political

1933); Dietrich Sandberger, *Studien über das Rittertum in England, vornemlich während des 14. Jahrhunderts* (Berlin, 1937). Some light is thrown on English chivalric ideas, as well as those common to Western Europe, in *Chivalry,* ed. E. Prestage (New York, 1928). F. Warre Cornish, *Chivalry* (London, 1901), and Leon Gautier, *Le Chevalerie* (Paris, 1890), remain, of course, standard works on the general subject, but strictly limited in their treatment of ideas, especially for England.

and social thought, on those issues, that is, that are immediately
and directly relevant to actual living. By the same token, the
sources that attract the historian will not always attract the
literary critic, nor will the monuments of literature, basic as
they are to the study of ideas, entirely satisfy the historian.
To the latter it seems at times sadly true that his literary
sources are useful in almost direct proportion to their unreada-
bility. He finds *The Boke of Noblesse* and Stephen Hawes'
The Pastime of Pleasure in many ways more revealing than
Morte Darthur.

Even more unfortunate, however, has been the general
failure to see these materials, attractive or unattractive, whole
or in fragments, as together the expression of a characteristic
outlook, something which, for lack of any better term, must
be called the chivalric mind. Generally speaking, students of
French chivalry have escaped this trap. But their very success
has made it more difficult for the student of English chivalry.
Too frequently the assumption has been made that English
chivalry reflected, if only as in a glass, darkly, the more mature
and sophisticated chivalry of France. In fact English chivalry
developed, like many other things English, atypically. Investigation in the field of late medieval English thought has been
directed, often with telling effect, toward the clarification of
religious, constitutional, legal, and social thought. But the
materials have been such as to emphasize the point of view of
the churchman or lawyer rather than the knight or, to be for
English conditions more accurate, the class of those capable of
bearing coats of arms—the gentry if you will. Until relatively
late, that class remained inarticulate. Even the chivalric tradition, in so far as it was preserved in writing, was handed
down to a large extent by clerks who happened to be more
than ordinarily familiar with the life of the aristocracy and
accordingly concerned with their needs.

Then too, the chivalric literature to which the researcher
must have recourse for the ideas of the period suffers from the

blight of translation. The Englishmen of the fifteenth and early sixteenth centuries, although capable of no little originality, especially in practical matters, had not yet developed the intellectual confidence necessary to establish a literature of their own. Their inveterate habit of leaning upon the writings of others makes it much harder than it would otherwise have been to evaluate the thought of either the author, his patrons, or his readers at large. The chivalric romances that still formed a large part of the English reading public's bill of fare are especially frustrating as source material for the study of contemporary ideas. At best, as in *Morte Darthur,* they are more or less faithful adaptations of versions neither native nor contemporaneous, significant largely by virtue of the degree to which they reflect in the process of adaptation the bias of their adapter, otherwise part of the common heritage of chivalric Christendom, unlikely to shed much light on that which is peculiar in the culture of fifteenth-century England.

The existence of such a thing as the chivalric outlook, something reaching beyond the narrower concerns of military and courtly life to encompass the entire secular activity of the governing class, has consequently been obscured. Yet a closer reading of the available literature reveals that there is a certain consistency in the attitudes of the ruling class of late medieval England toward all the larger issues of secular life, both private and public. To that complex of ideas and attitudes I have applied the term "chivalric." It is in a sense unhistorical, for the word itself was usually confined by the writer of that day to the strictly military aspects of the knightly life.[3] The historian must be pardoned for tracing relationships that transcended alike the vocabulary and the consciousness of a less analytical age.

There is still another difficulty. Those who have examined

---

[3] For a discussion of most working definitions of chivalry see F. J. C. Hearnshaw, "Chivalry and its place in History," *Chivalry,* ed. E. Prestage (New York, 1928), pp. 1-2.

this transitional era have not always given sufficient attention to what should be a familiar enough phenomenon, namely, a tendency for accepted values to change more slowly than the circumstances of society that ultimately condition them; and they have shown a concomitant willingness to read later attitudes into the words of an earlier period. The men of fifteenth-century England tended to evaluate the emerging society of capital and canon, centralized government and international rivalry, for the most part with reference to ideas inherited from an earlier age and hallowed by inveterate custom. The New Learning provided in time an inspiration to new thought and did much to facilitate the building up of a frame of reference more nearly in line with the new conditions. Meanwhile the intelligent Englishman adjusted himself for practical purposes to the changes in his environment without greatly altering the conceptual tools with which he was accustomed to attack such problems. Both the inertia of the old ideals and these practical adjustments in attitude are therefore factors of the utmost historical importance.

It has, for example, been customary to speak of the nostalgic spirit in which men like Malory and Caxton approach the subject of chivalry and to question the practicality, even the sincerity, of their apparent effort to restore a decadent England to chivalric virtue.[4] Such devotion to the quite medieval ideal of the knight could only, it is assumed, be romantic in a day when the knight himself had been forced to step down from his unique military position and when England clearly needed strong central government rather than a sentimental appeal to an outdated ethical ideal. This, however, is

---

[4] E. K. Chambers, *English Literature at the Close of the Middle Ages* (Oxford, 1947), pp. 185, 195-197; H. S. Bennett, *Chaucer and the Fifteenth Century* (Oxford, 1947), p. 200; Alfred T. P. Byles, ed., in *The Book of the Ordre of Chyualry*, E.E.T.S., O.S., No. 168 (London, 1926), introd., pp. xxxvii-xxxviii, in which the point is quite rightly made that later writers on chivalry looked back from the obviously decadent institution of their day to the period of the Crusades as the Golden Age of Chivalry; J. E. Housman, "Higden, Trevisa, Caxton, and the Beginnings of Arthurian Criticism," *Review of English Studies* (July, 1947), pp. 209-217. In the last-mentioned item the author questions the sincerity of Caxton's lip-service to the ideal of knighthood.

to exaggerate the perspective of history and to suppose that the ideals of late medieval society had kept pace with the maturing problems of national life. The chivalry of the late fifteenth century was not, like the chivalry of Spenser, or for that matter of Scott or Tennyson, truly romantic. Such romanticism carries ever with it the stigma of the lost cause, the fragrance of an irretrievable past. Caxton, and the author of *The Boke of Noblesse,* Malory, and perhaps Stephen Hawes as well undertook to reaffirm chivalry as a living ideal, sufficient for the life of those responsible for the physical welfare of the community, not to reinstate something that had been displaced.

The prevailing picture of late English chivalric thought has thus been far from complete or accurate. Like a medieval painting it has lacked perspective. The main figures, though perhaps a bit distorted, stand forth clearly enough; but the relationship between them is not clear, nor is the background more than perfunctorily indicated. To change the analogy, it must also be considered a moving picture, reflecting the realities of a changing society. Indeed the chief importance of research into the mind of the period is to clarify the processes by which the ideas and attitudes recognizably characteristic of medieval culture disappear and are replaced by those we are accustomed to call Renaissance. It was, after all, a transitional period in a sense more radical than is applicable to most other periods in the history of English culture.

This element of change must therefore be considered fully as important a subject for study as the chivalric habits of thought in their orthodox form. While recognizing the vitality that remained in the aging timbers of medieval thought, we must be careful not to overlook the seedling attitudes taking shape beneath and around them. In the stirring of new attitudes, not yet clearly articulated, often unrecognized at the time, we may find the beginning of ideas that matured in the century following and gave to the English Renaissance its peculiar quality. *Historia nihil facit per saltem;* nor did the Tudor concept of the gentleman-governor spring into being overnight. Its origins may indeed be traced well back in the history of fifteenth-century thought.

If these studies will in any way help to clarify the workings of the chivalric mind and throw some fresh light on the processes by which it underwent change, they will have served their purpose. They are studies in the history of chivalric thought rather than of chivalric practice, though it is at times neither possible nor desirable to separate an ideal from the external forms in which it achieves a palpable place in the life of the community. I have confined them for the most part to the writings of the period. Where examples from the earlier fifteenth century or from the latter part of the fourteenth prove particularly useful, I have, however, not hesitated to reach back beyond the mid-century mark. Similarly, in order to document the transitional processes through which a new ideal replaced the old, it has been necessary occasionally to move on beyond the era of Henrician revolution. I have also restricted these studies as much as possible to those writings that reveal more or less directly the thought of their authors. The existence of translations, and especially any evidence of their popularity, are, of course, facts of considerable importance. But if we would understand what was going on in English minds we must make the most of the few extant pieces of original expression, remembering all the while that in translating, or rather in the handling of borrowed materials, the medieval author felt free to adapt his source to fit his own sense of values. I can made no claim to the discovery of any new pieces. Rather I have undertaken to place those that are available and for the most part familiar enough (if in some important instances neglected) in fresh juxtaposition and to examine them in a fresh context.

I have treated the material in a series of more or less parallel studies. First of all attention is given to the question

whether there was, in fact, any perceptible revival of chivalry
in late fifteenth-century England, and an attempt is made to
indicate something of the nature and extent of chivalric
thought in that period. In the chapter that follows, the chivalric tradition is explored in relation to the strongly didactic
tendency in medieval thought. It is considered as an intellectual force calculated to shape the attitudes of the governing
class to the problems of secular life, a sort of secular annex
to the main structure of Christian thought. In the next chapter more summary treatment is given to the sources of intellectual inspiration out of which a new system of values arose
to replace the chivalric. Broadly speaking these latter may be
described as the example of classical antiquity interpreted in
the light of political and social reality, within the context of
the Tudor national state. The fourth chapter treats the relationship between the chivalric tradition and political reality.
Obscure as that problem unfortunately remains, it is nevertheless a very important one. For it is in its bearing on the
practical, largely political function of the governing class that
chivalry achieved the kind of relevance that is essential to the
life and health of any system of ideals. And, conversely, it
was when chivalric idealism ceased to serve as a scale of values
sufficient for the secular life of the ruling class, when, indeed
something new had already taken its place, that chivalry may
be said to have passed into the realm of romantic causes—and
only then. There follows a treatment of chivalric idealism as
a frame of reference for the discussion of dynastic policy and
the basic issues of war and peace. It was only natural that an
ideal in which fighting was glorified as the chief and highest
secular occupation of the man of knightly status or aspirations
should, as the bellicosity of the individual knight was absorbed
into the larger bellicosity of dynastic politics, provide in some
measures a guide to foreign relations. Finally the chivalric
tradition is evaluated as an educational ideal. Here in a sense
was the critical issue in the decline of chivalry, social in its

origin, political in its implications. It concerned the kind of education most suited to the needs of the English gentleman who was becoming more and more embroiled in the administrative work of government and increasingly aware of the duties of citizenship in the emerging national state. This question the chivalric tradition quite failed to answer, and it was left for the Tudor humanists to take all that was worth preserving in that tradition and to incorporate it into a largely classical education based on the following related assumptions: that the English gentleman was potentially a "governor" as well as the protector of society, that to fulfil his function he must have virtue and wisdom, and that those qualities could spring only from book learning, above all in the discipline of moral philosophy.

It will be evident that throughout these chapters I have concentrated primarily on those points at which the chivalric tradition touched the public concerns of the community. In an interpretative essay of this sort I have not felt obliged to deal with all aspects equally. In so far as there is anything new to add for this transitional period to the well-told tale of courtly love, for example, or to the familiar picture of the Christian knight, I have endeavored to make it an integral part of the argument. This decision arose from a steadily growing conviction that the vitality of the chivalric tradition depended upon the preservation of those points of contact between the ideal and the actual in the world of affairs. As soon as they were broken, the current of reality that is necessary for the life of a social ideal ceased to flow. That contact with the world of practical experience was maintained in the mind of the English gentry for a long time after the conditions of English society no longer warranted it. It was, indeed, not until new switches replaced the corroded ones that a fresh current was permitted to flow between the idealism of the governing class and the actual work it was to an increasing extent being called upon to do. Before that time it was still possible, and to a degree perhaps not always appreciated, for the English gentry to take chivalry seriously. After that time such was no longer possible. How seriously chivalry was taken, what replaced it, and how the change was effected are, then, the questions with which these studies are mainly concerned.

THE INDIAN SUMMER OF ENGLISH CHIVALRY

I

A CHIVALRIC "REVIVAL"

DESPITE THE FACT THAT BY THE MID-FIFTEENTH century the political, social, and economic foundations upon which chivalric idealism rested had to a large extent crumbled, the fact remains that chivalry was still able to evoke a lively response in the minds of Englishmen during the remainder of the century and even into the early years of the next. That such interest became more intense during this period is perhaps less certain. It must be admitted—it is usually asserted with confidence—that the trends of contemporary life and events were against anything of the sort. Together they were rapidly displacing the belted knight from his unique position in the political body. As a military force he passed away with the French wars and the Wars of the Roses, driven from his monopoly of the military profession by the yeoman archer, gunpowder, and the professional captain. The wars also contributed to those social and economic trends, powerful enough as they were, which compromised the exclusiveness of the aristocracy as a social caste, and by so doing removed one of the basic facts upon which the chivalric ideal had originally depended. In the confusion and maladministration of the mid-century the English gentry sought protection in shifting personal relationships, in a "bastard feudalism" which left little room for chivalric loyalty.[1] Those same conditions, rendered the more serious by the Civil Wars, pointed imperatively (or so it seems to the modern mind) toward strong

[1] K. B. McFarlane, "Bastard Feudalism," *Bulletin of the Institute of Historical Research,* XX (May and Nov., 1945), 161-180. The term "bastard feudalism" has recently come in for severe criticism on the part of some who feel that it reflects pejoratively on the society of the latter Middle Ages; see, for example, W. H. Dunham's review in the *American Historical Review,* LXIII (Jan., 1958), 387-388.

government as a remedy rather than toward idealism of any sort, let alone that of a decadent chivalry.

Knighthood in the stricter sense had, in fact, ceased to have anything necessarily to do with the political or administrative life of the community. Many men of importance in local affairs and in parliament preferred to avoid an honor not always commensurate with the financial onus that went with it. Even in the wars squires were considered virtually on a par with knights for use as indentured captains. Many there were, of course, who accepted formal knighthood as either an hereditary honor or one earned and to be valued. Many also no doubt sought it for the social prestige it still conveyed. Some were occasionally required to assume knighthood by virtue of the statutory liability of all men of forty pounds property to do so; and occasionally the king invoked the distraining power thus permitted him for the sole purpose of squeezing from such potential knights either a fee for the honor or a fine for its avoidance. The important fact is that knighthood as such had ceased to have much practical meaning. As Miss Thrupp points out, "the ideas associated with knighthood were . . . failing to kindle enthusiasm for the governmental work of the counties."[2]

But, safely insulated from the corroding effects of too close a relation to practical affairs, those ideas could still flourish in the less specific context of the ideal. The relatively large and apparently increasing number of books on subjects connected with chivalry is in itself a fact of considerable significance. It is one that needs to be interpreted carefully. When books were as scarce as they were then it is hard to generalize safely about the interests of the readers. If, as it appears, the volume of

[2] Sylvia Thrupp, *The Merchant Class of Medieval London* (Chicago, 1948), p. 276. On the relation of knighthood to administrative and governmental affairs, see also J. S. Roskell, *The Commons in the Parliament of 1422* (Manchester, 1954), chap. v, especially pp. 92-95, and also chap. vii; T. B. Pugh and C. D. Ross, "The English Baronage and the Income Tax of 1436," *Bull. Inst. Hist. Res.*, XXVI (May, 1953), 1-28; F. M. Nichols, "On Feudal and Obligatory Knighthood," *Archaeologia*, XXXIX (1862/63), 189-244; H. L. Gray, "Incomes from Land in England in 1436," *English Historical Review*, XLIX (Oct., 1934), 607-639.

chivalric literature increased, that fact could be laid as much to the rise in the total number of people capable of buying the books and reading them as to an increased interest in the subject.[3] Moreover, that literature must in this period be studied to some extent in relation to the other writings of the period, many of which reveal a nonchivalric turn of mind if not very often anything overtly antichivalric. Sir John Fortescue,[4] for example, and that faithful but obscure public servant, George Ashby,[5] could approach the problems of secular life in a spirit of practicality and realism that left small place for chivalric idealism even if they failed to express such explicitly antichivalric sentiments as those of their French contemporary, Commines.[6] Nevertheless, the quantity of books cannot be entirely dismissed. Not only is it evidence of interest among the governing class, it can help in some measure to account for the existence of that interest; for ideas can live for a long time in books and can be propagated by reading— sometimes long after they have ceased to derive much sustenance from real life.

Many writers wrote or translated or edited for publication treatises on the education and conduct proper to a knight and on the closely related subjects of warfare and heraldry. We know the names of some: Nicholas Upton, Stephen Scrope, William Worcester, Adam Loutfut, Sir Gilbert Hay, William Caxton, and John Tiptoft, Earl of Worcester.[7] To this list

[3] See H. S. Bennett, *English Books and Their Readers, 1475-1557* (Cambridge, 1952) on the general problem of the reading public.

[4] See especially his *Governance of England,* ed. C. Plummer (Oxford, 1885).

[5] *The Active Policy of a Prince* in *George Ashby's Poems,* ed. M. Bateson, E.E.T.S., E.S., No. 76 (London, 1899).

[6] *Memoires de Philippe de Commynes,* ed. B. de Mandrot (3 vols.; Paris, 1901-3). See also R. L. Kilgour, *The Decline of Chivalry as Shown in the French Literature of the Late Middle Ages* (Cambridge, Mass., 1937); W. J. Bouwsma, "The Politics of Commynes," *Journal of Modern History,* XXIII (Dec., 1951), 315-328.

[7] Nicholas Upton, *De Studio Militari* (written before 1446, translated by John Blount *ca.* 1500), ed. F. P. Bernard (Oxford, 1931); *The Boke of Noblesse* (attributed to William Worcester, see below, chap. v), ed. J. G. Nichols (London, 1860); Sir Gilbert Hay's translation of Bonet's *Arbre des Batailles* and of Lull's *Le Livre de l'Ordre de Chevalerie,* both done in 1456, may be found in *Gilbert of the Haye's Prose MS.,* ed. J. H. Stevenson, Scottish Texts Society (2 vols.; Edinburgh, 1901-14); *The Boke of the Ordre of Chyualry* (translated and printed by Caxton *ca.* 1484), ed. A. T. P. Byles, together with Adam Loutfut's transcript of the same original (made

might also be added Stephen Hawes, who wrote a noteworthy disquisition on the education of a knight under cover of an allegorical romance.[8] Related to the manual of knighthood, though bearing only indirectly on the subject of chivalry, was the "mirror of princes" literature, the familiar treatise *de regimine principum,* of which several appeared in England during the fifteenth and early sixteenth centuries.[9]

The writings of this period drew heavily on the chivalric literature of an earlier era, especially that of France. Malory, in his rendition of the Arthurian romances, and Caxton, in his translation of these and other pieces of chivalric literature,[10] set forth the values of chivalry in a form no doubt as inspiring to the secular thought of the reader as the lives of the saints were to his religious contemplation. The Arthurian legends, it is true, also fitted in nicely with the desire of the Tudor house to romanticize its British origins and thereby to enhance its prestige in the eyes of the English public.[11] But their popularity seems clearly to have antedated the rise of Tudor

in 1494), E.E.T.S., O.S., No. 168 (London, 1926); Caxton's *Fayttes of Armes and of Chyualrye,* ed. A. T. P. Byles, E.E.T.S., O.S., No. 189 (London, 1932); *The Declamation of Noblesse* (trans. John Tiptoft, *ca.* 1460, printed by Caxton, 1481), ed. R. J. Mitchell, *John Tiptoft* (London, 1938), Appendix I; *The Boke of St. Albans,* ed. W. Blades (London, 1881); *Knyghthode and Bataile* (1457-60?), ed. R. Dyboski and Z. M. Arend, E.E.T.S., O.S., No. 201 (London, 1936); *The Epistle of Othea to Hector* (or *The Boke of Knyghthode*) (trans. Stephen Scrope), ed. G. F. Warner (London, 1904); another translation of the *Epistle* was made at the end of the fifteenth or in the early sixteenth century, ed. J. D. Gordon, U. of Penn. diss. (Philadelphia, 1942). Several treatises on heraldry may be found in Evan Jones, *Medieval Heraldry* (London, 1945); H. S. London, "Some Medieval Treatises on English Heraldry," *Antiquaries Journal* (July-Oct., 1953), pp. 169-183. Two Scottish manuals of knighthood might be included in addition to Hay's translation of Lull, viz., *The porteous of noblenes* (1508), S.T.C. 20120, and *Buke of gude counsale to the king* (n.d.), S.T.C. 3307. This is not intended to be a complete listing. For additional material, especially on other manuscript versions, see the editorial introductions to the works cited in this note.

[8] *The Pastime of Pleasure,* ed. W. E. Mead, E.E.T.S., O.S., No. 173 (1928).

[9] The relation of this body of material to the chivalric tradition is dealt with more fully in chap vi below.

[10] *The Works of Sir Thomas Malory,* ed. Eugene Vinaver (Oxford, 1947). For a list of Caxton's translations and also for his own editorial comments, see *The Prologues and Epilogues of William Caxton,* ed. W. J. B. Crotch, E.E.T.S., O.S., No. 176 (London, 1928), hereinafter cited as Crotch.

[11] C. B. Millican, *Spencer and the Table Round* (Cambridge, Mass., 1932), pp. 7 ff.; Josephine W. Bennett, *The Evolution of "The Faerie Queene"* (Chicago, 1942), pp. 68-70.

fortunes; and it was more than likely an expression of the newly cultivated interest in all things chivalric—especially if those matters were at the same time indisputably English.

Less intimately related to the chivalric tradition, at least in its more active aspects, was the allegory of courtly love. Since the *Romance of the Rose,* however, it had become an integral part of that tradition, considered on its more distinctly literary and ethical side. It is worth noticing that it enjoyed something like an Indian summer of its own in the early decades of the Tudor era. Stephen Hawes[12] and the anonymous author of *The Court of Love*[13] breathed new life into a form, since Lydgate's *Temple of Glass* in a moribund condition. William Dunbar[14] and Gavin Douglas[15] carried on a tradition still green and flourishing in the Scottish kingdom.

And then there were the histories in which were described the fine feats of arms that appealed as directly to the imagination of fifteenth-century readers as they had to those of Froissart's generation. Unfortunately, the English chroniclers of the fifteenth century lacked the gift of their French contemporaries for vivid reporting. At times they seem deliberately to avoid expatiating on chivalric exercises—witness Fabyan's laconic treatment of the siege of Calais (1436): "and so the siege endured upon iii weeks, in which season many knightly acts were done and exercised upon both parties, which for lengthening of the time I pass."[16] But the brilliant reign of Henry V found at least one chronicler worthy of his subject in the Italian Tito Livio da Forli.[17] And in any case the English aristocracy could still be expected to read the French

---

[12] On Hawes and his *Pastime of Pleasure,* see below chaps. ii and vi.

[13] *The Court of Love,* in W. W. Skeat, ed., *Chaucerian and Other Pieces* (Suppl. to Skeat, ed., *Works of Geoffrey Chaucer,* Oxford, 1894-1900), pp. 409-447.

[14] William Dunbar, *The Golden Targe,* in *Poems,* ed. J. Small (Edinburgh, 1893), II, 1-11.

[15] Gavin Douglas, *The Palice of Honour,* in *Works,* ed. J. Small (Edinburgh, 1874), I, 1-82.

[16] Robert Fabyan, *The New Chronicles of England and France,* ed. H. Ellis (London, 1811), p. 610. On the extensive subject of the histories, see C. L. Kingsford, *English Historical Literature in the 15th Century* (Oxford, 1913).

[17] Tito Livio da Forli, *Vita Henrici Quinti,* ed. T. Hearne (London, 1716).

chroniclers. "Read Froissart," is Caxton's sound advice to them;[18] and, if he somehow failed to make that classic of chivalric history available in translated and printed form, that omission was rectified by John Bourchier, Lord Berners, in the generation following.[19]

Books belonging to all these categories found a place, and apparently an important place, on the not too capacious shelves of the knightly class.[20] Nor is there any reason for defining this public narrowly. The large and expanding class of those permitted to bear coats of arms could aspire as rightly to the chivalric ideal as that decreasing number of individuals who had been formally admitted into the order of knighthood. That class it was, too, that provided the patrons of the printing press from which most of the chivalric literature of the late fifteenth and early sixteenth centuries emanated. Caxton seems to have become the center of a considerable group of enthusiastic book-lovers, some drawn like himself from the London patriciate, but perhaps even more from the ranks of the aristocracy and gentry. These latter are the "many noble and divers gentlemen" who persuaded him to print Malory's Arthurian stories, and almost certainly helped inspire him to prepare for publication other monuments of the chivalric tradition.[21]

. . .

Secondhand as it was, this treasury of chivalric romance and equally chivalric chronicle constitutes in itself a major fact in the climate of opinion prevailing in England during the later fifteenth and early sixteenth centuries. It provides evidence of a heightened interest in things chivalric and was also the source of much-needed inspiration: it is both cause and

[18] Caxton, *Ordre of Chyualry*, p. 123.
[19] *The Chronicle of Froissart, translated out of French by Sir John Bourchier Lord Berners, annis 1523-25*, ed. W. P. Ker (London, 1901-1903).
[20] H. S. Bennett, *The Pastons and Their England* (Cambridge, 1932), p. iii and Appendix I; Thrupp, p. 249, and cf. pp. 161-163.
[21] See Crotch, pp. cxx-cxxi. Cf. H. R. Plommer, *William Caxton* (London, 1925), pp. 104 ff., 144-145. See also Bennett, *English Books*, chap. i.

effect of the Indian Summer of English chivalry. The supply of such materials, never plentiful in England, had fallen pitifully low by the time of the Wars of the Roses. England had been at once too close to the much more sophisticated chivalry of France to produce her own literature of chivalry and, during long periods in her history, too effectively insulated through the vicissitudes of language and politics to have made the rich culture of continental chivalry really her own. Until Chaucer and Gower undertook to interpret for English readers something of those riches, English chivalric literature remained pitifully weak in native treatments of chivalric romance, nor did England produce chroniclers of the type and stature of Joinville or Froissart. True, a number of romances appeared in various dialects of English during the late fourteenth and early fifteenth centuries.[22] For the most part, however, they were superficial in their rendering of their French originals. They missed much of the subtlety of chivalric thought as expressed in its classic form. They were nevertheless significant, for as much as anything else they account for the fact that chivalric idealism was kept alive and reasonably orthodox in an England where knighthood was rapidly losing its practical meaning. Some Englishmen no doubt read the French manuscripts; but they must have been relatively few despite a continued ability to use the language. It would appear, however, that by the end of the Hundred Years' War, although many still had direct access to French culture (Caxton's admonition to the young gentlemen to read Froissart would otherwise have been a more foolish remark than that astute old man was in the habit of making),[23] the English upper classes

[22] For example, *Sir Perceval, Sir Isumbras, Sir Eglamour,* and *Sir Degrevant,* all edited by J. O. Halliwell, Camden Soc., XXX (1844); *Sir Cliges, Lyfe of Ipomydon, Amis and Amiloun, Sir Amadas,* all edited by H. Weber in *Metrical Romances* (Edinburgh, 1810); *Sir Firumbras,* ed. S. J. Herrtage, E.E.T.S., E.S., No. 34 (1879); *Sowdone of Babylone,* ed. Dr. Hausknecht, E.E.T.S., E.S., No. 38 (1881); *Torrent of Portyngale,* ed. E. Adam, E.E.T.S., E.S., No. 51 (1887); *Sir Ortuel,* ed. S. J. Herrtage, E.E.T.S., E.S., No. 35 (1880); *William of Palerne,* ed. W. W. Skeat, E.E.T.S., E.S., No. 1 (1867).

[23] But cf. *ibid.,* p. 97, in which Caxton says most people in England do not understand French.

would have had little access indeed to this main current of chivalric culture had it not been for the efforts of Malory, Caxton, Berners, to say nothing—certainly less than they deserve—of De Worde and Copland, who followed in Caxton's footsteps as publishers of chivalric romance.

It might not even be too much to say that, from Malory to Berners, the most significant development in English letters was this rediscovery of the chivalric heritage through the translating, adapting, and publishing of the classics of continental chivalry.[24] The result, at any rate, became a temple of absurdly towering proportions for the veneration of an already decadent ideal; and it undoubtedly helps explain why that decadence for so long escaped the notice of contemporary Englishmen and why modern historians have found it hard to believe it could do so. It accounts especially for the fact that the court of Henry VIII, with all its Renaissance influences, its Erasmus, its More, its imported Italian artists and craftsmen, busily engaged in carving the profile of classical antiquity on walls and tombs, above all the Machiavellian realism of its policies, remained in many respects chivalric, its habits, like its buildings, still cut to the pattern of an earlier day. Henry himself "commanded" Lord Berners to translate Froissart, and it was to be another generation before strait-laced Protestants like Ascham turned against the *Morte Darthur*.[25]

To men of the period it may well have seemed that this recovery of chivalric literature constituted a "rebirth" considerably more impressive than the "rebirth" of classical culture then also taking place, and of so much more interest to the historian. The New Learning made its way slowly in England, and was still in the early years of the sixteenth century confined to a relatively small circle of humanists. Those scholars represented in most instances the better minds of the period, for chivalry failed to kindle the imagination or com-

[24] For some development of this idea, see W. P. Ker's introduction to Froissart, I, x-xii.
[25] See below, chap. ii.

mand the thought of the more original and realistic spirits. And humanism was fraught with the utmost significance for the future of English thought.[26] Despite its ingrained conservatism, it proved capable of adjusting to new conditions, whereas the chivalric ideal remained static, reactionary if anything in its relation to the problems of Renaissance England. But if the product of Caxton's press is any measure of the men who patronized it, the young gentleman of early Tudor England drew such notions as he had of secular society and of his own place in it to an overwhelming extent from this rich literature of chivalric chronicle and romance.

. . .

About their status in society the English gentry seem, indeed, to have been in this period just a bit more self-conscious than usual. Reflecting the actual complexity of society in a day when the old feudal relationships were everywhere being modified by the exigencies and opportunities of a money economy, when status was on all sides giving way to contract, the official documents after 1413 make more frequent use of terms denoting social status. It is at this point that the designation "gentleman" appears to have made its official debut, thus beginning a long and exceedingly useful career as a term of many-sided applicability especially suitable for reference to a governing class in which the formal titles of aristocracy were ceasing to have the precise significance they had once enjoyed. Those terms retained, however, a considerable degree of legal meaning throughout the century; and one gets the impression that they preoccupied the mind of England's legislators, perhaps even to the exclusion of more important matters. A statute of 1440 provided that candidates for election to parliament as knights of the shire be "notable knights of the same shires . . . or else such notable squires, gentlemen of birth, of the same shires as be able to be knights; and no man

[26] See below, chap. iii.

to be it that standeth in the degree of yeoman and beneath."[27]

Often there is implied in the literature of this period a belief that the whole social order needed defining—which it probably did. However precise the status of a knight may have been, the other orders mentioned in the statute just quoted remain shadowy. The theory of estates receives increasing attention, as does the question of the nature and origin of nobility.[28] And there appears to have been just the slightest tendency in this process of redefinition to emphasize the importance of the aristocracy for whose thought the values of chivalry provided the secular points of reference. In contrast to the popular fourteenth-century poem, *Cursor Mundi,* which deliberately left room among the secular classes for a middle class, neither noble nor "vile" in status,[29] the fifteenth-century *Boke of Saint Albans,* compiled in part to show "how gentlemen shall be known from ungentle men, and how bondage began," simplifies the picture by reducing society to gentlemen and churls.[30] Even in literature not ostensibly on chivalric subjects traces of this intensified class consciousness may be found. *The Dance of Death,* a poem popular throughout the century, portrays the life of the chivalric class—the baron, the knight, the squire and the lady—as gay, debonair, gallant, and in all things removed from the niggardly and avaricious life of the merchant and burgher.[31] Caxton, in his translation of Lull's *Le Libre del Ordre de Cavayleria,* alters his thirteenth-century original, to which for the most part he adhered with the utmost fidelity, in favor of a stricter definition of those

[27] *Statutes of the Realm* (London, 1810-28), II, 340, quoted by H. L. Gray, "Incomes from Land in England in 1436," *E.H.R.,* XLIX (Oct., 1934), 625. On the beginning of the term "gentleman," see Sir George Sitwell, "The English Gentleman," *Ancestor,* I (April, 1902); A. W. Reed, "Chivalry and the Idea of a Gentleman," in Prestage, ed., *Chivalry,* p. 209.
[28] Ruth Mohl, *The Three Estates in Medieval and Renaissance Literature* (New York, 1933), p. 294; Thrupp, p. 295.
[29] Part I, ed. R. Morris, E.E.T.S., O.S., No. 57 (1874), pp. 126, 128, 130. This part is discussed in considerably greater detail in Thrupp, pp. 295-297.
[30] Ed. W. Blades (London, 1881), "Liber armorum," sig. Ai.
[31] Ed. Florence Warren, E.E.T.S., O.S., No. 181 (1931), pp. 20, 22, 24, 26, 38, 40, 44, 54, 56. See also Thrupp, pp. 315-316.

eligible for knighthood;[32] and, burgher that he was, he insists stoutly that his book of chivalry is meant exclusively for "noble gentlemen."[33] Contrary as it was to social and political fact, the habit of dividing society into three estates died very slowly.

By far the most important evidence of chivalric revival lies in the writing of those who in the last half of the century would awake a once-proud England to an awareness of its rightful place of honor by restating the principles and precedents of the chivalric tradition. Largely implicit in Malory, this purpose becomes quite explicit in Caxton's editorial comments and in that bit of chauvinism in the guise of chivalry, *The Boke of Noblesse*. But of these more later.

. . .

Evidence of a continuation or possible revival of chivalric sentiment is not limited, however, to the literary sources. It is to be found also in the increasingly elaborate external forms in which chivalry found the visible expression without which it could scarcely have maintained its place in the life of the community. Heraldry became in this its "golden age"[34] an increasingly exact and colorful science, after 1417 the preserve of a highly professional group of heralds.[35] Tournaments, often patterned consciously after the romances of chivalry,[36] continued to relieve the tedium of court life and to mark important occasions.[37] The soldierly assumptions underlying chivalry and expressed characteristically in the tournament found expression also in the duel. The last judicial duel known to have taken place on English soil was fought in 1492;[38] but the private duel continued to reflect the notion that the knight

[32] *Ordre of Chyualry*, pp. 57-59, and introd. p. xxxix.

[33] *Ibid.*, p. 121.

[34] F. P. Barnard, ed., *De Studio Militari*, p. xii.

[35] On the whole subject of fifteenth-century heraldry, see A. R. Wagner, *Heralds and Heraldry in the Middle Ages* (London, 1939).

[36] Ruth H. Cline, "The Influence of Romances on Tournaments of the Middle Ages," *Speculum*, XX (January, 1945), 204-211.

[37] F. H. Cripps-Day, *The History of the Tournament in England and in France* (London, 1918), chap. v. On the related subject of armor, see Claude Blair, *European Armour, 1066 to 1700* (London, 1959).

[38] G. Neilson, *Trial by Combat* (Boston, 1909), p. 203.

must personally protect his honor and the justice of his cause. Nicholas Upton justifies both as legitimate martial acts. The private duel he even sought to justify on the broader and, we might think, morally indistinct ground that it was a way of gaining "renown and worship." Such duels are, he says, done "to prove one his strength and manhood, which manhood and fortitude is a moral virtue: yea, and also one of the cardinal virtues"; and, since they are not contrary to the "law general of all people," they should be permitted.[39]

True, there is about these practices the unmistakable taint of decadence. Through all runs the same self-conscious pursuit of form, often at the expense of the originally moving spirit. The tournament proper, the combat of many against many, the "mêlée" in which the knight liked to see the image of battle itself, had developed into something relatively tame. From an engagement in the open field, all but devoid of restriction or rules, differing from war only in that it was supposedly fought for the love of it rather than for any animosity to the opposing side and that it did not culminate in the loss or gain of territory, it had become little more than a spectacle, hedged in both by regulations and by wooden barriers, a courtly pageant. What Jusserand said of the fifteenth-century tournament in France could be applied without too much exaggeration to the English scene. They had, he said,

their rules and ceremonials carried to the last degree of perfection, complicated, couched in the 'flamboyant' style by masters of the art: they had no choice now but to disappear like the flamboyant style itself, supreme expression of the Gothic on the eve of its death. . . . Far, indeed, are the rough battles, fought in the open field, in the days of Philippe-Auguste and Henry Plantagenet. Despite blows, wounds, and death, they are now beautiful fetes, beautiful as manuscript illuminations, like miniatures come to life. 'Too much so to last' says popular wisdom. And, in fact, in the midst of this so well ordered splendor the tourney was doomed. The future lay with those jousts, those *'plaideries'* disdained by the free knights of the past.[40]

[39] Upton, pp. 9 and 16.
[40] J. J. Jusserand, *Les sports et jeux d'exercice dans l'ancienne France* (Paris, 1901), p. 98.

The joust had, indeed, become constantly more popular. At best less the simulacrum of battle than of the duel, it now lost all contact with the realities of warfare. The knights fought now on either side of a wooden fence, their weapons light and blunted, their armor so heavy, so ingeniously contrived for the special purposes of breaking lances that it was little more than an exceedingly expensive uniform of sport. The contestant could see nothing through the tiny slits of his helm except what was directly in front of him, and little enough of that. In a sense, this jousting armor symbolizes what had befallen the heavy-armed knight as he became more and more of an anachronism, increasingly helpless before the weapons of modern warfare. More and more the joust became a mere exhibition of personal prowess, part courtly exercise, part athletic contest. Its rules, like those of the tournament with which it was usually connected, became increasingly formal. They were established by a special Court of Chivalry,[41] and achieved their ultimate sophistication in the highly civilized and admirably clear *Ordinances for Joustes and Triumphes,* drawn up in 1466 by John Tiptoft, Earl of Worcester.[42]

As time went on, especially as we move into the sixteenth century, the athletic aspect of these once warlike games becomes more and more apparent. Appropriately enough, they share the bill of entertainment at large celebrations with the similarly decadent sport of archery.[43] In time, too, the tournament becomes more than ever a pageant, less than ever the image of war. Instead of imitating the chivalric romances with their honest, if tiresome, bellicosity, they tend to follow the hackneyed and intellectualized tradition of the courtly

[41] Mitchell, chap. vii; Cripps-Day, pp. 70-71; F. P. Barnard, "Heraldry," in *Medieval England,* ed. H. W. C. Davis (Oxford, 1928), pp. 195-244, 232-237. The fullest treatment of the subject is G. D. Squibb, *The High Court of Chivalry* (New York, 1959).

[42] Printed in Cripps-Day, Appendix IV.

[43] Col. H. Walrond, "Archery," *Shakespeare's England,* ed. Sir W. Raleigh (Oxford, 1926), II, 376-388.

allegory.[44] The *pas d'armes* lent itself especially to this kind of theatricality, certain knights, representing certain qualities, undertaking to hold the field or defend a position against certain contrary qualities. In this form, suitably purged of all relation to the practical business of soldiery, it was possible for the tournament to continue into the days of a wholly romanticized chivalry as the vehicle for that most sophisticated of court entertainments, the Elizabethan "triumph," more mask than martial contest. When we read of the festivities of 1581 in which four courtiers, "Master Philip Sidney" among them, calling themselves "the four foster children of desire," challenge the defenders of the "fortress of perfect beauty," who, after interminable allegorical pageantry and a very little combat in the lists, emerge victorious, we know we are in a new era, the age of a truly romantic chivalry.[45]

Yet this hardening process, so evident in the arteries of the chivalric body, had not yet paralyzed its mind. Upton's defense of the duel has in it a primitive frankness that may seem anachronistic but could hardly be *pro forma*. Malory's stories of combat, tiresome as they become to the modern reader, bear the authentic mark of the *aficionado*. The details he describes are like those he has seen in both real and simulated combat; and he relates them with gusto. We need not take the typical proclamation of a royal tournament at its face value when it says such "feats of the necessary discipline of Armes" are customarily done "to experience and enable nobles to the deserving of Chivalry, by the which our mother holy Church is defended, king and princes served, realms and countries kept and maintained in justice and peace."[46] It was a courtly

---

[44] Cripps-Day, Appendix IV, p. xlix.

[45] *Holinshed's Chronicles of England, Scotland, and Ireland* (London, 1808), IV, 435-445. Important light is shed on the vogue of chivalric forms in Elizabeth's reign in Sara P. Watson, "The Queen's Champion," *Western Reserve Bulletin*, N.S., XXXIV (Sept., 1931), 65-89, and in F. A. Yates, "Elizabethan Chivalry: The Romance of the Accession Day Tilts," *Jour. of Warburg and Courtauld Insts.*, XX (1957), 4-25.

[46] Cripps-Day, Appendix VI, p. xliii.

formula, its tone of high principle too often belied by the courtly frivolity that accompanied the event.[47]   But it is necessary to bear in mind that Caxton could still in 1485 look upon jousting in much this same light, as a practical and necessary training for war.[48]   Not, indeed, until the sixteenth century is it apparent that the tourney has ceased to have any real bearing on the practical business of soldiering.[49]

It would, in fact, be unwise for the historian to underestimate the importance of the tournament as a living symbol of chivalric idealism. As *imago Martis* it had served in particular to symbolize that aspect of chivalric idealism which was most relevant to the knight in his military, and hence in his primary, function.   Other symbols there were—the chivalric orders and the colorful paraphernalia of heraldry—and they all tended to proliferate as the practical function of knighthood disappeared; and they continued to serve the social pretensions of a nostalgic gentry for generations to come. In the clash of arms alone, however, could the illusion of reality be preserved. Moreover, the tournament slipped only very gradually into decadence. Its obsolescence passed largely unnoticed by contemporaries. It is hard even for the historian to be sure at what point the tournament ceased to be a truly martial game and became a dramatic event, in a sense the chivalric equivalent of the morality play. That process was probably farther advanced on the Continent than in England. But the English court maintained close relations with the most flamboyant centers of European chivalry.

. . .

The court of Burgundy provided in this as in many other respects an inspiration for the English court and a specific

---

[47] C. L. Schofield, *The Life and Reign of Edward the Fourth* (London, 1923), I, 418; Bentley, *Excerpta Historica*, p. 208.

[48] *Ordre of Chyualry*, p. 124.

[49] Cripps-Day, chap. vi; R. C. Clapham, *The Tournament, Its Periods and Phases* (London, 1919), chap. vi.

pattern for it to follow.[50] Situated in the most prosperous
burgher society in Northern Europe and owing much of its
brilliance (somewhat paradoxically) to the profits of Flemish
commerce and industry, the court of Charles the Bold nourished a peculiarly artificial kind of chivalry, colorful in its
pageantry, meticulous in the ceremonial with which it drama-
tized every function. It would have been surprising indeed
had not the English aristocracy found in it the most impressive
of examples. And many there were who made the trip across
the narrow sea, for Englishmen could usually find good reason
to visit the Burgundian cities. More often than not Burgundy
gave some sort of support to the English in their uneasy negotiations with France. There was in any event, a good deal of
diplomatic going and coming between the two courts.

It was in connection with negotiations of this sort in 1467
and 1468 that festivities were held the chivalric spirit of which
seems to have caught the imagination of contemporary observers to an extent unusual even in that day. In 1467 the
rapprochement between England and Burgundy was drama-
tized (one might also say popularized, so large and representative was the audience gathered in London) by a lavish affair
in which Antoine, the Bastard of Burgundy, jousted on successive days with Anthony Woodville, Lord Scales, brother of the
English queen.[51] It was all very magnificent, very much by
the book. It was prepared long in advance among the inner
circle of the court with all the courtly formality and frivolity
that could be dredged from the romances of chivalry. And it
was staged with all the display a prosperous London could
muster in honor of the Yorkist Edward IV, in whose policies
they had reason to be confident. The impression it made on
English spectators may be judged from the number of accounts
that have been preserved, and from the fact that, even a

[50] See O. Cartellieri, *The Court of Burgundy* (New York, 1929) for the standard
treatment of the subject.
[51] The best contemporary accounts of this affair are printed in S. Bentley,
Excerpta Historica (London, 1831), pp. 176-212.

generation later, the usually laconic Londoner, Robert Fabyan, still felt called upon to retell the story in full detail in his chronicle.[52]

The following year Edward's sister, Margaret, was married to the Duke of Burgundy. Again the festivities, this time in Bruges, were animated by the deceptively vigorous spirit of chivalry. Again things centered pretty much on the jousting.[53] More than one young English gentleman must have returned to England convinced that he had witnessed something quite genuine. One of them was, indeed, good enough to leave his impressions: "and as for the Duke's court, as of lords, ladies, and gentlewomen, knights, squires, and gentlemen, I heard never of none like it, save King Arthur's court."[54] If he saw but the glittering surface of the pageantry let us forgive him, for he had plenty to look at. Even the English champion, once again Lord Scales, pride of the Woodvilles, rode into the lists on a horse covered from ears to fetlock in cloth of gold trimmed with crimson and blue, and was followed by six pages almost as gorgeously attired as the horse.

It was not, however, the courtiers alone who maintained this line of contact with Burgundy. The basis of England's interest in the Netherlands was economic. If the splendor of Burgundian chivalry rested on the profits of Burgundian commerce, it was the wool and cloth trade that kept Englishmen constantly in touch with Burgundy and rendered them all the more susceptible to the chivalric pretensions of the Burgundian court. If many Londoners retained a very low opinion of their Flemish rivals, if, indeed, the burgher author of *Gregory's Chronicle* could recount only the niggardliness of the Burgundian hosts toward those who came in the retinue of the English court to the festivities at Bruges,[55] the example of Burgundian society could not but have made a profound

---

[52] Fabyan, p. 655.
[53] Bentley, pp. 223-240.
[54] *Ibid.*, p. 226.
[55] *The Historical Collections of a Citizen of London in the Fifteenth Century*, ed. J. Gairdner, Camden Soc., N.S., XVII (London, 1876), 238.

impression even on the merchant class. It was no accident
that Caxton, who for many years had held important positions
among the English merchants in Bruges, became in his later
years the most influential interpreter of the chivalric tradition
to the English reading public. Nor is it surprising that in
his printing ventures he should have enjoyed the patronage of
the Duchess Margaret.[56]

The wealthy commercial cities of Northern Europe are
rightly considered to have been the seed bed of transalpine
Renaissance culture. They also provided the conditions that
made it possible for the spirit of chivalry to enjoy its Indian
Summer. At least they made possible the vivid external forms
which by their lush extravagance masked for so long a time
the poverty of the spirit within. Lacking as yet any other
source of inspiration, any example of secular life other than
the chivalric, both Burgundy and England were for a few
generations content to carry to extremes the elaborate ceremonial that had at one time given expression to the idealism
of a truly feudal society. The English court was no doubt in
this respect but a pale reflection of the refulgent court of
Burgundy, but there are indications that it was trying to live
up to its illustrious neighbor.[57]

. . .

And it is important to remember that an interest in this
sort of thing was by no means confined to the court aristocracy.
Although chivalry was the product of a class system, and its
typical exponent only too often scornful of the burgher (the
later chronicles are full of tales of barbarity towards those of
lower birth which are never wholly redeemed by the more
orthodox stories of knightly courtesy), the prosperous burgher,
when he thought of such things, was willing enough to accept

[56] Crotch, p. lxxx.
[57] See, for example, *The Record of Bluemantle Pursuivant* (1471-72), in Kingsford, *Hist. Lit.*, Appendix XV, especially pp. 380-381.

the stereotypes of chivalry. Chivalric formalities must have been to him, as much as to the gentleman, the hallmark of the sublime life in this world. In England, where it was perhaps easier than in most places for a man of lower status to attain the dignity of knighthood through financial achievement, to many burghers the ultimate symbols of worldly success were still a coat of arms and a soldier's trappings.[58]

Even when those badges of gentility were not sought it was possible for the London merchants to take a lively interest in the pageants of chivalry surrounding the court. The Mayor and the city magistrates of London were given honourable seats at the famous tournament at Smithfield in 1467. Caxton shared with the "young gentlemen" of his acquaintance the same interest in the externals as well as the spirit of chivalry. The English merchant class, especially of London, had as yet no other measure of worldly sophistication than that provided by the forms of chivalry. At the very least, the pageantry of the court provided for the London citizens the best of shows and one ideally calculated to preserve in his mind a regard for chivalric traditions. He might deplore the extravagance of such demonstrations; and he might listen to the sermons at Paul's Cross[59] condemning alike the pride and vanity of the knight and his own tendency to cultivate that root from which all evil springs. More often, perhaps, he ignored the whole thing. But, like his nineteenth-century counterpart, he could not rid himself of a certain curiosity concerning the aristocratic life and a sneaking affection for a lord. He lived within a class system he normally accepted as God-given. Just as unquestioningly he accepted the chivalric idealization of that system.

. . .

[58] For a thorough analysis of the status and aspirations of the merchant class of London, no doubt typical of the class as a whole, see Miss Thrupp's book.
[59] See examples in G. R. Owst, *Literature and Pulpit in Medieval England* (Cambridge, 1923), pp. 331-338.

Occasionally a satirical note is sounded, reminding us that there were those in English society who were capable of laughing at chivalric formalities and treating knights rather more lightly than they were entitled to expect. The tournament receives very undignified handling in that bit of burlesque verse known as *The Tournament of Tottenham*.[60] Who wrote it we do not know. Perhaps one of those clerical writers who in their self-appointed function as public monitors frequently turned their hand to satirical verse.[61] Whoever its author may have been, it was composed in deliberate derogation of chivalric custom: "Of all these keen conquerors to carp is our kind [nature]." It tells of village lads who compete in mock solemnity for the hand of Tibbe, the Reeves's daughter, using flails instead of lances. Although not likely derived from the same social background or written for the same audiences, it speaks with somewhat the same accent of disrespect as characterizes the Robin Hood ballads in which, for example, Sir Guy of Guisbourne, hardly admirable as a person, is made to suffer the ignominy of defeat at the hands of the outlaw yeoman.[62] But these are instances that are noteworthy chiefly as exceptions. England produced no such critics of chivalry as appeared in France.[63] Malory no doubt understood only too well what the French original of his Sir Dinadan meant, and chose wherever possible to remove the barbs from his shafts of satirical common sense.[64] Nor did the England of this later period produce another Sir Thopas to burlesque a literary tradition that was already in the process of going to seed. Hard as it is to avoid the feeling that Stephen Hawes had his tongue in his cheek when he recounts the absurdly dull adventures of

[60] In Thomas Percy, *Reliques of Ancient English Poetry,* ed. H. B. Wheatley (London, 1927), II, 17-28. For William Dunbar's burlesque tournament, see "The Tournament," *Poems,* II, 122-126.

[61] G. F. Jones, "The Tournaments of Tottenham and Laffenhausen," *PMLA,* LXVI (Dec., 1951), 1123-1140. Cf. E. K. Chambers, *English Literature at the Close of the Middle Ages* (Oxford, 1947), pp. 126-129.

[62] "A Gest of Robyn Hode," *English and Scottish Popular Ballads,* ed. H. C. Sargent and G. L. Kittredge (Boston, *ca.* 1898), III, 39-88.

[63] Kilgour, chaps. viii and ix.

[64] See below, chap. ii.

Grande Amoure and La Belle Pucell, we are forced to accept the fact that he was playing the thing straight.[65]

. . .

Chivalric practices and pageantry continued to mark court occasions throughout the sixteenth century. It is, however, difficult to tell at what point they ceased to stand in the eyes of English observers for something real in the life of the nation and became, like the romances of Ariosto and Spenser, the expression of a conscious romanticism, freed from the hypocrisy and the absurdities inherent in an ideal that is merely outmoded. In a sense the last typically chivalric personality to occupy the English throne was Richard III. By training and temperament he belonged to the old order when the simple chivalric virtues of loyalty, prowess, and courage, of justice and liberality, still served the purposes of the knight, be he crowned or merely belted. Unlike his brother, Edward, or his nemesis, Henry Tudor, he could not adjust his coat to the rising winds of political realism. No doubt there were many about him who shared his views and his prejudices just as they had shared the kind of education he had received.[66]

Perhaps the critical period was the early part of Henry VIII's reign when the young monarch, though by no means a product of an exclusively chivalric education, delighted none the less to play the knight and encouraged his courtiers to do likewise. The years immediately following his coronation saw a continuous round of court entertainment in which the joust and tourney were prominently featured. If Hall, the chronicler, can be said to speak for the taste of the court, these chivalric shows were valued more for their color than for their martial significance. Yet to Henry they were an exhilarating pastime, an outlet for his animal energies, and withal warlike enough for him to take seriously as a soldier. "Ever desirous

[65] See below, chap. ii.
[66] See P. M. Kendall, *Richard III* (New York, 1955).

to serve Mars," Hall informs us, the King took part personally in these lance-breaking contests, to the alarm as well as to the admiration of his people.[67] In his tilting armor, fashioned for him by a French master, he looked even more massive than in his court dress, nearly every inch the champion of chivalric romance. That he saw himself as the reincarnation of those heroes of old is indicated by the care with which he nourished the Arthurian tradition. He saw to it that the "original" Round Table at Winchester was kept in good repair and liked to show it to visiting diplomats.[68] As his predecessors had done, he insisted that important diplomatic meetings be graced with chivalric games. In his rival, Francis I of France, he found a man of like tastes and between them they made the Field of the Cloth of Gold an occasion redolent of chivalric tradition.[69] To the uncritical observer it must have seemed as though things had changed very little from the days when another Harry won renown for English arms in combat with the flower of French chivalry and when Richard Beauchamp cut a figure among European knighthood scarcely less brilliant than the fabulous Burgundian, Jacques de Lalaing.

That he allowed the spirit of chivalric romance to affect his political decisions is, of course, more difficult to prove. Even in the days of his youth he had about him men of some common sense to supplement the store of it with which nature had endowed him. But, as we shall see in a later chapter, he was ready enough to commit English men and arms to a crusade against the infidel Moors dreamed up not entirely disingenuously by his far more sophisticated father-in-law, Ferdinand of Aragon.[70] And it is just possible that the war with France that followed he undertook in a spirit not unlike that in which Edward III embarked upon the Hundred Years' War—half dynastic realism, half knight-errantry.

[67] *Hall's Chronicle* (London, 1809), pp. 515-533, especially p. 520.
[68] Millican, pp. 22-24.
[69] Hall, pp. 605-622; see also Cripps-Day, pp. 115-118, for bibliographical information on this event.
[70] Hall, pp. 519-522.

Indeed it is very probable that the court of the young Henry VIII wore the clothing of chivalry more ostentatiously than did that of his father, whose tastes ran in less flamboyant directions and who began the search in Italy for the culture that was to transform the tradition of chivalry beyond recovery and in a large measure to replace it. In the days before the more serious affairs of state forced him to assume in grim earnest the role of a Renaissance prince, Henry VIII gave promise also of becoming a typical Renaissance patron of the arts and learning. As such, in their optimism, the small circle of humanist scholars that gathered around Erasmus liked to see him. And there is some reason for historians to call him the Lorenzo the Magnificent of England who carried to fruition the work begun by the old Cosimo, Henry VII. Yet the fact remains that, while Italian artists and craftsmen were carving the lineaments of classical antiquity on the walls of Hampton Court and creating self-consciously "Romayne" designs for the festive settings at the Field of the Cloth of Gold,[71] while Henry himself was walking with Thomas More in the latter's London garden in the ill-starred intimacy of temporarily shared interests, the prevailing color of the court remained chivalric. If Henry patronized Erasmus, he also "commanded" Lord Berners to translate Froissart. If Polydore Vergil continued to shed the cool light of his humanistic learning upon the record of English history, dwelling only incidentally on the festivities that accompanied the hard work of diplomacy, Edward Hall recounted with obvious relish and at incredible length the story of Henry's elaborately chivalrous meeting with Francis I,[72] and the "Translator of Livius" prepared for the king's reading the ineluctably chivalric saga of Henry V.[73] If the Earl of Surrey drew inspiration for his poetry from the newer courtliness of Italy, he comported him-

---

[71] For a discussion of the Renaissance elements in these designs, see J. Lees-Milne, *Tudor Renaissance* (London, 1951), pp. 23-25.

[72] Hall, pp. 605-622.

[73] C. L. Kingsford, ed., *The First English Life of Henry the Fifth* (Oxford, 1911).

self in a manner that reflected the deeply ingrained quality of his chivalric training, the characteristic prejudices of the medieval knight. And it is by no means of negligible importance that the pageantry of the court continued to lay a veneer of chivalric sincerity over a basically nonchivalric society.

Much of this veneer, perhaps a little of the chivalric spirit itself, continued throughout the century to add a touch of old-world color to that new society. But after the revolutionary events of the thirties a new England found it necessary to express its ideals in new forms and to derive from new sources of inspiration the values against which it must measure its policies and shape its conduct. Within the lifetime of Henry VIII it was possible for Roger Ascham to condemn in good set terms the literary tradition upon which the court in that monarch's earlier years drew so heavily for its forms and even for its ideals. That he condemned it as morally vicious is well known to all students of the period. It should be remembered that he also branded it as old fashioned, "English writers by diversity of time, have taken divers matters in hand." What suits one generation does not suit another. "Books of feigned chivalry," he implied, were, deplorably enough, the fashion of "our fathers' time," but can be so no longer.[74] As she had long since done in fact, so England was now in the process of outgrowing chivalry in theory. Having absorbed the New Learning and having adjusted themselves to the truly national meaning of the Tudor state, Englishmen could return to chivalry, however enthusiastically, only in a spirit of nostalgia and in an atmosphere of romance.

. . .

If something of a resurgence of chivalric feeling did, in fact, take place in the latter fifteenth century, what caused it? There was, as we have seen, little in the actual life of the day to make such a revival seem at all likely. But the ability to

---

[74] *Toxophilus,* introductory address, pp. xiv-xv.

separate the ideal from the actual is a basic characteristic of the mind of the period, and one that has failed to receive from the student of intellectual history the attention it deserves. Perhaps it can be explained as another expression of that deeply engrained habit of treating general concepts as realities which had filtered down in progressively simplified form from the schoolmen of "realist" persuasion to the level of popular thought, and which had achieved concrete form in the imagery, the allegory, and even the pageantry of popular culture.[75] The ideals and ideas connected with knighthood, once given a fictitious substance in the chronicles and in romances of chivalry, and a substance more accurately to be described as meretricious in the pageantry of the court, could maintain a life of their own largely independent of the facts of actual life.

The men and women of late medieval England were quite capable of, were indeed habitually given to, embalming general principles in traditional forms and thereby isolating them quite effectively from the contingencies of daily existence. In this way facts that aroused the anxiety of contemporary observers or in any way elicited from them a strong emotional response could be interpreted in the light of accepted values. And, by the same token, those tendencies which the historian finds most obviously working against the chivalric way of life could become actually instrumental in preserving the chivalric tradition, even perhaps in enhancing its significance in the eyes of all but the most hard-headed observers. What seems at first glance to be merely lip-service to chivalric idealism can thus be considered a quite honest response to the upsetting events of the fifteenth century.

Some part of this revived interest in the ideals of chivalry can be explained as the reaction of an aristocracy to social tendencies that threatened the exclusiveness of their estate.

[75] This, of course, is a well-known interpretation applied to somewhat different conditions by Johan Huizinga in his *Waning of the Midle Ages*. Though difficult to document and therefore to prove, it is provocative as a hypothesis and could, I believe, be developed so as to throw light on much that is obscure in late medieval English thought.

Chivalry had arisen as a code of secular values for the knightly class in a day when the simple pattern of the three estates bore a rough resemblance to the facts of social life. In England, to be sure, the boundaries of that class became progressively harder to define as the lesser aristocracy came to be linked by ties both of blood and interest with the commercial class of the towns. But the privilege of bearing arms and of aspiring to the order of knighthood remained none the less a jealously guarded possession, its ownership readily enough determined in any given instance. As time went on, however, new men found increasing opportunities in agrarian, commercial, and military life to rise in the social scale. Miss Thrupp's exhaustive researches into the anatomy of medieval society have revealed how frequent and how rapid could be the rise (and fall) of merchant families, and how readily wealth could flow from trade to the landed estates upon which any claim to gentility still to a large extent depended. These processes had been accelerated by the Hundred Years' War, through the opportunity it afforded the soldier of fortune and the dealer in supply to achieve a position of wealth and influence in the community. Although, as M. M. Postan once said, it left the anatomy of English society unaltered, the war affected the country's social metabolism.[76] It also fostered those centrifugal forces always inherent in medieval society, in England restrained only by the usually firm hand of the monarchy. Even among the landed families themselves considerations of local expediency and personal bargaining power tended to replace the old loyalty between lord and vassal which had been idealized in the tradition of chivalry.[77]

Especially alarming to the aristocracy, these changes presented a very unsettling picture to the thoughtful observer, whatever his status. No one in fifteenth-century England

[76] M. M. Postan, "Some Social Consequences of the Hundred Years' War," *Economic History Review*, XII (1942), 1-12, 10. See also Postan, "Revisions in Economic History IX—The Fifteenth Century," *Ec. Hist. Rev.*, IX (May, 1939), 160-167.

[77] *Ibid.*, p. 1; McFarlane, "Bastard Feudalism."

could think of society in terms of moving forces. Change still meant, as it had to Gower or Langland, decay within the ordained social structure, disease within the body politic.[78] It took a long time for even the most realistic observers of English society to appreciate the dynamic implications of those upheavals through which medieval society evolved into modern. In the middle part of the following century the "commonwealth men" made a most penetrating analysis of those moving forces, recognizing, as no one in English history had ever done before, the complexities of social cause; yet, in their practical concern for the welfare of the country, they appealed to English opinion in the name of the "very and true commonweal" which, with all its Platonic overtones, remained essentially the static organism of medieval theory, simply brought up to date and given local habitation in Renaissance England.[79] Less sophisticated than the commonwealth ideal, less able also to capture the best minds of the day, this reaffirmation of chivalry represents a similarly conservative reaction to the facts of an evolving society.

The social background thus helps to explain certain aspects of chivalric thought. But it is to the political events of the late medieval period that we must go if we are to place the chivalric thought of the late fifteenth century in its true context. The England of Malory and Caxton, of Scrope and Worcester, had but recently emerged from the century-long struggle with France, her continental territories reduced to a single port, her once respected claims to the French throne all but forgotten in the course of a galling and protracted defeat. The collection of papers concerning the later phases of the Hundred Years' War which William Worcester compiled, apparently as a documentary appendix to his revision of *The Boke of Noblesse,*

[78] The author is currently engaged in the preparation of a MS on this subject.

[79] A. B. Ferguson, "Renaissance Realism in the 'Commonwealth' Literature of Early Tudor England," *Journal of the History of Ideas,* XVI (June, 1955), 287-305. Cf. Caspari, pp. 114-115, where he takes issue with Allen on this point, emphasizing the Platonic element in the commonwealth ideal. J. W. Allen, *A History of Political Thought in the Sixteenth Century* (London, 1928), p. 134.

tells a uniformly depressing tale of dissolution and retreat, and one which must have affected him very deeply.[80] The civil wars also left many an Englishman in a pessimistic mood, his pride hurt, his prospects uncertain. One writer of political verse likens England to a garden which had been overgrown for years with weeds and calls upon all "true English people" to pray that Edward IV will clear the weeds away; and he points to Edward's military prowess as the chief indication of his fitness for the task.[81] Caxton was probably thinking of the naval and diplomatic defeat that England had just suffered at the hand of the Hanse when he broke off his translation of *The Game and the Playe of Chesse* (1475) to recall to his readers "how was renowned the noble realm of England. All the world dreaded it and spoke worship of it" and to contrast that happy situation with the current decline in England's prestige and prosperity.[82]

The deplorable state of the realm prompted some of the most penetrating comment on the political and economic realities of English life to appear before the efflorescence of pamphlet controversy under Henry VIII. Fortescue and Ashby explored the possibilities of reform within the royal administration.[83] An unknown verse-writer echoed the earlier *Libelle of Englyshe Polycye* in stressing the potentially favorable, but still far from realized, position England enjoyed in the balance of commercial and naval power.[84] But among these expressions of political realism may be detected unmistakable accents of chivalric idealism. Indeed, it was quite possible for both to emanate from the same source. Sir John Fastolf, honored by his secretaries as a paragon of knighthood, reveals in some of

[80] *William of Worcester's Collections*, ed. J. Stevenson, in *Letters and Papers Illustrative of the Wars of the English in France during the Reign of Henry the Sixth*, Rolls Series (London, 1864), Vol. II, Part II.

[81] *Political Poems and Songs*, ed. Thomas Wright, Rolls Series (London, 1861), II, 269.

[82] Crotch, pp. 14-15.

[83] See above, notes 4 and 5.

[84] Wright, II, 282-287. Cf. *The Libelle of Englische Polycye*, ed. G. Warner (Oxford, 1926).

his reports on the administration of the English holdings in France a truly statesmanlike appreciation of England's strategic position with reference both to the military and economic factors.[85] To modern eyes this seems the normal reaction of a troubled people to the problems it faced. For that reason, however, the modern observer finds it hard to believe that such a people could retain the notion of a ruling class the function of which remained simply that of protector.

But to the fifteenth-century reader the language of chivalry was more familiar than that of realistic policy. In the England of those days writers were accustomed to discussing political affairs in terms of the moral qualities of men. The tradition to which John Gower belonged and the author of *Mum and the Sothsegger,* to say nothing of the many sharp-tongued preachers and poets who had commented on the affairs of England and castigated the vices of the ruling class,[86] made it seem quite natural to seek a remedy for the ills of the realm in a return to virtue on the part of those in a position of power and influence. Usually that appeal to the conscience had been made in terms of the fundamental Christian virtues. Chivalric virtue had, however, long been accepted as a secular annex to the main ecclesiastical edifice, a sort of parish gymnasium built next the parish church. It was natural, then, that anyone convinced of the importance of chivalric values as a secular guide for the ruling class should see in their renewal a practical enough prescription for the sickness that was evidently sapping the vitality of England. Society, moreover, did not present to most men of the fifteenth century the problem of moving forces which must be harnessed or otherwise dealt with by means of constructive statecraft. The problem existed then as is has always done. But the mind of the day was accustomed to thinking in terms not of dynamism but of a world order

[85] Worcester's *Collection,* pp. 575-585, 723-730. Note especially his reference (p. 583) to the necessity of keeping the sea and his awareness of the relationship between trade and military strategy.

[86] The author is currently engaged in the preparation of a MS on this subject. See also G. R. Owst, *Literature and Pulpit in Medieval England* (Cambridge, 1923), pp. 210-470.

in which change was the product of human vice which manifested itself in the subversion of peace and justice. And it was to the maintenance of peace and justice that the true knight was bound to address himself.

The chivalric tradition was thus the last refuge in secular thought for a bewildered and bedeviled aristocracy. In fact it was the only one possible in the era of the civil wars; for if there is one generality that can safely be made concerning that kaleidoscopic period it is that the English were still living on cultural capital inherited from their ancestors. In their cultural, as in their economic life, the English upper classes were forced to make a relatively fixed income meet the increasing demands of an increasingly complex society. Chivalry had perforce to continue to do what it had been doing since the twelfth century, namely to supplement for the purposes of secular life the great body of Christian ethical teachings.

II

CHIVALRY TEACHING BY EXAMPLE

THE LITERATURE OF LATE MEDIEVAL AND EARLY
Renaissance England was in purpose overwhelmingly didactic.
The didactic habit was deeply ingrained in the medieval mind.
It was encouraged by the church, made inveterate by the
clergy, and had become so strong by the later fifteenth century
that it determined much of the literary activity of the increasingly large proportion of laymen then taking an active
interest in letters. It need not, however, be explained wholly
as the product of a clerically shaped culture. For it runs parallel to, and must surely have been related to, an equally marked
bent toward sheer practicality. A utilitarian bias characterized
alike those shrewd men who, like the Pastons, sought some
degree of order and security in the chaotic society of fifteenth-
century England and the humanistically trained pamphleteers
of the century following. More than has generally been
recognized this practical temper provides an element of continuity in English thought during an era of otherwise radical
transition. In one period it found expression in the traditional
forms of medieval culture: in the other it was conditioned by
the reinterpreted example of ancient Rome. It is perhaps the
temper most natural to Englishmen beset by many and urgent
problems. Small wonder, then, that the early printing presses
should have been devoted to such a large extent to the publication of books dealing with the problems of conduct in the
world and of salvation in the next (both, in their way, exceedingly practical), with questions concerning chivalry and heraldry, hunting and hawking, good governance and the law of
tenures, education and the wealth of England. Much of this

didactic and utilitarian literature was intended to serve as an example for the governing class, as a guide, that is, for the secular activities of those on whose shoulders rested the responsibility of government. During the century or so that elapsed from the Wars of the Roses to the early years of Elizabeth's reign the character of that example underwent a fundamental transformation. It changed from that of chivalry tempered by a sort of medievalized classicism to classicism tempered by a romantically conceived chivalry.

. . .

Curiously enough it was Caxton, the man of affairs, experienced in the realities of international trade and diplomacy, who more deliberately and consistently than anyone else whose writings have come down to us exhorted the English aristocracy to renew their dedication to the principles and practices of chivalry. And, somewhat more understandably, he did so out of a profound sense of patriotism, a vital concern for the commonwealth of England. Things had changed since the days when John Gower, also a layman, also experienced in the world of affairs, had likewise called upon the nobles and gentry of England to remember their duty to God and the community.[1] But Gower had not been disturbed about the prestige of England. On the contrary he saw in a foreign policy based on a sort of dynastic knight-errantry a factor only too likely to damage the welfare of the English people. And, like the preachers of his day, he castigated the search for military renown as potentially contrary to the spirit of Christianity.[2] By Caxton's day England was faced, not by a stalemate in a costly war, pursued in the interests of dynastic power, but by defeat, her prestige abroad seriously lowered, and her material

---

[1] Gower's views on the place and function of the knightly class may be found in *Mirrour de l'Omme*, in *Works*, I, lines 23593-24180; *Vox Clamantis*, in *Works*, IV, Liber V, chaps. i-vi, Liber VI, chaps. xiii-xiv, Liber VII, chap. iii; *In Praise of Peace* in *Works*, III, pp. 480-492.

[2] See especially *Vox Clamantis*, Liber VI, chaps. xii- xiv, and *Praise of Peace*, pp. 480-492.

fortunes rendered consequently precarious. Her domestic administration needed as never before the services of those dedicated to the general welfare. A time had come for spiritual regeneration, not solely for the good of men's souls—that was always an ultimate desideratum—but more immediately for the good of the country. To whom, then, could the patriotic publicist appeal but to the governing class? And on what other grounds than a rededication to the secular ideals of their order?

Perhaps Caxton meant his appeal in part to justify his publication (1484?) of *The Book of the Ordre of Chyualry*. But his choice of that work is in itself significant. And anyway, there is the ring of sincerity in the following lines which, though familiar to any student of the period, merit quoting *in extenso*:

Oh ye knights of England, where is the custom and usage of noble chivalry that was used in those days [the days of King Arthur]? What do ye now but go to the bagnios and play at dice? And some not well advised use not honest and good rule against all order of knighthood. Leave this, leave it and read the noble volumes of the Holy Grail, of Launcelot, of Galahad, of Tristram, of Perseforest, of Percival, of Gawain and many more. There shall ye see manhood, courtesy, and gentleness. And look in later days of the noble acts since the conquest, as in the days of King Richard, Coeur de Lyon, Edward the First and the Third and his noble sons, Sir Robert Knolles, Sir John Hawkwood, Sir John Chandos, and Sir Walter Manny. Read Froissart. And also behold that victorious and noble king, Harry the Fifth, and the captains under him . . . and many others whose names shine gloriously by their virtuous noblesse and acts that they did in honor of the order of chivalry.[3]

Lest his readers dismiss these words as the familiar scolding of the social critic, he proceeds to apply them to specific conditions.

I would demand a question, if I should not displease. How many knights be there now in England that have the use and the exercise of a knight. That is, to wit, that he knoweth his horse and his horse him. That is to say, he being ready at a point to have all things that belong

[3] *Ordre of Chyualry*, pp. 122-123.

to a knight: an horse that is according and broken after his hand, his armor and harness meet and fitting, and so forth et cetera.

Not content to let the matter rest at this point, his sense of the practical led him to make certain recommendations which he no doubt believed quite practical.

I would it pleased our sovereign lord that twice or thrice in a year, or at the least once, he would cry jousts of peace to the end that every knight should have horse and harness and also the use and craft of a knight and also to tourney one against one or two against two, and the best to have a prize, a diamond or jewel, such as should please the prince.

This, he concludes, should cause "gentlemen to resort to the ancient customs of chivalry" which, in turn, would have two beneficial effects. It would contribute "to great fame and renown," which, read in conjunction with Caxton's explicitly patriotic bias, refers undoubtedly to the prestige of England rather than to that of the individual knight as was usual in the earlier chivalric tradition. It would also make the English knights "always ready to serve their prince when he shall call them or have need." "This little book," he adds, should be read by "every man that is come of noble blood and intendeth to come to the noble order of chivalry," for it contains the "lore and commandments" necessary for the education of a knight. Indeed, he urges King Richard "of England and of France" to command that it be "had and read unto other young lords, knights, and gentlemen within this realm, that the noble order of chivalry be hereafter better used and honored than it hath been in late days past."[4]

It was, I believe, this same concern for the discipline of the English governing class, this same faith in the efficacy of chivalric literature for the planting of socially desirable virtues, that led Caxton to translate or otherwise edit for publication the several popular romances of chivalry. In his prologue to

---

[4] *Ibid.*, pp. 124-125. In connection with Caxton's patriotic bent it might be worth recalling his assertion that it is "necessaire to alle Englisshmen to knowe the propretees commoditees and meruailles of [the British Isles]." Crotch, p. 40.

his translation of *Blanchardin and Eglantyne* (1489) he argues that it is as necessary for young men and women of the aristocracy and gentry to read "Ancient histories of noble feats and valiant acts of arms and war . . . as it is to occupy them and study over mocle [much] in books of contemplation."[5] In the romances he saw also exemplified the virtues which found expression in knightly deeds. He undertook the task of publishing Malory's version of the Arthurian legends not only "to the intent that noble men may see and learn the noble acts of chivalry" but also to show how virtuous action led to honor and vicious deeds to punishment.

For herein may be seen noble chivalry, courtesy, humanity, friendliness, hardiness, love, friendship, cowardice, murder, hate, virtue, and sin. Do after the good and leave the evil, and it shall bring you to good fame and renown.[6]

Like Sir Philip Sidney, he believed that literature should inspire to action as well as give pleasure to the reader; but, whereas the Renaissance gentleman had in mind action in the service of the many-faceted Renaissance state[7] (his own many-sidedness was in large part a reflection of the increasing complexity of life in Tudor England), Caxton thought principally of chivalric action, of service, that is, performed by the knight in fulfillment of his traditional function as the protective arm of society.

A similar utility he found in history. In fact it is doubtful whether he drew a very clear line in his own mind between history and legend—or rather he considered the traditional heroes of romance, Godfrey of Boulogne or Charlemagne, for example, as historical figures unless, as in the case of Arthur, ironically enough the one Britisher among the Nine Worthies,

[5] Crotch, p. 105. Cf. Epilogue to *Godefroy of Bologne, ibid.,* p. 48. See also Eugene Vinaver, *Le Roman de Tristan et Iseut dans l'oeuvre de Thomas Malory* (Paris, 1925), pp. 139-140. See also M. Markman, "The Meaning of *Sir Gawain and the Green Knight,*" *PMLA,* LXXII (Sept., 1957), 574-586, for an interesting treatment of the didactic purpose underlying medieval romance.

[6] *Ibid.,* p. 94.

[7] Caspari, chap. vii.

he had reason to suspect his historicity.[8] The ancient worthies also reflected in their careers ideals which had already been given chivalric coloring by the time Caxton made their acquaintance.[9] In his prologue to *Polycronicon* (1482) he made as earnest a plea for the practical value of history, considered as experience, as any in the range of Renaissance literature—if not quite so gracefully put. The "feigned fables of poets" have stirred men to pity and justice, the eloquence of orators and "learned clerks" has pointed others to the paths of virtue, though they have sometimes lied.

But history, representing the things like unto the words, embraceth all utility and profit. It showeth honesty and maketh vices detestable. It enhanceth noble men and depresseth wicked men and fools. Also things that history describeth by experience much profit unto a rightful life.[10]

Yet it is chivalric virtue and chivalric action that Caxton sees most clearly reflected in the mirror of history. It moves knights not only to do noble deeds but to see through such "battles for the defense and tuition of their country and public weal"[11] the glory that is so high on the list of chivalric objectives. Indeed, Caxton considers achieving a place in history a primary objective of all human action. Since, he argues, the "fruits of virtue be immortal, specially when they be wrapped in the benefice of histories, then it must follow that it is most fair to men mortal to suffer labors and pain for glory and fame immortal."[12]

The chivalric tradition had always drawn heavily for its

---

[8] Housman, "Beginnings of Arthurian Criticism," pp. 209-217.

[9] See, e.g., Prol. to *Historie of Jason,* Crotch, p. 33; *Ordre of Chyualry,* pp. 121-122. See also Dyboski and Arend, eds., *Knyghthode and Bataile,* introd., pp. xxix-xxx, in which the point is made that the author tried hard to render Vegetius' Latin terms in chivalric equivalents.

[10] Crotch, p. 66. Cf. *Oeuvres de Froissart,* ed. M. le baron Kervyn de Lettenhove (Brussels, 1867-1877), II, 8. As H. S. Bennett noticed (*English Books and Their Readers,* p. 123), Renaissance writers in England were in the habit of quoting or paraphrasing the pronouncements of Cicero on the subject: "An hystore is the recorder of tymes passed: the lyght of verite: the maistress of mannes lyvenge: the presydent of memorie: the messanger of antiquite."

[11] Crotch, p. 66.

[12] *Ibid.*

nourishment on the stories of chivalric action. Those Englishmen who had contributed most to the popularity of chivalric
forms—Edward I, Edward III, and such famous knights as
Richard Beauchamp—had modeled their behavior quite consciously after the tales of a chivalric past.[13] This tendency
revealed itself most explicitly in forms that were in themselves
superficial enough: establishing round tables after the Arthurian manner, for example, or, like Beauchamp, engaging in a
three-day tournament exactly parallel in its form to certain
famous tournaments of romance. Could we but see into their
minds we would find that it had also colored in many subtle
ways the picture these men had of themselves and according
to which they undoubtedly shaped their more far-reaching
decisions. To this extent chivalry had always been romantic
in its appeal to the aristocratic imagination. In the fifteenth
century, with its social and economic foundations crumbling,
chivalry depended to an even greater extent on the example of
former heroes and the incentive of renown preserved in the
record of knightly, and largely military, action.

Lydgate, writing in the second decade of the fifteenth century, tells us he began his *Troy Book* at the request of Prince
Henry (later Henry V) who loved to read "books of antiquity"
so that he might be able "Of very knighthood to remember
again/ The worthiness . . . And the prowess of old chivalry."[14]
Indeed that most knightly of England's fifteenth-century rulers
kept, it would seem, a sharp eye out for his own place in the
historical record—perhaps more than he would have admitted,
since the true knight must demonstrate humility as well as
seek fame in arms.[15] On numerous occasions (if we may
believe his official biographer) he seems deliberately to have

[13] See above, chap. i, n. 33. A record of the exploits of Beauchamp is preserved
under the title *Pageant of the Birth Life and Death of Richard Beauchamp Earl of
Warwick*, ed. Viscount Dillon and W. H. St. John Hope (London, 1914); see also
Cline, "Influence of the Romance on Tournaments," p. 210.

[14] *Lydgate's Troy Book*, ed. H. Bergen, E.E.T.S., E.S., XCVII (1906), Prol.,
lines 72-89.

[15] Kingsford, *First Life of Henry the Fifth*, p. 65; Livio's translator writes that
after Agincourt he "refused the vane praising of the people."

played to the chivalric gallery. He decides, for example, to attack the most heavily defended tower at Caen instead of the weakest. Before that engagement, he challenges the Dauphin to personal combat so as to avoid additional bloodshed and a series of destructive sieges, a pious gesture we might be more impressed by if we did not know that similar challenges had been made at other critical points in the war with similarly negative results.[16] And he cultivates an exaggerated air of humility in the face of victory: after the fall of Harfleur he descends from his horse, removes his shoes and makes his triumphal entry on foot.[17] He was also quite capable of ruthless action on the basis of the most realistic appreciation of a tactical situation: in a tight moment at Agincourt he orders the English to slaughter their prisoners in cold blood.[18] But then chivalric virtue, like Christian charity, was in the fifteenth century honored as often in the breach as in the observance.

In times of stress Englishmen turned for patriotic as well as chivalric inspiration to the stories of his campaigns. At the request of Duke Humphrey of Gloucester, Tito Livio da Forli brought his training in the new scholarship of Renaissance Italy to bear on a life of Henry V which was almost certainly calculated to bolster English morale at a critical point in the chronic war with France. The resulting *Vita Henrici V*[19] (1437 or 1438) tells a tale curiously blended of chivalric heroism, typified by the king himself, of quite impersonal siege operations, and of a shrewd statesmanship worthy of a Renaissance despot.[20] This and other related versions of Henry's career served well into the sixteenth century to per-

[16] *Ibid.*, pp. 83-86. For references to this curiously disingenuous (or self-deluded?) custom, see Neilson, *Trial by Combat*, pp. 165 and 178; J. Huizinga, *The Waning of the Middle Ages* (London, 1927), chap. vii.

[17] *Chroniques d'Enguerrand de Monstrelet*, ed. J. A. Buchon (Paris, 1826), III, 326. See also E. Duncan, *The Story of Minstrelsy* (London, 1907), pp. 91-97.

[18] *Ibid.*, p. 344; *The Brut*, ed. F. W. D. Brie, E.E.T.S., O.S., No. 136, Part II (1908), p. 379.

[19] Ed. T. Hearne (London, 1716). On Livio, see Kingsford, *Hist. Lit.*, pp. 52 ff.

[20] See, for example, the story of the siege of Caen in Kingsford, pp. 83-95. For an estimate of Henry's statesmanship, see Edouard Perroy, *The Hundred Years' War* (New York, 1951), pp. 235-236.

petuate that image of the royal knight, the chivalric hero in a national setting which is the characteristic contribution of England to the history of chivalric idealism.

It was an image men of Yorkist leanings believed they had found embodied among their contemporaries in the person of the Earl of Warwick. In the days before the "kingmaker" had followed his fickle star into the tragic embroilments of his later career he could well have seemed to hopeful partisans the man ideally suited to the task of defending and restoring the honor and wealth of the kingdom. A chronicle, written shortly after the events of the fifties and early sixties, refers to "... that noble knight and flower of manhood, Richard earl of Warwick, shield of our defense."[21] Another chronicler of the period speaks of him more than once in language reminiscent of Malory's: "he was named and taken in all places for the most courageous and manliest knight living."[22] After his successful skirmish of 1459 with a Spanish merchant fleet in the Channel, he is pictured as the only man willing and able to defend the

honor and profit of the king and the land . . . for which manhood and his great policy and deeds of worship in fortifying Calais and other feats of armes all the commonalty of this land had him in great laud . . . and so repute and take for as famous a knight as was living.[23]

It is instructive to notice that Warwick's knighthood is here placed, with a Londoner's almost instinctive appreciation of the strategic importance of Calais and the Channel, in a context of national interest rather than of chivalric values. It is also interesting to notice that his tactics on the field of battle were, as Paul M. Kendall has pointed out, those more of the *condottiere* than of the knight. He preferred tactics that would win—the use of cannon and elaborate siege operations, the skilful deployment of yeoman archers—rather than the head-on

[21] *An English Chronicle,* ed. J. S. Davies, Camden Society, 1st Series, LXIV (1856), 93.

[22] *Six Town Chronicles,* ed. R. Flenley (Oxford, 1911), p. 144.

[23] *Ibid.,* p. 147. See also Paul M. Kendall, *Warwick the Kingmaker* (New York, 1957), p. 50.

clash of heavy-armed knights. His tendency to remain
mounted in the rear so as to manage the battle more readily,
though an eminently sensible thing to do, appears to have
drawn upon him the fire of the French chroniclers, who considered him a coward, despite the fact that he ordinarily led
his troops personally in their first charge against the enemy.[24]
In Warwick, as in Henry V, it is possible to see the historical
example of chivalry in action subtly changing its color during
the fifteenth century. Though few men of the day realized it,
the knight was already becoming transformed before their
very eyes into the Renaissance soldier.

· · ·

Chivalric romance, as we have seen, shared with the historical record of chivalric deeds the function of teaching by example. Among the several adapters and translators of such
romances, Sir Thomas Malory stands alone. His *Morte Darthur* (completed in 1469 or 1470) has become the most famous
of the chivalric tales that were so numerous and so popular in
the later fifteenth century. He stamped his own personality
on his work and, if we are willing to seek them out, some at
least of his own attitudes. And he did so to an extent that
makes *Morte Darthur* one of the most important of the not
too numerous sources of information concerning the state of
chivalric ideas in that period. The problem of interpreting
him is complicated by the fact that, especially since Eugene
Vinaver published his monumental edition of Malory, a great
deal of controversy has arisen over the literary aspects of the
work. The heat engendered has not always been accompanied
by a commensurate amount of light; and so there has at times
been a real danger of losing sight of Malory himself and, more
particularly, of the larger characteristics of his thinking. Let
us not, however, be deterred from rushing in where others

[24] Kendall, pp. 123-124. See also P. A. Jorgenson, "Alien Military Doctrine in
Renaissance England," *Modern Language Quarterly,* XVII (March, 1956), 43-49.

have picked their way more fearfully; for the literary critics have been something less than angelic, and the historian of ideas may perhaps find that he is on something more than a mere fool's errand.

It would seem that Malory shared with Caxton a desire to make the traditions of chivalry serve a didactic purpose and one rather closely related to the fortunes of England. It is hard to be certain about Malory's intentions because he seldom projected himself or his time directly into his writing. Indeed it is still difficult to speak with assurance about him as a person, so recently and imperfectly has he emerged from his former, all but nameless, obscurity.[25] There has always been reason to suppose, however, that it was in part at least a feeling that the England of the civil wars had deviated sadly from the great pattern of chivalry that prompted him to embark, in his later years and in circumstances of enforced leisure, on the stories of King Arthur's court. Certainly nothing in the literary heritage of the fifteenth century could better have served such a purpose than this "matter of Britain" which for generations had provided the inspiration and even to some extent the pattern, for the patriotic brand of chivalry characteristic of England. Very possibly, of course, the stimulus could have come from the opposite direction. If concern for the dolorous state of English fortunes did not turn him to the Arthurian materials, once embarked on the project he found himself dealing with themes that could very readily be given timely significance.

It is not necessary to look, as some scholars have done,[26]

---

[25] For data on Malory's life, see E. Hicks, *Sir Thomas Malory, His Turbulent Career* (Cambridge, Mass., 1928); A. C. Baugh, "Documenting Sir Thomas Malory," *Speculum*, VIII (Jan., 1933), 3-29; Vinaver's introduction to his edition of Malory's works.

[26] W. H. Schofield, *Chivalry in English Literature* (Cambridge, Mass., 1925), pp. 89-93; Nellie S. Aurner, "Sir Thomas Malory—Historian?," *PMLA*, XLVIII (March, 1933), 362-391; Vinaver, *Works of Malory*, I, xxv, xix-xxviii. Cf. dissenting views expressed in Mary E. Dickmann, "Characterization in Malory's Tale of Arthur and Lucius," *PMLA*, LXV (Sept., 1950), 877-895; R. M. Lumiansky, "The Question of Unity in Malory's *Morte Darthur*," *Tulane Studies in English*, V (1955), 29-39. This problem has become entangled with the purely critical problem of form and unity in Malory's work and has suffered accordingly.

for specific references or deliberately contrived parallels between the episodes of the *Morte Darthur* and those of fifteenth-
century English history. Malory was too good an artist, and
at the same time too little of a political pamphleteer, to indulge
in systematic political allegory. His work is not a *roman á
clef*. But, like many another Englishman of his day, he was
given to looking back to the reign of Henry V as a time when
English fortunes prospered under a truly knightly king. He
himself could remember Agincourt and the subsequent victorious campaigns in France. A similarity between this record
of victory under a man who took pains to gather about him
the trappings of the chivalric hero and the tales of King
Arthur, especially the story of Arthur and the Emperor Lucius,
could scarcely have escaped the imaginative and patriotic mind
of Malory. As Vinaver points out, Arthur becomes under
Malory's pen not a "mere abstract centre of the fellowship
of the Round Table, but . . . a political and military leader,
conscious of his responsibility for the welfare and the prestige of his kingdom."[27] Nor could Malory have failed to
see in the fratricidal struggle that destroyed the Round Table
and in the failure of the aging Arthur to dominate his kingdom a provocative parallel to the Wars of the Roses and to the
disintegration of the English monarchy he must have thought
was taking place around him even as he wrote. The "knight-
prisoner" was no doubt brooding over the fickleness of the
English public and the success of Yorkist policy when he in-
terpolated the following apostrophe into his account of Sir
Mordred's success in gaining popular support against Arthur
during the final climactic campaign:

Lo, ye all Englishmen, see ye not what mischief here was? For
he that was the most king and noblest knight of the world, and most
loved the fellowship of noble knights, and by him they all were up-
holden, and yet might not these Englishmen hold them content with
him. Lo thus was the custom and usages of this land, and men say

[27] *Works of Malory,* p. xxv.

that we of this land have not yet lost that custom. Alas! this is a great default of us Englishmen, for there may no thing us please no term.[28]

Such a specific appeal to the Englishmen of his day is unusual in Malory. But the context of the knightly examples he sets before them is always English. Camelot, he explains, is West-minster. Astolat is now Guildford, Joyous Gard "some men say it was Alnwich and some say it was Bamborough." The country of Logres, he assures his readers, is the country of England. And King Arthur takes pains to consult the Arch-bishop of Canterbury.[29]

In his early years, moreover, Malory had served under one of the last of those brilliant knights who had done so much to make the more successful phases of the Hundred Years' War an inspiration to the readers of English chronicles. Richard Beauchamp, Earl of Warwick, served for his entire generation as the model knight, the "Father of Courtesy." The Emperor Sigismund, no amateur in matters of chivalry, is reported to have exclaimed that, were all courtesy lost, it might be found again in him.[30] Beauchamp modeled his most famous jousting exploits self-consciously upon the pattern of Arthurian romance and may, in turn, have provided Malory with the specific pattern for his story of Beaumains and his successive battles with the Black, Green, and Red Knights.[31] Although he appears to have been more famous as the young international athlete who amazed and delighted the courts of Europe with his skill in the tilt-yard than as the diplomat and trusted administrator he became in his more mature years,[32] he must have served as a model also of the knight laboring in the service of his country, the worthy product of a bastard chivalry, the true "knight-governor." With such a patron as his personal

[28] *Ibid.*, p. 1229.
[29] Such references are especially numerous in the latter books. See also Schofield, p. 93.
[30] *Pageant.*
[31] Vinaver, *Malory,* p. 3.
[32] Compare the *Pageant,* an account of his life in word and picture meant obviously for the aristocratic public, with the historian's version in the *Dictionary of National Biography.*

"ensample" it was only natural for Malory to turn to the Round Table for "ensamples" of chivalric conduct to set before the bedeviled generation among whom his lot was cast in his later years. Whatever may have been the source of his inspiration, there is no denying the importance of the chivalric ideal in Malory's thought. The "high order of knighthood" was to him a very real institution, its values good and uniquely pertinent to the aristocratic society in which he lived. Without entering into the dangerous problem of artistic unity in the *Morte Darthur*,[33] the historian of ideas can readily see in Malory's devotion to both the institution and the system of ethical ideals in which it achieved social meaning an intellectual consistency that in itself binds the several stories into an organic whole and places upon it the distinct, if unobtrusive, mark of Malory's own convictions.

What, more specifically, those convictions were becomes apparent as his work in "reducing" his French sources into English is compared to the sources themselves. Like most medieval writers he reserved to himself the utmost freedom in handling his originals. By both omission and addition he made the resulting stories very much his own. Generally speaking, he interpreted the Arthurian cycle in terms of a chivalry quite different from the older and in many ways more sophisticated French tradition. In his hands it emerges as a practical code of conduct, limited to the needs and compre-hension of men who, like himself, were country gentlemen, who had perhaps served their country in the wars and had reason to look with more than romantic interest to the ex-amples of knighthood in action. It is the chivalry strictly of

[33] This is not the place for an extended bibliography on this hotly debated subject. Among recent studies, the following contain most of the pertinent biblio-graphical references: Lumianski, *op. cit.;* C. Moorman, "Malory's Treatment of the Sangreall," *PMLA*, LXXI (June, 1956), 496-509. This debate centers largely on Vinaver's thesis, stated in his edition of Malory's works, that Malory did not intend to write a single unified book, but tended to treat his material in eight related but self-contained books.

an agrarian and military caste, and interpreted as far as possible in terms of realism and common sense. It is not the chivalry of *courtoisie,* a tradition both too decadent by Malory's day to enlist his loyalty and too sophisticated for him fully to appreciate. Nor is it the chivalry of religious mysticism which had animated the French *Queste del Saint Graal.* Even less is it the chivalry of satire: it has in it none of the gently cynical realism occasionally expressed in the French prose *Tristan,* a realism born of disillusionment with the pretensions and postures of an overblown knight-errantry. Knighthood was to Malory "the practical function of a well established order . . . with its headquarters in the household of a great prince."[34]

Particularly revealing are the several alterations he made in the process of adapting the French prose *Tristan* in the speeches of Sir Dinadan, who appears so out of place in Malory's version even after large sections of his speeches have been deleted and their meaning altered.[35] He could not delete the character entirely, for it was too intimately involved in too many episodes. But he found Dinadan's humorous, satirical, slightly cynical sallies unquestionably embarrassing. He endeavored to pass him off as a scoffer and "japer," not to be taken seriously; but he could not entirely rid his remarks of their antichivalric venom.

Dinadan in the world of Arthurian adventure is almost as foreign, almost as anachronistic as the Connecticut Yankee. He sees absurdity in the aimless errantry of the Round Table knights, in their somnambulistic truculence, in the sublime lunacy of their unrequited love. Life, to him, is good, and its goodness is not likely to be enhanced by an artificial code of conduct. You fight only when you have to—a live coward is in reality better off than a dead knight.[36] Love is a natural

---

[34] Vinaver, *Works of Malory,* p. xxvii.

[35] In addition to the systematic comparison made by Vinaver in his edition of Malory, see his *Le Roman de Tristan et Iseut dans l'oeuvre de Thomas Malory* (Paris, 1925), pp. 131-148, and his *Études sur le "Tristan" en prose* (Paris, 1925), Appendix.

[36] *Works of Malory,* pp. 613-614 and 1482.

thing and enjoyable in its naturalness, so why pine in the service of one who is beyond your reach?[37]

Malory was no doubt quite capable of appreciating a good deal of Dinadan's practical realism—his refusal, for example, to fight a patently unequal combat: "it is ever worship to a knight to refuse that thing that he may not attain."[38] A healthy distaste for foolhardiness is, indeed, not uncommon in late chivalric writing. It appears, for example, with some emphasis in *The Boke of Noblesse,* probably as an echo of Sir John Fastolf's advice; for that very practical knight had at one point been accused of cowardice as a result of an engagement in which he had acted merely with common prudence.[39] Prudence had, indeed, been long recognized in the chivalric handbooks as a cardinal virtue, in battle as in other human endeavors. Only in the romances was the hero commonly required to adhere to an irrationally rigid standard of valor.[40] And Malory himself seems to have had little feeling for the courtly love tradition. But he could not help sensing that Dinadan's speeches, some of which are developed with Gilbertian humor and irony,[41] constituted a deliberate flanking attack on the institution he so greatly valued. Malory's mind had little capacity for humor and less for satirical irony. Perhaps no one possessed of a sense of humor could take the chivalry of the late Middle Ages with an entirely straight face.[42] But it is nonetheless a fact of importance that Malory was able to take his knighthood very seriously.

[37] *Ibid.,* p. 1477.

[38] *Ibid.,* p. 581, lines 24-26; p. 1476.

[39] On Fastolf, see account in *DNB* and in Kingsford, *The First English Life of Henry the Fifth,* pp. xii-xiii. Cf. Caxton-Lull, *Ordre of Chyualry,* p. 37.

[40] This point is discussed with useful references in M. A. Gist, *Love and War in the Middle English Romances,* U. of Pennsylvania Diss. (Philadelphia, 1947), pp. 177-178.

[41] *Works of Malory,* pp. 604-605, 1479-1480. See also pp. 614, 1482; pp. 1436-1437.

[42] Vinaver, *Malory,* pp. 64-66. Could the episode related in *Works,* pp. 1104-1105 be considered humorous? Cf. Schofield, p. 220. Chaucer, of course, was able to poke fun at the decadent chivalric romances in his *Tale of Sir Thopas* (*Works,* IV, 189-196), yet retain the utmost respect for the chivalric ideal, as witness his treatment of the Knight and the Squire in the Prologue to the *Canterbury Tales.* See also the Prologue to *Troilus and Cryseide.* Cf. C. S. Lewis, *The Allegory of Love* (Oxford, 1936), pp. 172 ff. A rollicking satire on the trappings of chivalry

It is essentially a simple ideal he nourished so assiduously: Malory's was a mind not given to analysis, nor was he always consistent. It finds expression, for example, in the contrast, more heightened than is warranted by his source, between King Mark, the poltroon, the cad, the embodiment of all that is foreign to the "high order of knighthood," and Sir Tristram, the doughty man-at-arms, the faithful lover, the model knight-errant. But it is an ideal that leaves small room for the more sophisticated chivalric conventions of courtly love. Tristram appears only too ready, love potion or no love potion, to be off with the boys adventuring and fighting; and it becomes a matter of only incidental significance that it is all done in the service of a lady.[43] In like spirit, Launcelot rejects a "noble maiden" because he is too busy to be married and too concerned for his success in the profession of arms to take paramours.[44] The courtly love ideal was, in fact, largely irrelevant, if not repugnant, to those of the provincial aristocracy who still held the basic principles of chivalry as guides to the actual business of living. Even in France, the home of *courtoisie*, the worthy Chevalier de la Tour-Landry warned his daughters to avoid the pitfalls of courtly love; and his stern and calculating attitude toward the place of women in society is nicely paralleled in the Paston letters.[45] Perhaps Malory himself, led

is contained in the ballad known as *The Turnament of Tottenham: or the Wooeing, Winning and Wedding of Tibbe, the Reev's Daughter there,* in Thomas Percy, *Reliques of Ancient English Poetry,* ed. H. B. Wheatley (London. 1927), II, 17-28. It may well have been of nonaristocratic origin; but cf. G. F. Jones, "The Tournaments of Tottenham and Lappenhausen," *PMLA,* LXVI (Dec., 1951), 1123-1140.

[43] *Works of Malory,* pp. 1435-1436, referring to p. 419.

[44] *Ibid.,* pp. 270-271 and commentary p. 1403. Cf. P. E. Tucker, "The Place of the 'Quest of the Holy Grail' in the *Morte Darthur,"* *Modern Language Review,* XLVIII (1953), 391-397. Tucker suggests that Malory had always been unhappy about the role of Launcelot as the traditional knight-lover: it was inconsistent with his emphasis on "knyghtly dedys and vertuous lyvyng" as the objective of true knighthood.

[45] *Le Livre du Chevalier de la Tour-Landry,* ed. Montaiglon, Bibliotheque elzévirienne (Paris, 1854), pp. 3-4. See Kilgour, pp. 108-122. Cf. S. Painter, *French Chivalry* (Baltimore, 1940), pp. 140-141. E. S. Bennett, *The Pastons and Their England,* chaps. iii-v; English writers seem, indeed, often to have underplayed the role of the knight as lover in preference to the man of military prowess, and to have taken a dour view of women. See, for example, Gower, *Vox Clamantis,* Liber VII, chap. iii; cf. Kelso, *Doctrine,* pp. 85 ff. Notice also Caxton's tongue-in-cheek treatment of Socrates' sayings on women, omitted by Rivers in his translation. Crotch, pp. 22-28. English versions of the life of Alexander stress the

on either by his French source or by his own inclinations (if we may trust the court records that bear his name, his relations with women were not notable for their courtesy),[46] was less conservative in matters of sex than many of his countrymen. Whereas the medieval romances, a form as likely as anything in literature to reflect the tastes and prejudices of their audience, are in England noticeably less tolerant of adultery than their French counterparts,[47] Malory seems never to have been able to make up his mind whether virtuous love was confined to the married state or could exist in a relationship marked merely by the steadfast loyalty of one lover to the other.[48] Ambivalent as Malory's sentiments on such matters may have been, the important fact is not their ambivalence but their subordination to those aspects of the chivalric tradition that were more relevant to the life of his class.

Although his knights are primarily soldiers, Malory occasionally allows us to see them also as country gentlemen. This at least is true of Sir Tristram, in describing whose accomplishments Malory goes considerably beyond his source. As the climax of his exploits, Tristram is welcomed by Arthur to the fellowship of the Round Table. In his speech of welcome Arthur hails him as one of the best and gentlest knights in the world and "the man of most worship"; and by way of evidence offers the following particulars: "For all manner of hunting thou bearest the prize, and of all measures of blowing thou art the beginning, of all the terms of hunting and hawking ye are the beginner, of all instruments of music ye are the best."[49] Even if we allow for the fact that Tristram seems to have done service in the hagiography of chivalric romance as a sort of patron saint of hunting, this is still a surprising list of qualities for one whose feats were in the stories mostly of arms.

---

soldierly aspect of his tradition to the eclipse of the courtly. George Cary, *The Medieval Alexander* (Cambridge, 1956), p. 241.

[46] Hicks, chap. x.

[47] Gist, pp. 7-8.

[48] R. T. Davies, "Malory's 'Vertuouse Love,'" *Studies in Philology*, LIII (July, 1956), 459-469.

[49] *Works of Malory*, pp. 571 and 1473. See also pp. 375 and 1445.

Nor is Malory so nearly unconscious of the value of money as the traditions of chivalric literature would lead us to expect. In a passage Vinaver believes unique in Arthurian romance, Launcelot is admonished that "it hath cost my lady the queen twenty thousand pounds the seeking of you."[50]

Comparatively practical as his approach to the chivalric tradition seems consistently to have been, it could not avoid the religious implications of knighthood. Nor should we expect it to have done so. Malory would not have been a man of his age if he had not accepted the close relationship between the chivalric and the Christian tradition. Indeed, on many points they were identical, so thoroughly had the originally somewhat barbarous ideal of the feudal warrior been assimilated into the Christian synthesis: to separate the secular from the religious elements in the resulting fusion is to reflect the modern historian's analytical capacity rather than the configuration of the medieval mind.

Although in emphasizing the practical bent of Malory's thought Professor Vinaver has called attention to an essential characteristic of his mind, in stressing also his secularity he may have overstated his thesis.[51] Malory's handling of the quest of the Holy Grail retains, it is true, little of the theological subtlety of the French source;[52] and he by no means shared the religious preoccupation of the French monastic author. Perhaps he failed even to appreciate the finer points of doctrine propounded by the latter. Certainly he condensed the theological argument wherever possible and added few points of his own. And it is hard to escape the feeling that Malory returned to the stories of Arthurian adventure with palpable relief after his sojourn on the spiritual heights of the Quest.[53] But he

[50] *Ibid.,* pp. 831 and 1518.
[51] See his introduction and notes to *The Quest of the Holy Grail.*
[52] On the French Queste, see Albert Pauphilet, *Études sur la Queste del Saint Graal* (Paris, 1921).
[53] On this highly debatable point, see E. K. Chambers, *Sir Thomas Wyatt and Some Collected Studies* (London, 1933), p. 33; Vinaver, *Malory,* p. 84, and *Works of Malory,* pp. 1521 ff. Cf. Moorman; D. S. Brewer, "Form in the *Morte Darthur,*" *Medium Aevum,* XXI (1952), 14-24.

seems also to have recognized the importance of the religious issue. It would have been surprising, indeed, if he had not. The medieval knight was as concerned as anybody else about his salvation—especially so in his later years when the affairs of the rough-and-tumble world had lost some of their power to excite. The elderly knight-turned-hermit is a stock figure in medieval literature. He is the man to whom the young knight in Lull's manual goes for advice on his worldly as well as his spiritual duties.[54] In real life we find Earl Rivers, the Anthony Woodville, Lord Scales, of the famous tourney with the Bastard of Burgundy in 1467, turning in his later life to the service of God, planning a voyage to Portugal "to be a day upon the Saracens," going on a pilgrimage to Rome, wearing a hair shirt, writing divers ballads "against the seven deadly sins" and occupying himself in the translating of other morally elevating works.[55] Both Henry V, the model of the crowned knight, and Edward IV, the would-be paladin, nourished the chimerical plan of a crusade—the former no doubt with greater sincerity than the latter, if sincerity may be at all accurately assessed where such conventional gestures are concerned. What, then, more natural than that the elderly Malory, deprived of accustomed freedom, with plenty of leisure to contemplate his own experience—perhaps with quite justifiable misgivings—would at least give some thought to the spiritual side of the knightly life.

What seems to the modern observer to be an element of instability in the medieval character, a tendency to oscillate, often with some violence, between extremes of worldly and spiritual endeavor, is in reality the result of a feeling that both are part, and a necessary part, of the life of the true knight. The man of the later middle ages recognized only too clearly the conflict, potential if not actual, between the concerns of the

---

[54] See also *Works of Malory*, p. 1074 for an example from Malory himself. It might also be worth remembering that Launcelot likewise ends his days as a man of God.

[55] *DNB*. See also Caxton's epilogue to *Cordyale* in Crotch, pp. 38-40.

world and those of the spirit; and there was more than a trace of morbidity in the tensions from which, as a result, he suffered. But he would have found any attempt to define a "secular mind" or a "secular civilization"[56] quite outside his intellectual experience. Secular interests, like the sins to which they were traditionally linked, could be separated from spiritual interests and the virtues that went with them; but they seldom were; for both had an essential part in the primarily ethical problem of human life. The City of God might preoccupy the religious enthusiast to the virtual exclusion of all else. The City of Man could never be considered in and for itself; and even the most worldly of medieval writers could only in the most extended sense of the word be termed "secular" in their thought.

And so Malory found himself facing quite naturally, as many another sinful old knight had faced, the problem of salvation. But let us not overemphasize his religiosity either. It is an open question whether he would ever have gotten around to this sort of thing had it not been for the fact that he had the French *Queste* in front of him as a burning example. And his reaction to the great questions of religion is not without equivocation. That fact should not surprise us too greatly when we remember that the Church itself had often equivocated in order to rationalize the life of the world, which, by strict definition, was one with the flesh and the devil and therefore evil; and it was committed to a kind of humane duplicity in its treatment of the necessity of such an evil as sex. Malory follows his French source in finding in the character of Galahad the embodiment of the heavenly chivalry to which no "earthly sinful" knight[57] could attain. Yet he refuses

[56] If Vinaver overstates his case regarding Malory's secularity of approach, Moorman (*op. cit.*) has erred even more in the opposite direction. The same argument, in other words, that makes one uneasy about Vinaver's position makes Moorman's contention that Malory's purpose was to chronicle the "rise, decay, and fall of a secular civilization" (p. 497) quite untenable. I am also at a loss to see, as Moorman asserts (p. 497 n. 4), that Tucker, Brewer, and Lewis share his conjecture on this point.

[57] See, for examples of the implied contrast between the sinless knight and the earthly, *Works of Malory,* pp. 863 and 948.

to condemn the terrestrial chivalry embodied in Launcelot, the best of earthly knights. Launcelot, despite his "instability"[58] and his sins of the flesh, was able to experience much of the exhilaration of the Grail quest and to retire from it with some solid satisfaction even though he came just short of his goal.[59] It is for him, and probably also for Malory, another adventure, the supreme adventure, in the life of the earthly knight, and one for which he was evermore the better for having undertaken.[60]

It may be that C. S. Lewis touched the heart of the matter when he suggested that Malory had a triple scale of values: the bad, represented by King Mark, the good, by Launcelot, and the best, by Galahad. Much of the confusion regarding Malory's thought has stemmed, he feels, from a failure to recognize this fact and therefore a tendency to force his ethical statements into the modern scheme of good and bad. This triple scale, he warned, would of course become "good, bad, worst" if read backward.[61] The important thing was, however, to understand that the earthly knight with whom Malory sympathized most deeply was a mixture of good and bad, like most other men. Malory does not condone the sin of Launcelot, neither his pride, his illicit love, nor his "instability." But he remains for him the best of "earthly sinful" men and his hero—a tragic hero, but one in whom the good greatly outweighed the bad. Like others of his cultural tradition Malory accepted the relative unattainability of the best without becoming dissatisfied with the good. To have done otherwise would have been to condemn and forsake the world which it was the part only of the saint or the absolute moralist to do.

---

[58] On Launcelot's "instability," which seems especially to have concerned Malory, see *ibid.*, pp. 948 and 1204 and p. 1551. See also introduction, p. lxxxvii. Cf. Moorman p. 503; Tucker, p. 394.

[59] *Works of Malory*, pp. 1523-1524.

[60] Cf. the somewhat less qualified statement by Vinaver, *ibid.*, p. 1522. Cf. Tucker, p. 396.

[61] Review of *Sir Thomas Wyatt and Some Collected Studies* by E. K. Chambers, *Med. Aevum*, III (1934), 237-240, 239.

Malory's practical mind replaced *"le chevaillerie celestiale"* of his French source with the practical formula "knightly deeds and virtuous living."[62] Yet he recognized that in this ideal of knightly conduct there lay the intimations of a perfection that transcended this unstable world.

Malory's mind, and no doubt also that of the late medieval English gentry among whom he lived, had little in common with the thirteenth-century Cistercian monk who wrote the French *Queste*.[63] That militant man of God accepted the concept of knighthood, but interpreted it in spiritual terms. He wrote at a time when monasticism still spoke in clear and absolute terms, drawing an inhumanly sharp line between the world and the spirit and proclaiming a spiritual crusade against the flesh and the devil. His was the era of the Knights Templar, of the crusading, semi-military orders that served as the shock troops of a militant Christianity. Yet he spoke also the language of the Church in its condemnation of fighting as a chivalric sport. The ecclesiastical authorities could not but recognize in the military ideal of chivalry and in the glorification of homicide that found expression in the epic romances of chivalry something thoroughly foreign to the Christian idealization of peace and the Christian prohibition of killing. They even saw in the tournament a mere rehearsal for manslaughter and war, and took steps—quite ineffective ones, it turned out—to stop them. The author of the *Queste* found in Galahad the perfect embodiment of the spiritual knight, the man of utter purity, uncontaminated by the worldly accretions that vitiated the chivalric ideal as it found expression in actual practice. His was essentially a monastic chivalry which emphasized the ascetic element, always a part of the mature chivalric ideal, to the point where it lost contact with the life

[62] *Works of Malory*, pp. 1522-1523; p. 891 and commentary, p. 1539. See also p. 931 and commentary, p. 1546; p. 934 and commentary, p. 1547; p. 945 and commentary, p. 1549; p. 955 and commentary, p. 1552; p. 1608; pp. 1276-1277. See also R. T. Davies "Malory's Launcelot and the Noble Way of the World," *Review of English Studies*, N.S., VI (Oct. 1955), 356-364.

[63] See the excellent analysis in Pauphilet, pp. 27-84, of the author's ideas and their place in the contemporary monastic system.

of ordinary sinful men—especially the life of the average knight who, if we may believe the preachers, was more than ordinarily sinful.

Malory accepted the idea that there was a heavenly chivalry that lay beyond the chivalry of worldly affairs; but he did not let the former preoccupy him to the neglect of the latter. He would, I think, have found it odd and incomprehensible that anyone should raise the question. Perhaps his position may become clearer if we examine it side by side with a more explicit statement made by his contemporary Stephen Scrope. In his dedication to Sir John Fastolf of a translation of *The Epistle of Othea to Hector* (a treatise on the knightly virtues) he suggests that that good knight who had spent his active life "in keeping and defending faith, the right of the church, the land, the country and the common welfare of it," as a result of which he had become "noble and worshipful among the order of chivalry," should now, with age and feebleness upon him so that he could no longer do the active work of a knight, occupy his time in "ghostly chivalry of deeds of arms spiritual, as in contemplation of moral wisdom and exercising ghostly works which that may enforce and cause you to be called to the order of knighthood that shall perpetually endure. . . ."[64] To Malory, as to Scrope, there could be no conflict between the knighthood of this world and the demands of the life everlasting. Only when the search for "worship" had degenerated into pride, the play of arms into mere homicide, and love into lechery, only that is, when the virtuous life which was common to both the chivalric and the Christian traditions had become compromised through the weakness of the flesh or the promptings of the devil could the chivalric life be held to imperil the soul.[65]

If it was, even incidentally, Malory's purpose to use the example of chivalric tradition to point the way toward a better

[64] Ed. G. F. Warner, Roxburghe Club (London, 1904).
[65] See the substantially similar position taken by Tucker, pp. 393 and 396-397.

England, he was undertaking an ambitious and from our point of view a not very realistic, task. H. S. Bennett was quite right when he said the age "was no fruitful soil in which to replant the ideal of chivalry,"[66] and E. K. Chambers no less so when he asserted that the England of the Paston letters needed a strong king, not a return to chivalry.[67] We must remember, however, that Malory himself was not aware of these difficulties. His own experience in the Wars of the Roses, we are told,[68] must surely have taught him the futility of such a project. But did it? Malory was, after all, a man of his day. He could not see, as the historian can, that he was already leaving the medieval countryside and nearing the outskirts of a new era. He was no more able than any of his contemporaries to recognize the signs of social change or to interpret the obvious decline of chivalric morale as anything more than the spiritual decay always to be expected in the society of sinful mankind, a society ordained in a fixed framework in which the only variable factor was the frail and fickle nature of man himself. If he looked to the past for the Golden Age of chivalry, that was no more than social critics did habitually in the later Middle Ages: when we see, for example, Langland or Gower exhort the men of their day to seek the Christian tradition in the days of its purity somewhere in a bygone Age of Gold,[69] we need not assume that they had given up as a bad job the attempt to perpetuate that tradition. It is very doubtful, indeed, whether Malory thought in terms of "replanting" chivalric ideals any more than the moralistic writers considered their task to be one of replanting Christian principles. Neither in fact, had been uprooted—ailing, yes; up-

[66] *Chaucer and the Fifteenth Century,* p. 200.
[67] *English Literature at the Close of the Middle Ages,* pp. 195-197.
[68] Bennett, p. 200.
[69] See for examples, Gower, *Confessio Amantis,* lines, 663-1088; *Vox Clam.,* Book VII, chaps. i and xxii (cf. Book VI, chaps. xix-xxi); Lydgate, *Minor Poems,* II, 844-845. Illustrations in fifteenth century manuscripts indicate that the artists were not without a sense of change, at least in the externals of knightly life. J. G. Mann, "Instances of Antiquarian Feeling in Medieval and Renaissance Art," *Archeological Journal,* LXXXIX (1932), 254-274.

rooted, no. Chambers is perfectly right in saying that Malory was no political thinker nor even a commentator. But he was none the less concerned with the ethical value of chivalry in his own day; and it would be well to place him, for historical purposes at least, in the company of such chivalric apologists as the authors of *The Boke of Noblesse* or Caxton himself rather than to picture him as a disillusioned soldier-turned-storyteller who, though he "occasionally exclaims against the times . . . for the most part . . . retires into a world of long ago."[70]

. . .

Although Malory and Caxton easily take precedence among those who, along with their many other objectives, sought in chivalric example the means of social regeneration, this chapter would not be complete without some mention of two men of a younger generation who carried some of the same chivalric prejudices into the less congenial atmosphere of sixteenth-century England. Stephen Hawes and John Bourchier, Lord Berners,[71] had in their youth absorbed the warmth of the chivalric Indian Summer. To the end of their days they spoke the language of a chivalric culture. But it is apparent that they had also felt the cooler breezes of the new intellectual season. They stand, in fact, just at the end of the era in which it was still possible to take chivalry seriously; and they already show signs of the coming tendency to treat its traditions either ro-

---

[70] Bennett, p. 200. E. K. Chambers also refers to the deliberate archaism of his return to the chivalric materials. *Sir Thomas Malory*, The English Association, Pamphlet No. 51 (Jan., 1922), p. 3. Cf. Vinaver, *Malory*, p. 55 and chap. v, *passim*.

[71] Biographical data on Hawes is so scanty as to be all but negligible. Such as there is may be found in W. E. Mead's introduction to *The Pastime of Pleasure*, E.E.T.S., O.S., No. 173 (1928), pp. xiii-xix. A survey of earlier scholarship and criticism concerning Hawes may be found in E. A. Burkart, *Stephen Hawes's "The Pastime of Pleasure"* (London, 1899). For Berners, the aristocrat, soldier, diplomat, and administrator. the situation is far otherwise. See *DNB;* S. L. Lee's introduction to *The Boke of Duke Huon of Burdeux*, E.E.T.S., E.S., XL (1882). Other critical treatment may be found in D. Greenwood's chapter in *Cambridge History of English Literature*, II, 332-340; R. M. Smith, *Froissart and the English Chronicle Play* (New York, 1915); W. P. Ker, ed., *The Chronicle of Froissart* (London, 1901-3), I, xiv-xxxiv.

mantically, largely for pleasure, or as something at best but supplementary to the broader vision of society of which the mind of Renaissance England was capable. They are in consequence difficult to assess.

Hawes, by far the more original and important of the two, is especially difficult to estimate in this particular connection. He entitled his principal work, and the only one we have any reason to study here, *The Passetyme of Pleasure;* and he prefaced it with some dedicatory verses to Henry VII (he wrote it in 1506 and the first printed edition appeared in 1509) in which he indicates that his chief purpose in writing "the feigned fable" is "to eschew idleness." Add to that his protestations of excessive modesty concerning his own ability to compose anything worth reading and his reiterated admiration for Lydgate as the "flower of eloquence," and the reader is prepared for anything or nothing. Certainly he is not prepared for the rather serious, very dull, and in many respects oddly original bit of didacticism that follows. He must remember that readers of that day would not have been misled by this false front of ineptitude, even of frivolity. It was, they would recognize, a conventional affectation, especially dear to the heart of Hawes's model, the "Monk of Bury." It was simply Hawes's way of saying that he was about to write a fictitious tale with a meaning attached. To eschew idleness was not merely to keep oneself busy, but to be occupied at something improving. The public of early Tudor England was in this respect as "Victorian" as that of the mid-nineteenth century.

Hawes was in fact experimenting with conventional forms, combining the allegory of courtly love, the romance of chivalric adventure, and the encyclopaedic bent of scholastic education, and working it all into the larger, but still familiar, pattern of the "pilgrimage of the life of man." The result was something thoroughly medieval in its components, yet in its totality foreshadowing, if only dimly, the kind of thing Spenser brought to mature perfection in *The Fairie Queene*.[72] The seriousness of his purpose becomes a little more apparent, too, when one reads the full title which, in the later editions at any rate, proclaims the "historie of graunde Amoure and la bell Pucel, called the Pastime of pleasure, containing the knowledge of the seven sciences, and the course of man's life in the worlde. . . ." To the 1554 edition the printer added his own introductory address in which he offers the book to the gentle reader specifically for his "better instruction."[73] A more exact idea of what Hawes himself had in mind by way of instruction appears in the course of the story when the ideal knight is urged

> . . . to renew that hath been long decayed
> The flower of chivalry.[74]

Hawes's purpose, like his materials, was medieval. On the virtues of chivalry and the need for some revival of chivalric virtue he and Caxton were explicitly at one. He planned simply to set forth chivalric examples in a form of his own composition rather than in translation. By so doing he incidentally made it a good deal easier for us to see the shape of his mind reflected in his writing.

As in the case of both Caxton and Malory it has been customary for critics and historians of literature to make Hawes a romanticist in his treatment of chivalry, a man whose "imagination has been stirred by the ideals of an earlier day," whose emotional commitment to the decaying institutions of chivalry prompts him to deliberate archaism and turns his attention from the present to the past.[75] This is more nearly a valid description of Hawes than of either Malory or Caxton. For a romanticist he was, by temperament if not by circumstance. He loves the hazy atmosphere of chivalric romance. He makes

---

[72] Murison, p. 228; C. S. Lewis, *The Allegory of Love*, p. 279; Mead, pp. xix and xliii.

[73] Mead, pp. xxxi-xxxiii.

[74] *Pastime*, lines 2985-2986.

[75] Mead, p. xix; Lewis, p. 279; W. J. Courthope, *A History of English Poetry* (New York, 1920), p. 91; Cf. Murison, p. 228.

the most of its emancipation from the precision of time and from the logic of plot. Perhaps, too, the ideals of chivalry appealed to him more for their archaism than for their immediate relevance. It is hard to be sure with Hawes. In his work, as in that of Dudley, Skelton, André, and most other English writers of the very early sixteenth century, there is apparent a baffling ambivalence, a combination of medieval and Renaissance qualities that makes it hard to interpret the author's mind and still maintain the familiar historical categories.

Yet it is dangerous to assume, even with Hawes, that a romantic turn of mind necessarily involves a deliberate effort to seek in a bygone age the satisfaction that cannot be found in the present. Conscious archaism implies a concept of history too modern for most Englishmen in the reign of Henry VII. It marks Spenser's choice of setting for *The Faerie Queene,* a setting no doubt as unreal to his Elizabethan readers at it is to us.[76] The medieval mind (and Hawes's was in most respects medieval) could ordinarily comprehend change only if described in terms of decay. Social development of the kind that in Hawes's own day was bringing a new order into being was quite another matter and one much more apparent to modern historians than to his own contemporaries. It was typical of medieval thought to look from a present in which things are not as they should be to a "golden" past which differed from the present only in that deterioration had not yet set in. To see in the past a different society, no matter how strongly it may appeal in some of its aspects to the imagination of the present day, is romanticism in its peculiarly modern form, the origins of which may be seen in the history of Renaissance ideas but hardly farther back than that.[77] Hawes, like Malory and Caxton, could be considered as one who seeks

[76] L. Bradner, *Edmund Spenser and "The Faerie Queene"* (Chicago, 1948), p. 7 and pp. 71 ff.

[77] The author has considered in one of its aspects the problem of the recognition of change in society in his article "Realism in the 'Commonwealth' Literature of Early Tudor England." It remains a problem worth more systematic investigation.

to "renew that hath been long decayed," rather than as one who would resurrect that which hath been long dead. There is a difference. Rather than insist upon so debatable a point, however, the sensible course would be to examine how Hawes actually treats the chivalric material. Such an examination will, I believe, reveal that the ideal knight Hawes had in mind is in many ways a different kind of person from the almost exclusively military figure envisaged by most of his predecessors.

Since for the very best of reasons *The Pastime of Pleasure* is nowadays seldom read, a brief interpretative summary of the story might be in order. Primarily an allegory of man's adult life rather than either a chivalric romance or an allegory of courtly love, it begins with a young man about to set out upon his career. Although not of the upper aristocracy, he is clearly of the gentry; and the initial decision he is free to make is between the active and the contemplative life. By the contemplative life we are apparently supposed to understand what had generally been meant by the term throughout the Middle Ages, namely, the life of clerical asceticism and religious meditation. We are in Hawes not yet to the point where, as for Thomas Starkey, the contemplative life could be considered that of philosophy in the Platonic sense, or of purely scholarly endeavor.[78] He hesitates, but chooses finally the active way, the way of worldly dignity, of chivalry, and courtly love. It is, then, to be an allegory of distinctly secular life. The young man, who, by the way, is called La Graunde Amoure, is told in a dream of the beauty and virtue of La Bell Pucell, a lady of higher degree than himself. He falls in love with her at once and decides to find her. But he cannot proceed immediately to the Tower Perilous where lives his lady. First he must render himself worthy through education—the education of a gentleman and knight. It turns out to be the standard education of the medieval schools, consisting

---

[78] See the debate on the subject in Starkey's *Dialogue.*

of the seven liberal arts: grammar, logic, rhetoric, arithmetic, music, geometry, and astronomy. Nearly half the poem is devoted to this for the most part conventional course of instruction. Midway through, in the first semester of his junior year, as it were, he finally meets La Bell Pucell in the Tower of Music. She returns his love with somewhat less than the usual courtly reluctance. Now it would not do at all to leave things in this highly satisfactory state, else the rest of the story would lose momentum. So for reasons which need not detain us they bid each other a tearful farewell and the young man works out his frustration on geometry. Having completed his scholastic training, Graunde Amoure seeks knighthood at the court of a king who promises to see that he gets instruction in arms. His progress is rapid—more so, to judge from the relatively brief treatment given it, than in the more cerebral sciences; and the king finally knights him and instructs him in the principles of chivalry. From then on, Graunde Amoure goes on a series of weird adventures, as befits a true knight-errant, including the usual fights with giants and monsters. It all somehow leads up to a reunion with La Bell Pucell whom he straightway marries. The rest of the story proceeds more rapidly through the knight's later years in which he takes a none too knightly interest in making money. Finally death catches up with him and we hear a few sententious closing speeches from Fame, Time, and Eternity.

Although Hawes reserves the word "chivalry" for the specifically military side of the knight's training, we are justified in considering his unusual, if uninspired, poem an allegory of the chivalric way of life. In that way of life the traditions of courtly love play a large part; and Hawes's mind was too conventional not to seize upon the ready-at-hand theme of the love allegory.[79] It is worth noticing however, that it fails to dominate his work to the extent that it does the earlier

[79] On this tradition, see C. S. Lewis's brilliant treatment in *The Allegory of Love*.

allegories or, for that matter the *Court of Love* and William Nevill's *Castell of Pleasure,* both roughly contemporary with his own poem. He absorbs the courtly love theme into an allegory of human life and enlivens it with the constantly popular element of knightly adventure in the realm of things strange and wonderful.

It would be tempting to conclude that Hawes's decision to paint a broader canvas reflects the taste of the court society for which he wrote. (He was groom of the chamber to Henry VII and no doubt kept at court because of his literary ability.) Perhaps it is true, as J. M. Berdan suggested, that "the old formal erotic allegory was out of touch with the ideas of the new age" and that the *Court of Love,* though artistically superior to *The Pastime of Pleasure,* therefore survives in only a single manuscript, whereas Hawes's poem went through several editions in the course of the century.[80]   But this conclusion, though comforting to our sense of evolutionary propriety, is a bit too facile. Nevill's allegory was even more conventional and much less readable, yet it seems to have enjoyed considerable popularity and was reissued at least once.[81] It is true that, in the dialogue between the printer and the author which serves as a prologue to the edition of 1518, Copland, the printer, professes to question the project from a business point of view. "Books of love innumerable printed be/ I mean of ladies and many a hardy knight." The trouble is that people do not buy books any more, but prefer to spend their money and time in all sorts of more or less disreputable amusements.[82] This, however, is simply the lament of a commercial printer, easily recognized by anyone who has had dealings with their modern counterparts. If anything it bears witness to the popularity of a genre which could still inspire "innumerable" publications. In many respects, indeed, Hawes was probably ahead of the

[80] Berdan, pp. 74-92.

[81] Roberta D. Cornelius, ed., *The Castell of Plesure,* E.E.T.S., O.S., No. 179 (1930), introd., pp. 43-50.

[82] *Ibid.,* lines 29-49.

popular taste of his day, incredible as that may seem. It is also true, of course, that courtly taste was in the process of rapid change in response to the many new stimuli arriving from the Continent, and especially from Italy. In any case, Hawes seems to have enjoyed a considerable reputation among the courtly class. Thomas Feylde, in the prologue to his *Conversation between a Lover and a Jay,* written not too long after this time, wrote with real respect of both Nevill and "Young Stephen Hawes" who "treated of love so clerkely and well."[83]

But the problem is more than one of mere literary tradition. Hawes spoke to a generation to which chivalric ideas still meant something. Like Malory, Hawes's readers were likely to demand of chivalric institutions some practical bearing on life. They were not yet able to accept those traditions in an entirely romantic spirit. Nor was Hawes, I think. The courtly love tradition becomes in *The Pastime of Pleasure* almost a bourgeois convention. The two principals in the romance look forward not to the sort of guerrilla action against society common in the older, especially the French literature, their not quite licit love maintained against the stiffest of social odds, but to marriage. More than that they live happily. As his passions wanes with the years, Graunde Amoure simply falls back unchivalrously on the aging man of the world's second line of defense and devotes himself wholeheartedly to the amassing of wealth.[84] He and his wife become, then, the typical married pair, the embodiment of the "middle class" values already typical of the English gentry. There had been a tendency in this direction in English thought for a long time— even before, as C. S. Lewis put it, Chaucer "brought the old romance of adultery to the very frontiers of the modern . . . romance of marriage."[85] The authors of the Middle English romances seem not to have been deeply influenced by the

---

[83] The poem was printed by Wynkyn de Worde (n.d.) and reprinted for the Roxburghe Club by T. F. Dibdin (1818). Burkart, p. 11.

[84] *Pastime,* lines 5348-5382.

[85] Lewis, *Allegory,* p. 197.

French concept of courtly love and where they treat the subject
it tends to be in a context of marriage rather than of adultery.[86]
Such an attitude agreed with the prevailing practicality of
the late medieval English mind. Malory, as we have seen,
did not put himself out greatly to develop the courtly theme in
the *Morte Darthur,* if indeed he was much interested in it.
And Caxton took pains to publish the Knight de la Tour
Landry's quite anticourtly advice to his daughters who, like
those of the English Pastons, had too much to do in getting
husbands and working out with them some sensible *modus
vivendi* to be much concerned with the romantic artificiality
of love "by the book." In Hawes's work the story culminates
not only in marriage, but in bourgeois marriage. In it the
"wild Provençal wine"[87] has been tamed indeed, and more
than a little watered.

For our purposes, however, the important fact about
Hawes's treatment of the chivalric values is not his handling
of the courtly love theme but his emphasis on the education of
the knight. As I have suggested at an earlier point in this
study, the courtly tradition had, like the Christian element,
been grafted on the parent stock of a basically feudal chivalry
and could again be separated from it. Both could thrive on
their own roots, for they stood for needs more nearly universal
in Western society than those of the feudal knight whose practical function could not long survive the medieval society he
lived to protect. What marks the critical point in the decline
of chivalry, the point, that is, at which it ceases to be a deterioration within a still accepted, largely unchallenged complex
of ideas and institutions, and becomes merely the decorously
conservative clothing worn by an entirely new person, is the
passing of the feudal knight as the ideal of aristocratic society.
On this point, if we take the trouble to look for it, Hawes can
provide considerable food for thought.

The education of Graunde Amoure occupies, as we have

[86] Gist, pp. 7-8; Davies "Malory's 'Vertuouse Love.'"
[87] Lewis, p. 197.

seen, a very large part of this allegory of the life of man—or, to be more exact, of the gentry. Admittedly the dullest part of the poem,[88] it is also one of the most original when considered in the context in which Hawes places it; and it may well have been the part closest to Hawes's own interest. I shall have more to say about it in a later chapter, for it is worth more than a passing glance.[89] For the moment, however, certain points should be noticed. Here again Hawes reveals his ability to give to a fundamentally medieval tradition a peculiarly Renaissance twist. The idea of including general information in an allegory of love was an old one. Jean de Meun, who continued the *Romance of the Rose* begun by Guillaume de Loris, could not resist the temptation to work into his poem the encyclopedic erudition of the medieval schools. It is doubtless to this, the classic tradition of erotic allegory, that Hawes believed he was contributing. The system of education he describes is, moreover, of the same scholastic variety, still the standard curriculum of the English universities. Yet it is not introduced as a digression or, as in de Meun's work, a series of digressions in an allegory primarily of love, but as an integral part of an allegory encompassing the entire life of a gentleman. Its purpose is not simply instruction, but the instruction directed not to the end of courtly success but to that of success in the complex world of Hawes's own England.

To recognize this is to become aware of the distance that Hawes has traveled beyond the chivalric education traditionally prescribed in the late medieval manuals of knighthood. That the knight must be educated in the liberal arts is a considerable step in advance. Such education, formerly confined largely to clerks, was now to an increasing extent sought by men of the governing class who, like the hero of Hawes's poem, had chosen the life of action in the world of affairs. That Hawes refers repeatedly to the practical application of the liberal arts, especially that of rhetoric, to the affairs not only of the knight

[88] *Ibid.*, p. 282.
[89] See below, chap. vi.

himself (whose worldly activities, be it remembered, extended well beyond those of the medieval knight), but of the commonwealth as well, places him with the new generation of humanistically trained men who during the earlier half of the sixteenth century gave to English education a new orientation toward the vastly enlarged demands and opportunities presented by the Tudor state.

Hawes is thus one of the finest specimens of that perennial hybrid, the "transitional figure." The term is often abused, being made to label with some show of scholarly respectability that which has defied analysis. But with Hawes we are on reasonably solid terrain because we have at hand what bears all the signs of being the distillation of his entire social philosophy. The case of Lord Berners is more difficult and, unfortunately, not so rewarding. For Berners was simply a translator—a good one, but not one who injected much of himself, except his sense of style and a love of his subject, into his work.

One classic of medieval history, one especially famous as a mirror of chivalric action and the source of chivalric inspiration for generations to come, Caxton failed to make available to his contemporaries in their own tongue. He advised the young gentlemen of England to read Froissart's chronicles for the example of knightly deeds they contained, but he did not print or translate them. No doubt he preferred the more "English" and certainly popular *Brut* or the more general history of the world contained in Higden's *Polychronicon*. The task of translating Froissart was therefore left to a later hand. In 1519 Lord Berners, "a martial man, well seen in all military discipline," undertook it, and in 1523 the first edition issued from Pynson's press.

Whether this translation is for our purpose more important as evidence of the lively interest in things chivalric at the court of the young Henry VIII or as the vehicle by means of which chivalric example was passed on to successive generations of the English gentry, thus contributing, as it certainly did, to the romantic vogue of chivalry in the era of Elizabeth, is a moot question. That its publication was an important event in the history of chivalric thought is, however, uncontestable. For, to a greater extent than most of the other chronicles the men of early Tudor England were likely to read—Fabyan's, for example, or, to use one of a very different sort, Polydore Vergil's—that of Froissart was a record of chivalric action, and, by implication if not otherwise, a commentary on chivalric ideals. Only the histories of Henry V's reign, especially the translation made in 1512 of Tito Livio's *Vita Henrici V,* could begin to rival Froissart as a source of chivalric inspiration, and even there the national or patriotic element tended to outweigh the pure tradition of knight-errantry. Froissart's mind dealt by preference with the chivalric moment, the "fine feat of arms" rather than with the clash of national interests, with the knightly motive rather than with policy.

Froissart himself was quite explicit as to his purpose in writing the chronicles: it was, to quote from Berners' translation, "to the intent that the honorable and noble adventures of feats of arms, done and achieved by the wars of France and England should notably be registered, and put in perpetual memory, whereby the prewe [gallant] and hardy may have example to encourage them in their well doing."[90] Neither Caxton nor Berners was willing to restrict the scope and the purpose of history to such an extent. Indeed it is fully as important that they both insisted on the service of the historian to the national community as it is that they hoped to derive chivalric example from the record of the past. In his general preface Berners goes even farther than Caxton in demonstrating the value of history, considered as the stored-up experience of the ages, for the civil life of a country. He also recognizes the possibility of deriving benefit from "the monuments of writing," apparently other than history, through

[90] *Froissart,* I, 17-18.

which "many men have been moved, some to build cities, some to devise and establish laws right profitable, necessary, behooveful for the human life; some other to find new arts, crafts, and sciences, very requisite to the use of mankind." Here we get just a whiff of that faith in the creative intelligence of man which was to be a characteristic of much pamphlet writing in the early Tudor period, and which far transcended the feudal and chivalric conception of government and the governing class as essentially protective in their function. Berners' preface[91] seems, indeed, oddly out of line with Froissart's, the breadth of its outlook to some extent belied by the relatively narrow gauge of the translation to follow.

By the time he wrote the preface to his second volume,[92] Berners seems to have reverted to a more traditional, more limited, and more distinctly chivalric, perhaps also a more congenial point of view. He congratulates himself for having put his time to good account in translating Froissart. The wars between England and France therein recounted are, he maintains, far superior to other wars "for knightly feats, manhood, and humanity." He is pleased that "my noble countrymen of England" take pleasure in reading the "worthy and knightly deeds of their valiant ancestors." Above all he finds satisfaction in the encouragement given him by Henry VIII, who had originally "commanded" the work, and who shared this interest in the record of knightly deeds: "and herein his Highness taketh singular pleasure to behold how his worthy subjects, seeing in history the very famous deeds, as it were images represent their valiant ancestors, contend by vigorous virtue and manhood to follow, yea to pass them if they may." To Berners, as to Caxton, and perhaps Henry VIII himself, history is still to an overwhelming extent a matter of chivalry teaching by example.

If Berners had written only a few years earlier (he was born in 1467 or 1469) he would probably have worked with Caxton,

[91] *Ibid.*, 3-7.
[92] *Ibid.*, IV, 3-4.

for he was of the same breed as those "many noble and divers gentlemen of this realm of England" who, Caxton says, talked him into printing the stories of King Arthur's court. We do not, of course, know who these men were, but we may assume they were interested alike in the history of England and in the example of chivalry. Caxton certainly stresses both in his prologue to *Kyng Arthur*. In his early years Berners breathed the same social and political atmosphere as did Caxton and his patrons. He was, in a sense, one of the last of that line of pre-Reformation knight-scholars who by virtue of their scholarship point to a new era in English culture, but by virtue of their preoccupation with chivalric values belong in the waning Middle Ages.[93]

We would, however, miss the subtler problem presented by Berners if we look only at his translation of Froissart. He also translated *The Boke of Duke Huon of Burdeux, The hystory of the most noble and valyant knyght Arthur of lytell brytayne, The Castell of Love,* and *The golden boke of Marcus Aurelius*.[94] These he completed, along with the Froissart, while he served in his later years as deputy general of Calais. With plenty of time on his hands, and no compelling reason to devote himself to scholarship, he set to work on the kind of things that he and the several members of the English aristocracy who, he says, suggested the titles, would find to their taste.

With the exception of the *Golden Book of Marcus Aurelius,* they all belong to the chivalric tradition. *The Castell of Love* is a courtly allegory in the familiar form. The two chivalric romances, *Duke Huon* and *Arthur of Little Britain,* belong to the period in which that genre had become rather heavily encumbered by the magical and supernatural element—so

---

[93] Anthony Woodville, Lord Rivers, is a good example: in his youth a famous jouster and soldier, in his mature years a diplomat and scholar, and one of Caxton's most respected patrons and collaborators. Except for his interest in the culture of Renaissance Italy, Tiptoft would be another.

[94] The *Duke Huon* is available in the E.E.T.S. edition of S. L. Lee; see n. 71 above; *Arthur of lytell brytayne* (1555), S.T.C. 807; *Golden boke of Marcus Aurelius* (1535), S.T.C. 12436; *Castell of Love* (1540), S.T.C. 21740.

much so indeed as to remove the chivalric element also to some
extent from the realm of reality. Berners professed to be
bothered about this supernatural quality. Concerning the
Arthur of Little Britain, "wherein seemeth to be so many im-
possibilities," he expressed particular doubt. Like Hawes, he
felt it necessary to justify writing such "feigned matter" on the
broad ground that it helped in "eschewing idleness," which
is "the mother of all vice."[95] He retained, it would seem, some
of that skeptical and utilitarian habit which was so deeply
ingrained in the English mind. Malory had for the most part
underplayed the supernatural, the marvelous element in the
romances he adapted;[96] and Caxton had treated all the romances of chivalry with the seriousness of one who looks to
literature only incidentally for the sheer pleasure of reading.

But it is a question how seriously Berners and his friends
took these pious protestations. The matter of the *Arthur,*
Berners argues, is after all no more unebelievable than that of
many other stories of knightly adventures he has read. Despite his naïve concern with the distinction between truth and
fiction, he loves the story; and so presumably did the other
people for whom he wrote, for the romances continued to be
popular in England throughout the century. Amusement was
for him, much more than for his predecessors, a worthwhile
reason for translating such material; and we are at liberty to
believe that he labored as much for this purpose as to preserve
in the memory of his countrymen "the chivalrous feats and
martial prowess of the victorious knights of times past."[97] We
are watching at this point a development in the English mind
of considerable significance: namely, the gradual rise of that
truly romantic attitude toward the chivalric heritage which in
the course of the century made it possible for a basically nonchivalric society to take the liveliest interest in chivalric tales.
The Elizabethan reading public could thank Berners not so

[95] *Arthur of Little Britain,* preface.
[96] Vinaver, *Works of Malory,* III, 1276-1277.
[97] *Arthur of Little Britain,* preface.

much for the example of chivalric values in action as for such stuff as chivalric dreams are made on.

As for the *Golden Book of Marcus Aurelius,* it represents an equally significant interest in the nonchivalric example of antiquity. Though a forgery perpetrated by the Spaniard, Guevara, and presenting a most specious picture of Roman thought, it was immensely popular in sixteenth-century England and points toward the new classically oriented culture of the Renaissance. Here again we are able to watch the mind of early Tudor Englishmen in all its rich ambivalence. The chivalric example was wearing out from too much hard use in uncongenial terrain. The chivalric romance was on the verge of a final emancipation from reality. Both no doubt retained some validity for the English gentleman; but he was seeking new sources of inspiration, and was willing to contemplate new examples.

The winds were blowing strongly from Italy in those days and they were such as to clear away the lingering vapors of the chivalric Indian Summer. A new example was being sought and found, and this new didactic inspiration was to be studied in a new context—the national state of Tudor England. Henry VIII himself, in his response to the religious, political, and administrative problems of his more mature years, did much to provide the new context. His unmarried daughter was to do even more. The English humanists were largely responsible for preparing and presenting to the English reading public the example of a newly appraised, reinterpreted antiquity. Some forerunners there had been. Even among those deeply concerned with the problem of a revived chivalry there had been signs of an interest in the new subject matter. John Tiptoft, Earl of Worcester, whom we shall have to consider in more detail in a subsequent chapter,[98] is the principal example. An accomplished knight, and officially in charge of the chivalric ceremonies of the court, he sought in Italian culture a new

[98] See below, chap. vi.

criterion for gentility and found the answer in Buonaccorso's *Controuersia de Nobilitate,* as nonchivalric a story as one could imagine, yet dealing none the less with a major preoccupation of the late medieval aristocracy. In the next chapter we shall examine some aspects of the new example and the new context. The ideas of Tudor England have been for the most part fully and ably analyzed. I shall concentrate therefore only on those general problems which will provide a sort of *terminus ad quem* for the investigations that have preceded and a frame of historical reference for the chapters that follow.

III

A NEW EXAMPLE AND A NEW CONTEXT

HOWEVER IRRELEVANT THE CHIVALRIC IDEAL may have been to those forces the historian sees at work remodeling English society in the late fifteenth and early sixteenth centuries, there is no question but that it still meant something to the men of that day and that it was capable of evoking more than a romantic response. But one cannot help feeling, as one watches apologists for the chivalric way trying to breathe life into the old system of values, that they were using the example of chivalry largely for want of one more suited to the new society even then taking shape. That new society would in the long run have produced its own myths and created its own historical precedents—and, in a sense, it did. In the meantime, however, some new source of intellectual inspiration was necessary to tide the English mind over the rough transition from medieval to modern thought. In point of fact that new source of inspiration, the new "example," came to a large extent from the outside, in the form of humanism.

The evolution of a new *Weltanschauung* did not, of course, depend entirely on such outside stimuli. Those English minds that were at all alert to what was taking place in the society around them had immense capacity for realistic appraisal and practical adjustment. Sir John Fortescue, for instance, was able to fit a predominantly medieval pattern of thought to new political situations quite without the help of any outside influence except, perhaps, the example of current history he saw in the France of Louis XI and Philippe de Commines. And in the early Tudor period a number of pamphleteers adapted both medieval and humanist concepts to meet the challenge of the even more revolutionary events of that era, exploring cause and effect in economic and social life with an empiricism that was none the less significant for being largely unconscious.[1] Realism and applied common sense were not, however, likely by themselves to do more than prepare the way for a new outlook. At best they diverted attention from the intellectual stereotypes to the actual instance, from the myth to the reality. In so doing they helped to weaken the hold of chivalric concepts over the English mind.

Something more nearly approaching a new positive ideal came with the growth of Tudor nationalism. As it emerged from the revolutionary happenings of the thirties and forties, the nation-state provided as never before and to an increasing extent the practical frame within which ideas must be set if they are to have more than conventional meaning. Now we have seen that English thought, English chivalric thought in particular, had for a long time been conditioned by a growing national consciousness. England was ahead of the rest of Europe in that respect, owing in part to her insular position and in part to the historical fact of the Norman conquest with its sequel of a highly centralized feudalism. But, as far as chivalric thought is concerned, that sense of nationalism centered upon the person of the king rather than upon the nation as we know it: the interests it recognized were dynastic rather than economic or strategic. Some there were, to be sure, like the author of the *Libelle of Englyshe Polycye,* who were able to think in terms of a nascent mercantilism by no means unrelated to the economic problems that preoccupied the "commonwealth men" of the following century; but they were rare, and they form no part, except as negative evidence, of the history of chivalric thought. The chivalric mind could respond

[1] See the author's essay, "Renaissance Realism in the 'Commonwealth' Literature of Early Tudor England."

to a patriotic appeal. But it was not national; rather it was dynastic, centering upon the person of the king.

Not until the latter part of Henry VIII's reign did the nation begin to impinge upon the minds of Englishmen in its modern rather than its medieval form. Then a truly national administration emerges from the royal government typical of the preceding period. Then the Anglican Reformation sets England apart from the body of medieval Christendom and places her irrevocably, and to all concerned quite apparently, among the sovereign powers then beginning to compete in that grand free-for-all which is the modern state system. Then, too, the pamphleteer and the propagandist, the antiquary and the chronicler find their pens moving more and more along the lines of national interest, tracing the shape of those controversies that were to condition English history for the rest of the century.

. . .

It is here, in the pamphlets of the period, that we see in the process of growth a state of mind to the more pressing concerns of which the values of chivalry were largely irrelevant. Perhaps the new attitude may best be seen in the work of those public-spirited commentators who, in the name of a deceptively medieval "commonwealth," explored the relationship between government and the well-being of society and who exhorted all responsible citizens to discharge the duty of their citizenship by placing their minds as well as their bodies at the service of their country. These "commonwealth men"—Morison, Starkey, Hales, to name only the better known—saw that, as far as the health and wealth of the body politic was concerned, the process of government involved the manipulation of ponderable forces, economic interests in particular, by means of constructive policy. This required the pooling of intelligence on the part of all intelligent citizens. The implication that arises from such comment is that citizenship is something in which all may have a part. The welfare of society "requireth every man's counsel," not exclusively that of the aristocracy, despite the idea not unnaturally cherished by the latter that they were the natural counsellors of kings. Moreover, the measure of citizenship is mind. These men recognized, albeit for practical purposes rather than for the purposes of political theory, that the national state had outgrown the primarily protective function commonly assigned to it in the earlier period. The knight could no longer be considered simply as the sword-arm of the political body. Nobility had now to be evaluated to some extent by the measure of citizenship, and citizenship by the demands of a dynamic society.

Examples of this attitude are plentiful for the reigns of Henry VIII and Edward VI.[2] A few of those that bear directly or indirectly on the status of knighthood will have to suffice. Elyot's emphasis on the education of the gentry as "governors" rather than as mere soldiers, or even as courtiers in the sense made popular by Castiglione, is especially pertinent and will have to be referred to again at a later point in these studies.[3] Possibly the most useful example, and one in this connection not sufficiently appreciated, is *A Discourse of the Common Weal of this Realm of England,* composed about 1549 and now commonly attributed to John Hales.[4] For his

[2] *Ibid.* See also, for example, Thomas Starkey, *Dialogue between Cardinal Pole and Thomas Lupset,* ed. J. M. Cowper, E.E.T.S., E.S., XII (1871), especially p. 21; Robert Crowley, *The Way to Wealth,* ed. J. M. Cowper, E.E.T.S., E.S., XV (1872), especially p. 132; Henry Brinkelow, *The Complaynt of Roderyck Mors,* ed. J. M. Cowper, E.E.T.S., E.S., XXII (1874), especially p. 10; *Pyers Plowman's Exhortation, unto the Lordes, Knightes and Burgoysses of the Parlyamenthouse* (1530), S.T.C. 19905; *Policies to reduce this Realme of Englande vnto a prosperous Wealthe and Estate,* in *Tudor Economic Documents,* ed. R. H. Tawney and Eileen Power (London, 1924), III, 312-345, especially pp. 312 and 345. Contrary opinions, to the effect that the king's business was not to be meddled in by every man, but only those of his own council, were also expressed, and bear equally eloquent witness to the new ideal of active citizenship; e.g., Sir John Cheke, *The hurt of sedition* (1549), S.T.C. 5109, sig. Fiii.

[3] Sir Thomas Elyot, *The Boke named the Gouernour,* ed. H. H. S. Croft (London, 1880), especially Proheme, p. cxcii, Book I, pp. 23-24, Book III, p. 433. Cf. Elyot's *The Image of Governance* (1541), S. T. C. 7664, preface and sig. Aiii. See also Caspari, chap. iv, and below, chap. vi.

[4] Ed. E. Lamond (Cambridge, 1929). Miss Lamond made a substantial case for the authorship of Hales. Some doubts have been expressed by Jean-Yves Le Branchu in his *Écrits notables sur la Monnaie* (Paris, 1934) and by E. Hughes, "The

discussion Hales assembles a set of characters chosen in good medieval tradition as representatives of the functioning members of the body politic—a knight, a merchant, a doctor, a husbandman, and a craftsman. The knight, as befits his dignity, leads the discussion. So far there is nothing to warn the reader that he is about to be served anything more palatable to modern taste than the earlier dialogue *Of Gentylnes and Nobylyte* (*ca.* 1523) or Heywood's interlude, *The Weather*[5] (1533), in both of which the knight simply personifies his estate and voices its peculiar interests. The knight indeed plays this role for Hales as well. He is a landlord, with the special grievances and interests of his class.[6] We gather that he has also received a basically military training.[7] In short, he is the typical knight. At least he is typical of that prosaic and practical knighthood which had grown up in the circumstances of late medieval English society and which bore only a formal relationship to the graceful and high minded knight-errant so dear to Chaucer's heart. But it soon becomes apparent that we have to deal with something quite different even from the knight of *Gentylnes,* despite the claims made by the latter to nobility on the grounds of his own and his forbears' service to the state as soldiers and feudal lords.[8] Certainly he resembles in no way whatsoever the inspired monomaniacs in Malory's pages who fight their way with a sort of aimless obstinacy through a political vacuum.

Hales, it appears, has something very important to say concerning the commonwealth. He chose, he says, the dialogue form because the problems he had in mind were such as lend

---

Authorship of the Discourse of the Commonweal," *Bull. John Rylands Lib.,* XXI (1937), 167-175.

[5] *Of Gentylnes and Nobylyte,* ed. K. W. Cameron, in *Authorship and Sources of "Gentleness and Nobility": A Study in Early Tudor Drama* (Raleigh, 1941). *The Weather,* in *Pre-Shakespearian Dramas* ed. J. Q. Adams (Cambridge, Mass., 1924), pp. 397-422.

[6] See, for example, his arguments with the Husbandman on the matter of rents, and his complaint about the high cost of maintaining the "conntenaunce" of a gentleman, p. 19 and pp. 38 ff.

[7] Vegetius has been his textbook, so the Doctor assumes. *Discourse,* p. 26, lines 24-25. On his military experience, see p. 22, line 25, and p. 84, line 17.

[8] *Gentylnes,* lines 36-39, 224-234.

themselves to debate rather than direct statement. (It was a form for which ancient letters provided ample precedent and one especially popular among the humanist writers.) And he has chosen his characters not because they represent universal types in a static society but because they represent "every estate that find themselves aggrieved nowadays."[9] The problems are those which affect the wealth and power of the English nation and they are primarily economic. This in itself is a very significant fact. Like most of the other "commonwealth men," Hales considered the government not simply as a protective agency but as one that exists basically for the sake of manipulating the economic forces in English society in the interests of the common "wealth."[10] This function involves the most careful inquiry into facts, into the interests of all concerned, in an effort to find the causal relationships. Having found the causes of the nation's ills—immediate, tangible causes, not ultimates, the cloth trade, for instance, rather than the will of God or the innate sinfulness of man—it becomes then the duty of those in whose hands the state is entrusted to devise constructive policies to remedy these ills and lead the country to wealth and prosperity.

In this exploration of economic cause the Knight takes the liveliest interest. He asks all the leading questions—and they are often more penetrating in their search for social causation than anything in the earlier political literature of England with the exception, perhaps, of More's *Utopia*. He does not give the answers. That, also significantly, is the role given to the Doctor who, however, is not the scholastically trained and theologically preoccupied person one would expect to find a generation earlier, or even in the mid-century for that matter, but rather the humanist, eager to turn his classical learning to the practical uses of his country. He it was about whom More

[9] *Discourse*, p. 12.
[10] One of the first to develop this interpretation was J. W. Allen. See his *History of Political Thought in the Sixteenth Century* (London, 1928), pp. 151-152. See also the author's "Realism in the 'Commonwealth' Literature."

and Starkey wrote in dialogues of their own, the wise man, who, in the words of Starkey's Thomas Lupset, has not allowed himself to be tempted by the "sweetness of his studies, and by his own quietness and pleasure" to abandon "the cure of the commonwealth and policy."[11] He represents the Platonic ideal of the learned man who, in the absence of a philosopher-king, feels obliged to place his wisdom at the disposal of those immediately responsible for the actual working of government. It is as a member of this latter group that the knight finds his true place in the social system. He is a soldier, yes, but it is as a Justice of the Peace and as a Knight of the Shire that he performs his principal service. He knows at first hand the problems of the countryside, having served in the commission on enclosures.[12] He has experience also in parliament; and he indicates quite specifically his intention of bringing the Doctor's wisdom to the attention of parliament when next he sits with that body.[13]

He is, indeed, the personification of a new secular ideal, the gentleman as governor. Although it is the Doctor who has the answers and who comes nearer to that combination of the active and the contemplative life upon which Starkey set such store, the Knight is the natural custodian of good counsel. Indeed, judging from the shrewdness of the questions he poses to the Doctor, he is quite capable of doing a bit of constructive thinking on his own account. It may be that he represents the position of Hales himself who stated his purpose in writing and, incidentally, his own ideal of active citizenship, in the following words:

Considering the manifold complaints of men, touching the decay of this Commonwealth and Realm of England, . . . Albeit I am not of the King's council, to whom the reformation and consideration thereof doth chiefly belong, yet knowing myself to be a member of the same commonwealth, and called to be one of the house, where such things ought to be treated, I can not reckon myself a mere stranger to this

[11] See More's *Utopia*, Book I, Starkey's *Dialogue*, pp. 2-24.
[12] *Discourse*, p. 13, lines 1-3.
[13] *Ibid.*, p. 110, line 20, p. 111, line 2; cf. pp. 67 and 125.

matter. . . . Therefore, having now some vacation from other business, me thought I could apply my study to no better thing than to make some discourse with myself. First, what thing men are grieved with, then what should be the occasion of the same. And that known, how such griefs may be taken away, and the estate of the commonwealth reformed again.[14]

Here then is the portrait, Tudor style, of the knight in action. If it is not the complete picture, it is at least a striking profile. If it leaves out the still fashionable, though subtly metamorphosed, courtly features, it includes all that the more serious-minded of contemporary observers, including Elyot, thought of primary importance. There is scarcely a trace in it of the chivalric characteristics familiar to readers of late medieval literature—or for that matter to those of Hales's own contemporaries who in apparently large numbers continued to find satisfaction (or escape) in the most fanciful of chivalric romances. Still medieval in his view of a society of estates in which the aristocracy enjoys pre-eminent power and privilege, this good gentleman of England has come to accept the fact, without always appreciating its philosophical implications, that society is a complex of moving forces. Still conscious of his military responsibility, he is becoming aware of the overriding importance of policy in directing those forces. Still willing, though to a rapidly weakening extent, to leave learning to clerks (no doubt as a means of enlisting the interest of his "gentle" readers in what are to be the highly sophisticated arguments of a learned man, Hales has his Knight quiz the Doctor sharply on the usefulness of book-learning), he is eager to discuss affairs with the trained and philosophical mind and listen respectfully to its advice.

One or two additional examples of this new notion of its social function held by the governing class, and we shall have to move on. In another of these semidramatic conversations, so popular among those who wished to argue the issues of the day, entitled *A Proper Dyaloge betwene a Gentillman and a*

[14] *Discourse,* p. 10.

Husbandman[15] (1530), the "gentleman" represents a stage of development between that of the Knight in *Gentylnes* and that of Hales's Knight. But he is engaged in a discussion, vigorous if thoroughly tendentious, concerning the need for ecclesiastical reform which had become a problem of national rather than class concern. He expresses in particular the views of the landed class. He dwells at some length on how the clergy had appropriated the estates of his ancestors by playing upon their fear of purgatory. In this dialogue it is possible, however, to see the gathering shadow of the Anglican Reformation, that most disturbing of coming events which did more than anything else to focus the attention of the English people, regardless of class, on a matter of the common welfare and on the national government as the only possible source of remedial legislation and constructive policy.

Again this new national orientation becomes apparent in the pamphlets, more specifically in the military books of the sixteenth century. In that category one might expect to find, if anywhere, the familiar combination of chivalry and patriotism that passed for nationalism in the fourteenth and fifteenth centuries. Again, however, it is the national interest rather than the dynastic policy of the crown that is the central issue; and the military man tends increasingly to express himself in terms of the duty common to *all* Englishmen to defend their country rather than the duty peculiar to the knightly caste alone. This is a subject that will require separate attention later on.[16] For the moment it will be enough to notice how, in *An Exhortation to Styrre all Englysshemen to the Defence of theyr Countrye* (1539), Sir Richard Morison lays special stress on the duty of all subjects "of what degree soever they be, to serve their country in such sort, as their prince and head shall appoint them,"[17] and concludes that if his countrymen "fight this

[15] S.T.C. 6813. Notice that the terms "gentleman" and "knight" were used for practical purposes interchangeably. In Hale's *Discourse* the Knight is made to represent the interests of the "gentlemen" as a whole. See, for example, pp. 18 ff.
[16] See below, chap. v.
[17] S.T.C. 18110, sig. Aiiii.

one field with English hands, and English hearts, perpetual quietness, rest, peace, victory, honor, wealth, all is ours."[18] The nation in arms has here replaced the ideal of patriotic knighthood as the concept governing the defense of the realm.[19]

Morison, it must be remembered, was one of those humanistically trained publicists whom Cromwell gathered about him for just such services in formulating and presenting to the English public the essentials of Tudor policy.[20] Indeed, as we have seen in the preceding pages, it is impossible to separate the new national consciousness at all clearly from the influence of humanism. Humanism throughout Northern Europe tended toward the application of classical precept and example to the utilitarian purposes of social reform. In England that tendency finds its characteristic expression within the particular context of the Tudor state.

· · ·

The story of early English humanism is too long and too familiar to retell in any detail here;[21] nor is it in itself part of the problem immediately before us. Yet the part played by the new studies in supplanting the chivalric outlook is so important that some attention will have to be devoted to it both at this point and in subsequent chapters.

The example of antiquity was peculiarly fitted to serve as the raw material for a new social ideal. Athens and Rome,

[18] *Ibid.*, conclusion.

[19] See also *ibid.*, sig. Bv, where the idea is expressed that each Englishman should be equipped and ready to defend his country.

[20] On these men, see W. G. Zeeveld, *Foundations of Tudor Policy* (Cambridge, Mass., 1948).

[21] On fifteenth-century English humanism, see R. Weiss, *Humanism in England during the Fifteenth Century* (Oxford, 1941), W. F. Schirmer, *Der englische Frühumanismus* (Leipzig, 1931). Caspari's book begins with an excellent chapter on the social and intellectual foundations of English humanism. In his *John Skelton, Laureate* (New York, 1939), pp. 4-40, W. Nelson calls attention to the significance of the group of lesser humanists who were attracted to the court of Henry VII and whose reputation has perhaps suffered unduly in comparison with the towering figures of Erasmus and More. For early Tudor humanism, see, among many dealing in one way or another with the subject, Caspari; D. Bush, *The Renaissance and English Humanism* (Toronto, 1939); Zeeveld.

indeed, were in many respects closer to the realities of early Tudor England than anything envisaged in medieval social theory. The English knights had, as we have seen, long since ceased to enjoy a special legal position in the English state and had lost their monopoly of the military profession. By the sixteenth century they shared with the gentry, from whom they were distinguished only by the somewhat arbitrary title they bore, the multifarious duties of local government. Together they became part of the lesser aristocracy upon which the Tudor monarchy depended to an increasing extent for its judicial and administrative talent. The English knights had thus for the first time come to bear some of the characteristic features of the Roman *equites,* especially as that class of lower nobility had been refashioned by Augustus and readapted to the needs of the imperial state. In early Tudor society the gentleman tended more and more to combine the functions of guardian and thinker, formerly divided between the knight and the clerk, to become as never before part of a truly governing class. To an increasing extent, therefore, he was able to find the source of cultural inspiration most suited to his life, the example he so badly needed, in the writings of the ancient world, which were directed toward an entire governing class, rather than in the chivalric writings which were meant primarily, if not exclusively, for the military aristocracy.

The English humanists were eclectic in their use of classical sources. Plato they found especially stimulating. During the fifteenth century the Italian humanists had seen in him a suitable successor to Aristotle as *the* philosopher. His ideal of an aristocratic society, organized into a good and just state, ruled by a philosopher-king with the help of an elite of guardians and men of learning, a society in which the ultimate good lay in virtue and in which virtue must be cultivated by learning, all appealed strongly to the English humanists. They also drew nourishment from the Roman ideal of the citizen. That ideal, combining "the precepts of Greek philosophy with

Roman political experience,"[22] they were able to study in the works of Cicero and Quintilian with their emphasis on active participation in public affairs, eloquence as the means, and virtue and learning as the essential requisites. In Cicero also, and in Seneca, they could find the Stoic belief in the power of men's natural reason as the supreme authority in purely human affairs and as the most powerful of tools for the reform of human society. It was, we might add, a belief with which chivalric idealism could have little in common. In particular, the "reasonable" attitude of the Erasmian humanists toward war left no room at all for the chivalric idealization of fighting as the finest secular endeavor of the knightly class.[23]

The example of antiquity could thus act both as a model and as a solvent, as an example of an attitude toward society more fitted to contemporaneous life than that of medieval tradition and at the same time one which did much to loosen the hold of tradition on men's minds. The immediate result was less the formulation of new ideas than the adoption of new attitudes. But, however traditional the basic assumptions may have been, however conservative the trend of humanist thought, the approach to human society, and to English society in particular, made by the English humanists was fresh and vigorous and gave eloquent evidence of the stimulating effect of the new classicism.

Much of the classical literature had, to be sure, been available to English scholars for a long time; and in a sense the example of antiquity had been familiar, and very useful, to the medieval man of letters since the days of John of Salisbury. But the classics had been made to serve the peculiar ends of medieval society. They were considered either ancillary to scholastic philosophy or illustrative of the Christian-chivalric ethical system. And they were interpreted strictly within the Christian scheme of history and cosmology. Medieval society

[22] Caspari, p. 15.

[23] See below, chap. v. See also R. P. Adams, "Designs by More and Erasmus for a New Social Order," *Studies in Philology*, XLII (April, 1945), 131-145.

was not consciously imitative. Its writers adapted whatever they found inspiring in the literature of antiquity or of the early Christian era to fit their own picture of society without the slightest sense of historical incongruity. And so they missed the peculiarly moving inspiration that was to come from a recognition of the unique character of ancient society. For them the Roman military heroes remained "chivalrous paynim knights,"[24] identical except for their paganism with the knights of medieval Christendom. The Nine Worthies, the stock-in-trade of every court poet, were alike in their exemplification of chivalric virtue—Joshua and Hector and Julius Caesar as well as Arthur and Charlemagne and Godfrey of Boulogne.[25] As Lydgate, by no means a stranger to classical learning, put it,

> Knighthood in Greece and Troy the City
>   Took his principles, and next in Rome town,
> And in Carthage, a famous great country,
>   Record [witness] of Hannibal and worthy Scipio;[26]

And it was in large part a medievalized antiquity that Caxton relayed to the English readers at the very threshold of the new era. These men of fifteenth-century England were unable to see that the society of Athens and Rome was distinct from that of their own, yet related to it by ties of intellectual and temperamental compatibility and by a wide variety of common experience and common interests.

This the men of Tudor England were able in varying degrees to appreciate. Sir Thomas Smith (apparently in this instance echoing William Harrison) could, for example, throw a provocative light on English institutions as they were in the early years of Elizabeth's reign by comparing them to Roman;

[24] *Boke of Noblesse,* pp. 4 and 75. Myron P. Gilmore discusses the emergence of the sense of anachronism, with valuable bibliographical references, in *"Fides et Eruditio:* Erasmus and the Study of History," in *Teachers of History: Essays in honor of Lawrence Bradford Packard,* ed. H. S. Hughes (Ithaca, 1954), pp. 9-27.

[25] See, for example, *The Minor Poems of John Lydgate,* Part II, ed. H. N. MacCracken, E.E.T.S., O.S., No. 192 (1934), pp. 627, 784 (line 92), and 811.

[26] *Ibid.,* p. 777, lines 41-42. Cf. p. 784. On Lydgate's "humanism," see Schirmer, *Lydgate.*

yet he was also able to see that the *equites Romani* were not quite the same sort as the English gentry. Indeed it is in their administrative function, their place in the complex machinery of a state, that he finds the chief similarity between them and their classical counterparts, not in their military capacities, which had seemed to the medieval mind to all intents and purposes the same.[27] Later in the century Sir William Segar made a similar distinction, even more notable for the awareness of historical development implied in it. Ordinary knights, he said, resemble what the Romans called

"Equites Romanos . . . differing in a sort, but in some other sort doth agree with it; for seldom in all points one commonwealth doth agree with an other, nor long any state accordeth with itself."[28]

Chronicle writers and the several translators of histories, most of whom insisted upon the utilitarian nature of their endeavor, justified history as the storehouse of human experience, the source of mature wisdom, and tended increasingly to stress the example of classical antiquity. In his translation of Quintus Curtius' *Historie of . . . the actes of the greate Alexander* (1553), John Brende advocates strongly the translation of all "histories" from foreign tongues into English, but "specially the histories of antiquity, which both for the greatness of the acts done in those days, and for the excellency of the writers have much majesty and many examples of virtue."[29] The habit of applying the terminology of chivalry to the example of ancient history continued, and it is difficult always to be sure where literal meaning ends and mere linguistic habit begins. Morison's *Exhortation* includes the best medieval and chivalric precedents for patriotic action as well as those drawn from antiquity and the Scriptures. But his purpose is in accord with the new, distinctly national policy. Thomas

---

[27] *De Republica Anglorum,* ed. L. Alston (Cambridge, 1906) Book I, chap. xviii. On the question of Smith's borrowings from Harrison's *Description of England,* see *ibid.,* pp. xvi-xxi.

[28] Sir William Segar, *The Boke of Honor and Armes* (London, 1590), S.T.C. 22163, Book V, p. 19.

[29] S.T.C. 6142, sig. Aiiii.

Berthelet wrote a preface to Sir Anthony Cope's *Historie of
... Anniball and Scipio* (1544) in which he finds both ancient
generals models of chivalry; and Cope is himself not above
using such terminology. But the context of his book is clearly
that of Renaissance power politics. And Cope, moreover, seems
to be quite aware of the fact that warfare "then" and "now"
are two different things.[30]

The task of the humanists and the many men of affairs
trained in the humanistic studies was, then, to reappraise the
classical heritage and prepare it for the consumption, if not of
the public at large, at least of the governing class. It was a
reappraisal conducted in the spirit of the man of affairs rather
than of the dilettante, with the welfare of the community as
the chief end. Although obviously derivative, it was by no
means slavishly imitative. The example of classical antiquity
supplied the inspiration, not the blueprint for a new social outlook. It was simply the most influential of the outside influences on the English mind; and it was especially so when interpreted within the framework of the national state and
when, as in the case of More and of the younger generation
of pamphleteers like Starkey, Morison, and Hales, it was
accompanied by a remarkably keen appreciation of the nature
of social and political forces. In this respect especially it is
hard to exaggerate the significance of early Tudor humanism.[31]

. . .

The movement took a long time to get started in England.
That outpost of medieval culture remained more inaccessible
to the cultural influences emanating from Italy than did the
other transalpine countries. In the fifteenth century, moreover, the English universities, watched over carefully by a
church frightened into intellectual reaction by the specter of

[30] S.T.C. 5718. The pagination of this copy is not clear.
[31] With reference to Spenser's political writings, Caspari (p. 205) speaks of the
failure of Elizabethan commentators to maintain the subtle insights into social
forces apparent in More's *Utopia*.

heresy, were scarcely the soil in which to plant the seeds of a new learning. Not until the enlightened patronage of Duke Humphrey of Gloucester induced a few English scholars to study in Italy during the middle part of the fifteenth century can England be said to have been open to the new intellectual currents. Even then, however, they extended little beyond the small circle of ecclesiastics who still enjoyed a virtual monopoly of book-learning. And, even more important, the new classical studies were for a long time used as a means to an improved scholasticism rather than as an end in themselves.[32]   The laymen touched by them before the last decade of the century were very few: Duke Humphrey and John Tiptoft were exceptions of great significance, but exceptions that eloquently proved the rule. When Thomas Fuller remarked that the axe that beheaded Tiptoft cut off at one blow more learning than was left in all the heads of all the surviving nobility of England, he was not indulging in unpardonable hyperbole.[33] Perhaps the chief effect of the new studies on the chivalric tradition during the fifteenth century lay in a growing appreciation of the practical usefulness of classical learning in diplomacy and what we should nowadays call public relations. A Ciceronian style was rapidly becoming a fashionable requisite for the orator and official letter-writer. The formal oration occupied an important part in diplomatic meetings, its importance deriving less from its content than from the grace of its style. Pageants of chivalry, tournaments, and elaborate heraldic displays still made up much of the magnificence of such occasions. The Dukes of Burgundy, Charles the Bold in particular, employed the resources of their prosperous burgher economy in outdoing all other courts in this respect. Even Henry VIII's extravaganza at the Field of the Cloth of Gold would have delighted the heart of Froissart. But prestige was becoming increasingly attached to the subtler sophistication of rhetoric.

[32] Weiss, pp. 22 and 182.
[33] Thomas Fuller, *The History of the Worthies of England,* ed. P. A. Nuttall (London, 1840), I, 234.

Especially in dealing with the papal curia, it became essential to show such humanistically oriented pontiffs as Pius II that even an out of the way country like England could produce a graceful orator or dispatch a letter of impeccable latinity.[34] Thus learning, if only for the sake of form, came to be sought after in the courts of princes, and classical training came more and more to be acknowledged as a stepping stone to royal preferment.

Henry VII seems to have been especially sensitive to the prestige appeal of classical learning.[35] Whether for strictly utilitarian reasons or because he had a keen ear for a well-phrased speech or for a poem full of classical allusion, the fact is that Henry went to some lengths to draw to his court men of humanistic learning. If necessary, as it seems to have been, he imported them. And, tight-fisted as he undoubtedly was, he was willing to pay for them. In scholarship as in art he looked for talent primarily among the Italians; but he made Bernard André, the blind poet of Toulouse, his laureate and patronized the unbridled and all but unclassifiable genius of the very English Skelton. André was especially important as a pioneer of that court humanism the Tudors made famous. Unlike John Lydgate, who served in a similar capacity under Henry VI and who, though by no means ignorant of classical letters, tended still to use the examples of antiquity in a chivalric context, André was able to give his master's affairs a classical setting almost entirely devoid of chivalric coloration.[36] And, like Polydore Vergil, who also shared Henry's patronage, he was able to recognize in that monarch's far from showy policies the hard-headed statecraft of a Renaissance prince.[37]

[34] Nelson, pp. 8-9. The best treatment of Renaissance diplomatic practice is G. Mattingly, *Renaissance Diplomacy* (London, 1955). See especially pp. 55-63.

[35] See Nelson, pp. 4-40 for a discussion of the scholars at Henry VII's court.

[36] See, for example, *Les Douze Triomphes de Henry VII*, in *Memorials of King Henry the Seventh*, ed. J. Gairdner, Rolls Series (1858).

[37] *Annales Henrici VII*, in *Memorials*, pp. 82 and 83-84. See also below, chap. v. It is possible that Lydgate may have foreseen dimly what André recognized clearly, that is, the importance of a peaceful mercantilist policy. Schirmer, at least, believes so: *Lydgate*, p. 202.

In general, however, these early humanists were concerned rather with the form than the spirit of the new learning. That, certainly, was what they were being paid for. Their contribution was an important one. They spoke directly to the aristocracy and gentry. They demonstrated that learning had a place in secular affairs, that it could be given specific value as part of the front a prince had to keep up if he was to stay in the highly competitive game of power politics. But it remained for the Erasmian humanists to seize and interpret for the broader English public the spirit of humanistic learning. Somewhat ignored by Henry VII in favor of the more pliable and perhaps less disconcertingly original court scholars, the group of which More and Erasmus were the leading figures had their opportunity when the succession of young Henry VIII precipitated a general reshuffling of places and patronage.[38]   The Erasmian humanists not only absorbed much of the classical attitude toward life but, what was still more important, were able to use the classical inspiration as the stimulus to highly original criticisms of actual society.

. . .

It is, of course, hard to estimate the exact extent to which these influences hastened the decline of the spirit of chivalry. In the chapters following, some suggestions will be made concerning the relation between the chivalric tradition and this first, relatively pure infusion of humanism into the cultural bloodstream of England, especially in the matters of war and education, both vitally involved with chivalric values. On the whole, however, the influence of humanism must be considered of basic importance in the formation of a new, nonchivalric social outlook.

The early Tudor humanists set for half a century the pattern of cultivated thought and set it in radically nonchivalric

[38] Nelson pp. 31-33.

form. They did not like the chivalric way of life and they distrusted its values. Erasmus and Vives both brought to England a strong prejudice against chivalric romance as suitable reading matter for the young. More satirized the notion that war was in any way a noble or exhilarating endeavor. And, a generation later, Ascham delivered himself of a condemnation of the chivalric tradition in literature more bitter than that of Erasmus or of Vives, its humanistic bias now reinforced by his Protestant suspicion of pre-Reformation culture. Much of this antipathy toward the chivalric tradition stemmed from the humanists' sense (justified or not) of being culturally superior to their medieval predecessors. But much of it can also be laid to the broad chasm of principle that separated them from the heritors of the earlier tradition. Chivalric ideals were antithetical to everything the Erasmian humanist stood for. And it must be remembered that this earlier generation of humanists were still just a bit too close to the day when chivalry really meant something to be as tolerant as most of their contemporaries, or even as the more sophisticated of Elizabethans, toward the chivalric romance.

Yet it would be easy to exaggerate the degree of conscious conflict that took place between the humanistic and the chivalric traditions. English humanism was nonchivalric rather than consciously antichivalric. Even Erasmus and More manage for the most part to ignore chivalry or at best to satirize chivalric pretensions simply as part of the irrationality they believed they saw in the life around them rather than to attack it as an enemy of the first order. Elyot in his *Book named the Governor* demonstrated how readily those aspects of the chivalric tradition which retained some validity in Tudor society could be retained in a system of education meant for the English governing class.

Indeed, one of the striking facts about the mind of Tudor England is its ability to retain much of the courtly and the ornamental flavor of chivalry and even some of its ethical principles while adopting attitudes toward society and government that were quite new and quite foreign to the spirit of chivalry as it existed in the days of its undisputed ascendancy. As we have seen, this development was no doubt facilitated by the fact that chivalry had by the sixteenth century lost any embarrassing connection with political or administrative reality. Its gradual attenuation into an aesthetic mannerism or a code of purely personal conduct was thus rendered all the simpler. An intermediary stage in that process may possibly be seen in the poems and the career of the Earl of Surrey.[39] A member of the old aristocracy, brought up in the traditions of his class, and in part at least trained in the education still considered suitable to that class, he wrote poetry in the courtly love tradition and in his military career comported himself in a consciously chivalric manner. Yet his is the demedievalized, sophisticated chivalry of Castiglione's Courtier. It is Italian in origin, Neoplatonic in its intellectual coloring, in general immensely broader in its horizon than that, say, of Stephen Hawes. With him we are well on the way toward the romantic, humanistically oriented chivalry of Spenser and Sidney.

. . .

Closely related to both the "example" of antiquity and the compelling pressures of the national state was the Anglican Reformation. As a factor in the decline of chivalry it might be called an unsettling influence, the chief, in fact, of the problems that arose in considerable number during the early Tudor period to upset the equilibrium of medieval thought. Its contribution in this regard consisted less of an attack on things medieval than of a preoccupation with a controversy which was in the process, only partially recognized at the time, of breaking down the accustomed categories of medieval life and

---

[39] See F. M. Padelford, *The Poems of Henry Howard, Earl of Surrey* (Seattle, 1928), pp. 83-85, for Surrey's own references to his education and youthful environment. A critical treatment of his poetry may be found in Berdan, chap. vi.

in particular of focusing attention on the problem of national unity and welfare. Its influence on chivalric thought was therefore indirect. The concept of the "commonwealth" was in part the creation of the humanistically educated pamphleteers of early Tudor England and in part also the social ideal within which the Anglican Reformation achieved some sort of domestication in English culture. In either case it was one in which the ideal of chivalry could have little meaning beyond that of a guide to personal conduct. Chivalric attitudes toward the place and function of the governing class became increasingly irrelevant to it. Beyond this it is difficult to go with any certainty. Protestantism was as nonchivalric as humanism, but no more given to clearly antichivalric expression. Like humanism (if indeed it is possible to separate them: most of the early Reformers were, after all, humanists) it contributed to the new intellectual climate in which the chivalric ideal, prolonged beyond its normal span of life by the Indian Summer of late medieval life, could no longer maintain itself in anything approaching its original form.

It is, however, worth noticing in passing that the reformer had as much reason to oppose the chivalric tradition on the grounds of his protestantism as on those of his humanism. Protestantism had as little in common with the spirit of chivalry as it did with that of medieval Catholicism. The extreme Protestant was prone to see the two, not without historical justification, as parts of the same body and one which they would cheerfully have seen interred. Roger Ascham gave expression to this attitude when he made the following classic evaluation:

In our forefathers' time, when Papistry, as a standing poole, covered and overflowed all England, few books were read in our tongue, saving certain books of chivalry, as they said, for pastime and pleasure, which, as some say, were made in monasteries, by idle monks, or wanton canons: as one for example, *Morte Arthure:* the whole pleasure of which book standeth in two special points, in open manslaughter, and bold bawdry: In which book those he counted the noblest knights, that do kill most men without any quarrel, and commit foulest adulteries by subtlest shifts: . . .

And he laments the day when "God's Bible was banished the Court, and *Morte Arthure* received into the Prince's chamber."[40]   The above quotation is so familiar that, but for its extreme usefulness, I should hardly dare to use it again.   Not quite so familiar is that fact that Ascham had already in the introductory address prefixed to *Toxophilus* made substantially the same point.[41]   He apparently felt strongly on the subject. In the homes of the more convinced Protestants the Bible, and to a lesser degree Foxe's *Book of Martyrs,* supplanted the chivalric romances as effectively as they did the *Legenda Aurea* as repositories of edifying example.

It is also true, however, that the reformers returned in their search for authority, and to some extent also for congenial company, to the world of medieval culture.   Their concern for theology was more scholastic than humanist.   Their morality, especially among those who foreshadowed puritanism, could be as ascetic as that of monasticism in the days of its pristine zeal.   But in neither respect did this reaction involve the ideas and institutions that fall within the meaning of the term "chivalry."   A preoccupation with theology and with the traditional system of Christian ethics was in itself only too likely to become nonchivalric: even the medieval church had been able to rationalize chivalry only with the greatest difficulty, and then found it necessary to issue sporadic denunciations of the homicide too often attendant upon tournaments and to do whatever possible to stem the baronial warfare that allowed the same spirit of bellicosity to develop into a game played strictly for keeps.   At best the reformer hoped, like Luther himself and Wyclif before him, to find in the Christian nobility of the nation the secular force necessary for reform;

[40] *The Scholemaster,* in *English Works,* ed. W. A. Wright (Cambridge, 1904), pp. 230-231.
[41] *Toxophilus,* in *ibid..* pp. xiv-xv.

and he was able, like Erasmus, to make use of the "Christian Knight" as the protagonist of righteousness in the warfare which was life, an analogy hallowed by long tradition stretching back beyond the crusading orders to St. Augustine's ideal of the Christian soldier.[42]

The analogy remained, however, an analogy and little more. As for the ascetic attitude toward man's existence, the problem is complicated by the fact that the chivalric ideal also encompassed a strongly ascetic element. The idea of the Christian knight could lead to the life of chastity and self-denial exemplified in Galahad and aspired to somewhat over-optimistically by Launcelot.[43] And among the earnest apologists for the chivalric ideal in the fifteenth century there is especially discernible a suspicion of wine and women and of self-indulgence in any form. But this is the asceticism of the dedicated soldier. It is part of the morality of the camp and is concerned immediately, if not in the final accounting, with those vices that make for poor soldiering.[44] Though obviously related to Christian asceticism, it was rather a sort of "Spartanism," as common among fighting castes as mortification of the flesh has been among Christians of all periods. The Protestant was likely to feel little in common with it, either in its monastic or its Spartan manifestations. Not until the break with the universal church had been made complete and loyalty toward the national church had become identified with loyalty toward the Queen herself and to the newly unified national state of her creation could a Spenser once more find in chivalric tradition, despite its ingrained Catholicism and its implied universality, a vehicle for moral instruction in a protestant and Erastian England.

. . .

[42] P. Smith, *Erasmus* (New York, 1923), p. 56. On the religious aspect of chivalric thought in the early Middle Ages, see Painter, chap. iii.

[43] See below, chap. iv.

[44] See below, chap. v.

Something of the complexity of the forces at work under-mining the chivalric ideal in the first half of the Tudor century may be seen in the strange adventures encountered by the Arthurian legend. The story has been told more than once,[45] and I propose to add nothing of a substantive nature to it. The tales of King Arthur and his Knights of the Round Table had, however, occupied a place very close to the heart of the chival-ric myth; and their fate during the era of early Renaissance controversy and intellectual ferment is consequently by no means irrelevant to this study of chivalric decline. It was through them that both Malory and Caxton hoped to make their appeal to the English gentry in the interests of a revital-ized chivalry. Indeed, since the days when Edward I sought to make an English hero out of the hero of Celtic legend, Arthur had served to symbolize the more or less patriotic chivalry that was being secreted in the interstices of English feudal practice.[46] In the early sixteenth century Englishmen could still feel their pulses quicken at the mention of Arthur.[47] Henry VIII was careful to feature him prominently in the pageantry of the court, especially in the earlier part of his reign. While there is in Henry's Arthurianism a large streak of the theatrical which seems to relate it more to the taste of his daughter[48] than to the more sober and utilitarian concern of Malory and Caxton, it serves nevertheless to express a re-markably consistent theme in the court life of the period.

But there is also a certain ambiguity in the early Tudor vogue of King Arthur. Arthur and his knights served a double purpose. On the one hand they typified the values of chivalry. On the other they stood for things British, and hence, accord-

---

[45] See, especially, C. B. Millican, *Spenser and the Table Round* (Cambridge, Mass., 1932); J. W. Bennett, *The Evolution of "The Faerie Queene"* (Chicago, 1942), chap. vi; E. Greenlaw, *Studies in Spenser's Historical Allegory* (Baltimore, 1932), chap. i. The use made by the Tudor chroniclers of the Arthurian material has been traced in R. H. Fletcher, *The Arthurian Material in the Chronicles* (Boston, 1906), chap. xi.

[46] E. K. Chambers, *Arthur of Britain* (London, 1927), pp. 127 ff.

[47] Millican, chap. ii.

[48] *Ibid.*, pp. 22 and 24; Bennett, chap. vi; Cripps-Day, chap. vi.

ing to prevailing tradition, English. The interest displayed by the Angevin kings in the Arthurian tradition unquestionably had already in it something of both. As we have seen, English chivalry had from a very early date taken on a strongly patriotic color; and that color was probably not the least of the attractions the legends had for Malory and Caxton. But until the latter part of the fifteenth century the chivalric element tended to outweigh the patriotic. It remained for the early Tudors to turn the vogue of Arthur so strongly to nationalistic uses as largely to overshadow its chivalric implications. Henry VII may have been sensitive to it chiefly on account of his own Welsh background; for, despite the Anglicization of Arthur, he remained a hero of especially compelling prestige among the people of the Celtic Fringe. The young Prince of Wales was christened Arthur; and Bernard André professed to see in him the return of Arthur prophesied in Welsh legend.[49] Henry VIII seems to have had little interest in the Welsh background of Arthur, but continued to make much of his memory for the purposes of a patriotic Englishry. By this time the national element had begun to predominate rather clearly over the chivalric.

The story, however, cannot be left in this relatively simple setting. By the latter 1530's the chivalric element in the Arthurian tradition becomes thoroughly confused with a variety of other factors—political, religious, and academic. Scholars had found it increasingly hard to accept the adventures of Arthur as historical fact. While accepting him as an historical personage, they rejected the stories of his marvelous accomplishments, including his defeat of the Roman Emperor. There was not, they pointed out, enough evidence among other chronicle writers to confirm the stories told by Geoffrey of Monmouth. Polydore Vergil applied to the problem his Italian training in historical criticism. He flatly rejected many of the stories told of Arthur and marveled at the "common

[49] *Memorials of Henry VII*, p. 44.

people" who admired him so greatly and "extole Arthur unto the heavens."[50] He had been preceded in his doubt by Ralph Higden, whose *Polychronicon* was probably responsible for the conflict that seems to have existed in the mind of honest old Caxton between his admiration for the Arthurian material and his respect for historical accuracy,[51] by Robert Fabyan, who expressed even greater skepticism, and by John Rastell, who, in the characteristic spirit of Renaissance scholarship, carried Fabyan's criticism still further. This critical attitude continued to mark the chronicle writing of Cooper, Grafton, and Stowe.[52]

Vergil's skepticism seems to have entered him temporarily in Henry VIII's bad books, where his name remained until the early 1530's. Then Henry found other aspects of his historical interpretation so valuable as to outweigh the anti-Arthurian heresy into which he had fallen. In the Act in Restraint of Appeals, passed in 1533, the king contended that "this realm of England is an empire," its ruler competent therefore to make decisions in all aspects of national life. This, so the preamble reads, is declared "by sundry old authentic histories and chronicles."[53] Here it was that Vergil's respected scholarship came in very handy. Despite his skepticism concerning Arthur, he was able to trace the English monarchy to the Emperor Constantine with sufficient cogency to strengthen Henry's propaganda arm, especially among European scholars. And so his *Historiae Anglicae Libri XXVI,* denied publication since 1513, was in 1534 given printed form in Basle with the "imperial" blessing of the English king.[54]

But there were those in England whose patriotism transcended the immediate demands of Henry's propaganda cam-

---

[50] *Polydore Vergil's English History,* ed. Sir H. Ellis, Camden Society, XXXVI (1846), I, 29. See Millican, chap. ii, for an account of the battle of books that was precipitated by Vergil's judgment.

[51] Crotch, p. 93.

[52] Bennett, pp. 64-65.

[53] 24 Henry VIII, c. 12.

[54] R. Koebner, " 'The imperial crown of this realm': Henry VIII, Constantine the Great, and Polydore Vergil," *Bull. Inst. Hist. Res.,* XXVI (May, 1953), 29-52.

paign and who were shocked by Vergil's refusal to believe in the historicity of Arthur. Some, too (usually the same people) saw in Vergil an alien and a Catholic who mischievously unseated the idols of a Protestant and patriotic England. Poor Vergil accordingly came in for a degree of abuse that seems quite out of proportion to his offense. He was even accused of spiriting away documents unfavorable to his interpretation. For a century his name continued to be linked with a truly perfidious anti-Albionism. The attack was led by John Leland, the royal antiquary, whose labors, like those of his contemporary John Bale, were animated by a strongly national sentiment and a Protestant bias.

Yet Protestants, as such, found, as we have seen in the case of Ascham, little that was congenial in the Arthurian stories.[55] Those tales smacked too much of the "superstitions" of popery. The historical facts (Leland sought to supplement the questionable evidence of Geoffrey by data collected by himself from local legends and archaeological remains) lay imbedded in masses of fiction, especially in the still popular version of Malory-Caxton. And fiction, by virtue of its independence of fact, the literal mind of the extreme Protestant took to be little better than lies. If "feigned matter" could give the not very religious old soldier, Lord Berners, a moment of pause, what could it do to a Reformer?

By the mid-century English opinion was becoming increasingly indifferent to the memory of Arthur. Although the *Morte Darthur* and other romances of similar pedigree continued to be printed and read among "the common people," there was little fresh treatment of the theme; and it ceased to play the part in royal pageantry under Edward VI and Mary that it had under the first Tudors. It was not until after 1580 that the Arthurian stories regained their favor in court circles where they provided food for the reintegrated national feeling of Elizabethan England. With a newly aroused sense of their

[55] For further reference in the early Elizabethan period, see Bennett, pp. 74-76.

nation's greatness and, in particular, with a new vision of imperial expansion taking shape in their minds, the writers of the period following Drake's return in 1580 from his trip around the world turned frequently to the conquests of Arthur as precedents of more than historical importance.[56]   Perhaps in response to this same revival of interest in the legendary reaches of England's past, Spenser undertook to find in Arthurian chivalry a source of literary inspiration.   And not only literary inspiration; for, despite the antipathy hitherto expressed by the more extreme Protestants to these relics of a Catholic Christendom, it was now possible for him to turn the chivalric romance once more to didactic ends.

Thus the fortune of Arthur and his knights rose and fell and rose again as a result of forces more complicated and frightening than any they met with in the pages of Malory. The patriotism never far removed from English chivalry had matured from the simple dynastic loyalty of the Hundred Years' War to a complex and sophisticated loyalty to the national state, and had in the process largely outgrown the chivalric system of values.   Humanistic scholarship had questioned the legends to which fifteenth-century apologists for the chivalric way of life had looked for their most cherished examples.   Protestant opinion had for a time created an atmosphere antithetical to an ideal so deeply immersed in Catholic culture as that of chivalry.

In addition to these factors there is, I believe, another that is implied in this whole process, namely a radical change in the attitude of Englishmen toward chivalry itself.   By the middle decades of the sixteenth century it was no longer possible for the intellectually alert Englishman to accept chivalric values as a system sufficient for the secular needs of the governing class.   New examples, drawn with scholarly imagination from the teeming storehouses of antique culture, disturbing and preoccupying events in church and state, the emergence

[56] See especially Bennett, pp. 71-79.

of a society oriented as never before toward the national government as the creative custodian of truly national interests, all combined to render irrelevant those aspects of the chivalric tradition that had any immediate bearing on the activities of the knight considered in his capacity as citizen. The new ideal of the gentleman-governor, while not necessarily antichivalric, was so much broader than the chivalric ideal as to supplant it for most practical purposes. Little wonder, then, that the stories from which the didactic example of chivalry was so largely derived were for a while neglected by men struggling with the revolutionary forces of a new era.

That tales of chivalry had not lost their evocative power in this process is, however, more than demonstrated by the eagerness with which the Elizabethan reading public once more welcomed them. But by that time it is clear that chivalry had become a romantically contrived affair, bearing little more similarity to the chivalry of Malory's ideal than did the similarly contrived, equally evocative chivalry of *The Idylls of the King*. Still powerful as a source of inspiration for personal conduct, still the accepted vehicle for expressing the sense of glory and the personal idealism that is connected with the notion of *noblesse,* it has lost any necessary connection with the life of the gentleman considered as a functioning member of the body politic. Legend and history which at one time had been considered mainly as chivalry teaching by example now serve the purposes of a national spirit, newly integrated and immensely broader in its scope than the example of chivalry.

IV

CHIVALRY AND THE COMMON-WEALTH

AT AN EARLIER POINT IN THESE STUDIES I HAVE
suggested that the continued existence of chivalric idealism as
a living scale of values depended on the ability of the ruling
class to see in knighthood a unique and necessary organ of the
political body. As long as it was possible to maintain this
functional concept,[1] to preserve, that is, the myth that in
knighthood alone could the community find its defense against
both aggressors and transgressors, it was possible to take chivalry seriously as a code sufficient for the secular concerns of the
governing class. When those concerns so far outgrew the protective function traditionally ascribed to the knight that the
discrepancy became apparent even to the conservative mind of
that class—and not until then—chivalry can be said to have
passed over the great divide that separates medieval and
modern society and to have entered that bourne of romanticism
from which there is no return.

It is, then, to this military-political aspect of chivalry that
we must turn if we are to understand the decline of chivalric
thought. All other aspects retained a certain vitality, even a
certain validity, long after the knight considered as the ideal
protector of the community had become merely a romantic
figure. All other aspects could be separated to some degree

---

[1] E.g., *Select English Works of John Wyclif*, ed. T. Arnold (Oxford, 1869-71),
III, 145-146; John Wycliffe, *De Civili Dominio*, ed. I. Loserth (London, 1900), II,
253-254; John Gower, *Mirour de l'Omme*, lines 23593-24180, and *Vox Clamantis*,
Liber V, chap. i, especially lines 1-18; John Lydgate, *Fall of Princes*, Part II, ed.
H. Bergen, E.E.T.S., E.S., No. 122 (1918) p. 223; Lull-Caxton, *Ordre of Chyualry*,
pp. 14-42, and cf. the somewhat original version of Lull's book by Gilbert Hay,
pp. 11-34. These are only representative examples. Many others could be found.

from the harsh reality of affairs: the quasi-religious color of chivalry, its aesthetic values, its ideal of personal conduct, to say nothing of the snob appeal of heraldry, could exert a powerful influence over the imagination of later generations. Even the military ideal continued to inspire Englishmen long after the heavy-armored knight had been submerged in the technical complexities and lost in the collectivism inherent in modern warfare. The aristocratic soldiers of Elizabethan days—Sir Philip Sidney is the classic example—tried hard to comport themselves in accordance with the chivalric ideal.

Yet the career of Sidney illustrates very nicely the transformation that had overtaken even the military-political aspect of chivalry. To him, military activity was only one type of action, albeit a peculiarly suitable one, for the man of gentle breeding, and military training quite secondary to education in *litterae humaniores* as preparation for a career in the service of the state.[2] Even such an Elizabethan apologist for the military life as Barnaby Rich, writing in "doleful dumps of deep despair" at the decline in the prestige of the soldier's profession, makes no attempt whatsoever to equate that profession with the function of the governing class, much less with the order of knighthood, strictly interpreted.[3] The governing class had, moreover, by that time far outgrown the protective function it had assumed in the simpler environment of feudal England. The Tudor gentleman, Elyot's "governor," could no longer consider himself merely the sword-arm of the body politic. Like the Knight in Hales's *Discourse,* he is becoming one who is either actually or potentially engaged in the business of government. If his typical duties in local administration may not always leave room for the formulation of constructive policy, he may be asked to serve on royal commissions or as a member of the commons assembled in parliament where his opinion will be valued and he will have the opportunity of

[2] See Caspari, chap. vii, for a thorough discussion of Sidney in this context.
[3] *Allarme to England* (London, 1578).

sharing, either directly or indirectly, in the task of shaping policy to meet the unprecedented demands of Renaissance life. The positive, constructive role of governor was becoming especially apparent in economic affairs where, given the assumptions of a nascent mercantilist doctrine, the task of government was clearly that of harnessing social forces and by means of intelligently concocted policy manipulating a mechanism of cause and effect of which the alert Tudor citizen was becoming to some extent, and to an increasing extent, aware.[4]

A curious fact in this transformation of the medieval knight into the Tudor "governor," and one which will require a little more explanation than has already been offered in these studies, is that the functional concept of knighthood lasted long after the knight, considered as one who has formally entered the order of knighthood, had ceased to have any necessary or prescriptive part in the task of government, or for that matter in military life, and after the gentry, more broadly considered, had already taken over many of the complex duties they were to perform as "governors" in the Tudor state. Indeed, paradoxical as it may seem, it was probably because of that separation of fact and concept that the ideal of knighthood could continue for so long its inspirational and evocative existence in the minds and hearts of that same class.

. . .

Chivalry had from its origin carried with it strong political implications. It did so, if for no other reason, because it was primarily a military ideal. It had arisen in answer to the need for something beyond the specifically Christian values to guide the *bellatores* whose duty it was to fight for the protection of the other estates. The literature of medieval England is full of references to this protective function of knighthood. Once the analogy of the human body had suggested itself as a means

[4] Ferguson, "Realism in the 'Commonwealth' Literature."

of describing the state, it became a commonplace to picture the knights as the arms of the body politic. All agree, and moreover, constantly reiterate, that the knight's duty is to defend Holy Church, protect the widow and orphan (the classical examples of those in need of protection), maintain justice, and repel aggression. Even when a writer adds, as Gower for example did, the more general prescription that the knight must labor for the common good, he is still thinking of the knight as the sword-arm of the political body, one whose task is not only to fight external enemies but to enforce rights in the community itself, to preserve *le common droit* by virtue of his ability to apply, if need arise, the ultimate sanction of force, and in so doing to promote peace.[5]

It is at this point that the military function of the knight merges with his civil duties as a governor. Or, more accurately, it is at this point that it is possible for the modern observer to recognize that the knight had also a civil function to perform which was closely related to his original soldierly function. For the medieval mind was not prepared to make any great distinction between the military and civil capacities in which the knightly class was called upon to serve. It considered the maintenance of peace and justice to be the true and chief end of all secular government. To that end the king and the lords and the lesser aristocracy, all knights in the functional sense however much they might vary in their rank and title, must labor together. The king differed from the rest of the ruling class in that he alone possessed general jurisdiction.[6] All shared the responsibility for good governance; and good governance was normally equated with the maintenance

---

[5] See n. 1, above.

[6] The author of *Mum and the Sothsegger* addresses his pamphlet of political criticism to "the king and the lords," R-fragment, prol., line 49. In the *Mirour,* Gower devotes separate sections to knights, kings, and other lords. In *Vox Clamantis* he follows the simpler division of society into clergy, knights, and laborers. Even in the *Mirour,* however, he treats the familiar Nine Worthies, regardless of their exact station, as ideal examples of knighthood (lines 23869-23871). Cf. *Piers Plowman,* B-Prol., line 112.

of rights, the rights of all classes against those who in their avarice or vainglory would override them.[7]

Although no doubt always bearing within itself the germs of mythology, the *mystique* that in the twelfth and thirteenth centuries grew up around the institution of knighthood still bore by the mid-thirteenth century a close working relationship to political and social fact. The English knight had long since ceased to be merely the mounted soldier of the early Norman armies, with nothing to recommend him but elementary training in arms. He had become a member of a self-conscious aristocracy of birth and wealth as well as of military prowess. He was usually a substantial landowner, related by ties of blood or interest or both to the greater baronial families with whom he shared his chivalric code of values. He had become, willy nilly, an administrative power in his locality, holding one or more manorial courts, maintaining actually and within limits not always clearly marked off from the broadening power of the Crown that "justice" which it was his theoretical obligation to do. He might, if his ambitions ran in that direction, serve as steward or escheater for the king, or even as sheriff. In any event he bore the burden of local justice and administration, exercising broad powers among his own tenants and serving in a dozen ways as the agent of the central government in the local districts. So dependent were the Angevin kings on a constant supply of lawful knights that they were at pains to insist by statute that those who could qualify by the holding of property should undergo the ceremony of knighthood and so become responsible for its civil as well as its military duties. "The ultimate reinforcement of the king's own council by knights elected in the shires was really implicit in a system which had already brought the knights of all shires into continual association with the central government."[8]

[7] See below.

[8] F. M. Stenton, "The Changing Feudalism of the Middle Ages," *History*, XIX (March, 1935), pp. 289-301, p. 299. I am indebted for the general interpretation

Despite his increasing immersion in civil affairs, the thirteenth-century knight remained very much the soldier. It was for such a career that he was almost exclusively trained, and he undoubtedly considered it the true mark and prerogative of his rank. For he was now not merely a soldier but a very specialized one, no longer the mere cavalryman of Norman times, but a member of a relatively small (and apparently decreasing) group of highly trained, expensively equipped brothers-in-arms, the flower of the king's "chivalry," who shared the *mystique* of a closely knit and ineluctably military caste. Although, as R. F. Treharne has pointed out, the knight of this period was in fact a "landed proprietor, with an essentially civilian mode of life, and a predominantly administrative occupation,"[9] it was as a belted knight, one girt with sword (*gladio cinctus*), that he received official recognition and enjoyed prestige in the community. In the thirteenth century the assumption could still be made without too great violence to the facts that the military virtues and the qualities of citizenship were closely related and tended to reside in one and the same class of people. All the administrative responsibilities that devolved upon the knight could be considered in one way or another connected with his protective function and with his monopoly of the means of enforcing justice. From his land might derive his legal status, but from his sword sprang his authority. It was, moreover, as a professional man-at-arms that the knight

of the knight's role in medieval England to this and the following works: R. F. Treharne, "The Knights in the Period of Reform and Rebellion, 1258-1267; A Critical Study in the Rise of a New Class," *Bull. Inst. Hist. Res.*, XXI (May and Nov., 1946), 1-12; N. Denholm-Young, "Feudal Society in the Thirteenth Century: The Knights," *History*, XXIX (Sept., 1944), 107-119; K. L. Wood-Legh, "Sheriffs, Lawyers, and Belted Knights in the Parliaments of Edward III," *E.H.R.*, XLVI (July, 1931), 372-388; M. R. Powicke, "Distraint of Knighthood and Military Obligation under Henry III," *Spec.*, XXV (Oct., 1950), 457-470; H. L. Gray, "Incomes from Land in England in 1436," *E.H.R.*, XLIX (1934), 607-639; R. M. Nichols, "On Feudal and Obligatory Knighthood," *Archaeologia*, XXXIX (1862-63), 189-244; J. S. Roskell, *The Commons in the Parliament of 1422* (Manchester, 1954); T. B. Pugh and C. D. Ross, "The English Baronage and the Income Tax of 1436," *Bull. Inst. Hist. Res.* (May, 1953), 1-28.

[9] Treharne, p. 5.

of this period saw himself, and it was as such that he appealed to the popular imagination.

Certainly it was as such that he appears in the literature in which the *mystique* of chivalry was then receiving its classic expression. Thus stated, the idea of chivalry came to be a not too inaccurate way of rationalizing a social order in which the ruling class was also, and in a real enough sense primarily, a military caste. So it appears in that most influential of medieval treatises on chivalry, Ramon Lull's *Le Libre del Ordre de Cauayleria,* written during the latter part of the thirteenth century. Though unfamiliar with the peculiar conditions in which English knighthood was developing—the unusually centralized administrative system which enlisted the support of the local knight directly in the service of the king and the generally peaceful circumstances of English life which induced the aristocracy to cultivate more than was common in thirteenth century Europe the skills of civil life—Lull nonetheless spoke for a generation in which knighthood retained much of its international or nonnational character; and he wrote concerning the nature of knighthood, and of the ideals, education, and institutional forms pertaining to it. In his pages the knight is clearly the protector of the community, the secular arm through whose protective and coercive power justice is rendered and wrong undone.[10] Lull was even willing to allow the knight to act as judge if need be; but he gave implicit recognition to the distinction so fundamental to medieval thought between the clerk and the soldier. Clerks could be looked to for the legal learning necessary for the administration of justice, but the courts remained under the protection and lordship of the knightly class.[11]

---

[10] See Caxton's version, published under the title *The Book of the Ordre of Chyualry,* pp. 14-46. On Lull and his relation to both his own day and the fifteenth century, see *ibid.,* introd.; Painter, *French Chivalry,* pp. 76-84.

[11] *Ordre of Chyualry,* p. 30. Cf. *Boke of Noblesse,* p. 77. Lydgate preserves the separateness of function explicitly in *Fall of Princes,* Part I, pp. 223-224. Honoré Bonet in his *L'Arbre des Batailles,* translated and edited by G. W. Coopland as *The Tree of Battles* (Cambridge, Mass., 1949), p. 131, lumps the occupa-

Naturally enough it was almost exclusively as a military figure that the knight made his appearance in the romances and chronicles which served more than we are always willing to admit as the mirror and model of social idealism, however much they might deviate from actual practices. In the romances especially we may see reflected not what the knight was but what contemporaries, himself included, thought he should be. From both it is possible to deduce the ethical ideals which were growing up around the institution of knighthood and which, taken together, gave to the chivalric mentality its characteristic shape.[12] At first glance the image we are able to see seems curiously unpolitical except for the obvious military character of the knight. As such he dominates the pages of Froissart. The mounted and armed knight moves through the romances as through a political vacuum, a limbo symbolized by the ever present and boundaryless forest in which he seeks adventures equally isolated from the recognizable context of organized society. His is a simple and individualistic code of conduct reflecting, if anything, the personal relationships of a primitive feudalism. Yet these ethical ideals are not incompatible with the function traditionally ascribed to the knightly class in the more formal treatises on chivalric conduct. Nor were they likely to be considered so by people in an age when political life was actually conducted on very personal terms and was popularly envisaged in an even more personal light. It was an era in which little clear distinction was made between the private and public capacities in which people were called upon to act.[13] Those qualities which made for right living in private life were accordingly indistinguishable from those that would be appropriate to the discharge of

---

tion of the lawyer with those of tiller of the soil, tender of vines, and keeper of beasts—any of which will cause a knight to lose his knightly status.

[12] See G. Mathew, "Ideals of Knighthood in Late Fourteenth-Century England," in *Studies in Medieval History presented to Frederick Maurice Powicke,* ed. R. W. Hunt *et al.* (Oxford, 1948), pp. 354-362.

[13] Cf. S. B. Chrimes, *English Constitutional Ideas in the Fifteenth Century* (Cambridge, 1936), pp. 34-35.

public responsibilities. And so the man whose duty it was to protect society and to join with others in the discharge of that duty would naturally be expected to exhibit military prowess (the term usually signified not only skill at arms but that quality of rashness which was both the glory and the folly of so many famous knights) and loyalty to his feudal lord or to his brother-in-arms. The knight must also show mercy and pity. Those virtues could be and were illustrated in the quite personal relationships into which the knight wandered. They were also capable of being applied on a broader scale more nearly approximating what we should now recognize as public. The knight in other words must demonstrate that concern for the righting of wrongs which is essential to the performance of his social responsibility as "Justicier."[14]

Scarcely, however, had the simpler realities of medieval knight service found ideal expression in the chivalric code when English knighthood itself began to lose its practical significance, and the idealism embodied in that code began to lead a life of its own and one increasingly unrelated to political reality, if not downright antagonistic to it. These related processes together constitute the most baffling thing about English chivalry, and more than anything else explain why the generalizations appropriate to European chivalry do not always serve for England. They raise one question in particular: How was it possible for chivalric idealism to outlive the day in which it at least approximated actuality and to retain a certain freshness for so long that it could still be taken seriously, if only *faute de mieux,* in the late fifteenth century?

· · ·

Of the general trend of political and social history there is little doubt, although many aspects await the kind of research that traces the myriad history of individuals. Even in the

[14] Mathew, p. 360.

thirteenth century there were not enough knights available for all the administrative duties the king looked to their class to perform. Men of substance were finding that influence and social status did not necessarily depend upon formal admission into the order of knighthood. Such a distinction involved, indeed, military obligations that were more than the lesser landlord wished to be saddled with as a regular thing. It also involved a considerable amount of expense. Knighthood brought with it a scale of living that became increasingly elaborate at a time when few incomes from land were expanding to any corresponding extent. Administrative duties also followed knighthood almost automatically, for the king looked first of all to the knights for such services and beyond them only when there were not enough knights to fill the bill. It is not surprising that the king had already resorted to the expedient of "distraint," that is, of requiring those men who held enough property to warrant the dignity of knighthood to accept the formal honor or pay a fine. And it is equally natural that many preferred to pay the fine rather than accept the honor. During the fourteenth century distraint of knighthood seems to have been resorted to mainly in order to secure money. And belted knights were specified as desirable in the writs of summons to parliament largely in time of military emergency. Meanwhile the administrative services theoretically performed by knights came more and more to be performed by men like Chaucer's Franklin who were not knights at all and could, indeed, be contrasted effectively to the Knight himself, who among Chaucer's pilgrims typified the older and purer tradition of military knight-errantry. The knights of the shire had, indeed, by Chaucer's day achieved a position in which the term "shire" had outrun in significance the term "knight."

During the fifteenth century this tendency for knighthood to lose its close and necessary connection with the machinery of government continued unabated. As J. S. Roskell has

shown in connection with the Parliament of 1422, belted
knights were by no means a dominant part of the shire representation in the fifteenth-century commons.[15]   Although most
of those returned as shire-knights were liable to distraint by
virtue of their property holding, only half were in fact knights.
Of these, most followed the profession of arms in the time-
honored fashion.   Equally significant is the fact that between
a fifth and a quarter of the Commons in this first parliament
of Henry VI's reign were men of law, trained in the relatively
new and rapidly developing profession of politics.   Nor was
there by that time any clear social distinction between the
representation from the shires and the borough.   The former
still were considered the senior partners in the evolving House
of Commons,[16] but members of the country gentry were seeking election as borough representatives and all alike shared
the privileges and responsibilities that went with membership
in that body.

Although knighthood retained its meaning longer as the
ordo militaris than it did in what had always been its secondary
responsibility in the service of civil government, even in that
respect events were removing the knight from his preferred
place.   Weighted down by the increasing poundage of his
armor as well as by the increasing expense of maintaining it,
he lacked the flexibility of the yeoman archer or the less pre-
tentious man-at-arms.   Nor in the new era of siege artillery
could he retain the independence he once had when he could
assert his local interests behind a virtually impregnable fortress.
The wars, too, had wrought changes in his status as a military
captain.   Since the early fourteenth century recruitment had
been by indenture rather than by feudal obligation.[17]   Now in

---

[15] Roskell, chap. v.

[16] S. B. Chrimes, " 'House of Lords' and 'House of Commons' in the Fifteenth
Century," *E.H.R.*, XLIX (July, 1934), 494-497.

[17] On this subject, see B. C. Keeney, "Military Service and the Development of
Nationalism in England, 1272-1327," *Spec.*, XXII (Oct., 1947), 534-549.   See also
N. B. Lewis, "The Organization of Indentured Retinues in Fourteenth-Century
England," *Tr. Royal Hist. Soc.*, 4th Ser., XXVII (1945), 29-39.

a sense a military entrepreneur, the captain thus became a professional soldier in the more modern meaning of the term; and this status extended to the men contractually engaged to fight with him. Furthermore, as too few knights were available to serve the purpose, squires came to occupy a position in no practical respect different from that of the dubbed knight.[18]

Both in his civil and military capacities, the knight was being forced to serve in ways increasingly difficult to reconcile with the traditional ideals of his order. His expenses tended chronically to outrun his relatively stationary income; and so he turned to occupations not traditionally considered knightly. He might become a full-time landlord, for example, preoccupied of necessity if not by choice with the "clerkly" problems of finance and litigation. Or he might become a career administrator on the estates of a magnate or in the royal service. If his family connections or the vagaries of fortune led him in that direction, he might even take part in the mercantile life of London. Even if he remained a soldier, the French wars had taught him that there was in the profession of arms itself more than renown and high adventure. And, having returned with money in his pocket to an England divided into armed factions, and having there taken up land, he was often at pains to sell his support to the highest bidder. To his new lord he owed a somewhat brittle allegiance, compounded less of the old chivalric loyalty than of a newer, contractual obligation.[19] Like the late medieval clergy, the late medieval knight was becoming entangled in the affairs of a world his order was not constituted to cope with; and, like them, he found his scheme of values in consequence strained to the uttermost. Both the knights and the clergy, however, retained those values and in the latter fifteenth century may have recognized anew the necessity of re-emphasizing them.

Moreover, the values of chivalry remained the secular

[18] Roskell, p. 92.
[19] K. B. McFarlane, "Bastard Feudalism," *Bull. Inst. Hist. Res.*, XX (1945), 161-180. Cf. N. B. Lewis.

values of the governing class as a whole. Despite the fact that formal knighthood had come to include only a fraction of those who constituted that class—the squires and that broad and ill-defined category of substantial citizens now beginning to be called "gentlemen" greatly outnumbered the knights and the nobility—all shared in varying degrees a common gentility. Indeed, with the partial exception of the nobility, there existed little difference of birth among these classes. The English social structure, constructed on the exceedingly flexible, constantly moving principle of primogeniture, made possible the existence of a governing class remarkable for its community of interests and for the homogeneity of its values.

.   .   .

In this process the scope of chivalric idealism came to be correspondingly enlarged. While lagging far behind in the march of time it did not stand still. It suffered from the fact that it had in a sense achieved a rigid orthodoxy, even a stereotype, in the standard manuals. Although two centuries old, and never wholly in accord with the peculiarities of English society, Lull's treatise appears to have appealed strongly to fifteenth-century English readers. Indeed, it reached its widest public as far as England is concerned during that century. It appeared in the form of several translations and adaptations, the most important being those by Hay (1456) and Caxton (*ca.* 1484). It unquestionably continued during that period to serve as the standard theoretical work on the subject; and, the age being much addicted to standard works, it no doubt helped to imprint on the chivalric "revival" an even more archaic stamp than it might otherwise have borne. But it also emphasized just those practical aspects of the chivalric tradition that seemed to fifteenth-century Englishmen to promise some sort of regeneration in public as well as private life. Like them,

Lull was, even at that early date, troubled over the decay of knightly virtue. Like them, he looked back to a Golden Age of Chivalry not as from a time when chivalry had lost its social function but as from a time when it had merely fallen on evil days.

Lull's was, nevertheless, a distinctly medieval outlook. He was capable of focussing only with difficult on the state as it emerged from the actual localism and the theoretical universality of feudal Europe. It would therefore be surprising indeed if the adapters of the fifteenth century, conservative as they were, had accepted his work totally without comment. In the Scottish version, compiled by Gilbert Hay, it is possible to see how this thirteenth-century statement of the chivalric ideal could be adapted to the need, increasingly felt at the close of the Middle Ages, for a concept of citizenship that would give expression to the increasingly complex duties of the governing class. More original than Caxton, and certainly more advanced in his political awareness, Hay enlarged considerably on the brief and general statement of the knight's function made by Lull and followed faithfully by Caxton.[20] Whereas in the latter it is simply stated that "in seignory [lordship] is much noblesse," Hay must needs spell out the point: "A man is not a lord suppose he have never so much of worldly goods: but he is a lord that has seignory and jurisdiction upon other men, to govern them, and hold law and justice upon them when they trespass."[21] More than that, he emphasizes the duty of the knight to the community. He can, it is true, demand service from those of servile status so that he may lead a gracious and leisured life; but he must also see to it that a complex society is maintained: he must

. . . govern and keep peaceably the laborers, and save them from force and wrong, so that clerks might peaceably study in sciences, men of

[20] On Hay and his relation to Caxton, see *Ordre of Chyualry*, introd., pp. xxxv-xlii.
[21] Hay, p. 14; cf. *Ordre of Chyualry*, p. 19.

church work in God's service, merchants in their merchandise, and other crafts working at lords' devices.[22]

In another editorial comment he asserts "the office of knighthood should have stark [powerful] place in governance . . . For the office is founded aye on good and profitable works that are speedful to the common profit."[23]

Now there is nothing new in this idea that the knight must labor in the common interest. It is present in Lull's own work.[24] It was indeed a commonplace of medieval thought. Initially an attempt to idealize the personal relationships that characterize feudal society, chivalry was soon drawn into the more sophisticated intellectual atmosphere of the medieval schools, and there colored to some extent by light reflected from the classical notion of the *respublica*. The idea of a "body politic" in which the knightly class had an appointed place and for the good of which it performed a prescribed function gave to the ideal of knighthood a setting much broader than that of the feudal relationship. It introduced the concept of the "commonwealth" which proved henceforth a constant and ineradicable element in Western European thought. Chivalric theorists could hardly be expected to have grasped all the implications of John of Salisbury's classical learning, of, especially, his prematurely humanistic understanding of antique culture; but they seem to have felt the need to link knight service in some way to the welfare of the community. In thirteenth-century England the rebellion of the barons is justified in terms of the "*communitas regni*"; and chivalric idealism is expanded to include the "regement of princes."[25]

New or not, a vague ideal of service to the commonwealth seems to have preoccupied chivalric apologists to an increasing

[22] Hay, p. 15; cf. *Ordre,* pp. 32-41.
[23] Hay, p. 28; cf. *Ordre,* pp. 41-42.
[24] *Ordre,* p. 213. Cf. Lydgate, *Minor Poems,* Part II, ed. H. N. MacCracken, E.E.T.S., O.S., No. 192 (1934), p. 844.
[25] F. M. Powicke, *Henry III and the Lord Edward* (Oxford, 1947), II, 689-690.

extent in the late medieval period. It led Hay frequently to enlarge on his original. Caxton gave an equally significant place to it, but in his prologues and epilogues[26] rather than in his generally faithful translations. It became the form in which was expressed that crude sense of citizenship which had always been inherent in the ideal of chivalry, which tended always to redeem it from the anarchical tendencies likewise inherent in the tradition of knight-errantry, and which, as the modern state began to take shape and the tempo of its life to accelerate, came increasingly to approximate the modern notion of citizenship.

It had, of course, to be broadened considerably before it could be made to fit this emerging pattern of modern life—more so, in fact, than the ideal of chivalry itself could stand. To the simple idea that the knight had a public service to perform as the protector of the community had to be added some notion of service to the national community, of which Lull had no knowledge,[27] and also an appreciation of the need for trained intelligence in government, which was lacking in most chivalric writings. Even before it became at all clear to contemporary observers that the state was a dynamic thing, that society was a complex of moving forces, and that it was the part of government to direct those forces by the use of creative statecraft, it had already become apparent that the complexities of government required the services of a highly educated, specially trained ruling class, men whose primary duty it was to serve in a secular capacity and who must to an increasing extent take the place of the clergy as the brains of the body politic. Almost imperceptibly, therefore, the medieval concept of service to the community could be and was broadened to include active statecraft and at the same time reduced to more specific terms (one might almost say nar-

---

[26] E.g., Caxton's prologue to *Tullius of Olde Age,* Crotch, p. 41; prologue to *Book Callid Caton, ibid.,* p. 77. Cf. Lydgate's *Fall of Princes,* Book VIII, line 2760; *Boke of Noblesse,* pp. 57, 66, 75.

[27] *Ordre,* introd., pp. xxxvi-xxxvii.

rowed) to fit the requirements of the national state. This was, to be sure, the work of the sixteenth century—at least for England. But it is instructive to see the extent to which the late medieval expression of the chivalric ideal was made to include the simple, traditional, seldom qualified notion of public service. And we may, I believe, safely assume that the simplicity of the traditional idea in some degree masked the stirrings of a new awareness of political reality.

. . .

It is also instructive to notice that in Lull's work and in the fifteenth century translations of it the ideal of knighthood is expressed almost exclusively in terms of those moral qualities upon which, according to the Christian tradition, the welfare of society depends. The Christian tradition was not the only source of this moralism, it is true. Classical examples were also popular in fifteenth-century England. Classical culture gave birth to a more mature notion of citizenship than any to be found in that of medieval Europe. Although the chivalric writers were generally unable to distinguish clearly between the medieval knightly class and the Roman *equites*,[28] they may well have carried over into the chivalric ideal some of the antique notion of service to the *respublica*.[29] But it remained an essentially Christian system of ethical values to which the medieval writer of chivalric manuals habitually turned. Now it may be argued that Lull, being a man of religion who, like St. Augustine, had put behind him the secular follies of his worldly youth, does not fairly represent the secular ethos of chivalry at its most typical. Nevertheless it remains a fact of some importance that, in a treatise which for Englishmen of the fifteenth century had become the standard work on knighthood, there is no trace of

[28] E.g., *Boke of Noblesse*, pp. 57, 66, 75. Sir Thomas Smith was able to do this in the mid-sixteenth century: *De Republica Anglorum*, Book I, chap. xviii.

[29] Translated by Caxton as "the comyn prouffyght," Crotch, p. 41. See n. 25 above.

those aesthetic and erotic elements that bulk so large in the romances of chivalry, and for that matter also in contemporary practices.[30]

To those who were preoccupied with the apparent decay of medieval society, to those who were concerned with the ills to which France and England were in particular subject, chivalry could have meaning only as an ideal through which the governing class could find regeneration. To them, in short, it was an ideal set in a political context. It was this attitude, for example, that caused Alain Chartier during the 1420's to appeal to the French aristocracy in the name of a chivalric ideal stated in terms of as mature a concept of patriotic citizenship as any to be found in pre-Renaissance literature.[31] If Chartier was in this respect a voice crying in the wilderness of a disorganized and demoralized France to which the chivalric ideal could have little meaning beyond the courtly and aesthetic,[32] the English apologists spoke to a society in which, it would seem, those more frivolous aspects of chivalry had a limited appeal. The chivalric romances remained, it is true, popular among fifteenth-century English readers. But it is worth remembering that, in the most popular of them all during the later period, namely the Arthurian stories as told by Malory, the courtly aspect was, no doubt deliberately, played down. And the more serious treatises continued to breathe that atmosphere of Spartan discipline which chivalric literature had absorbed from the long tradition of medieval moralism, with a few reinforcements drawn from the classical authors.[33]

[30] *Ordre*, p. xxxvii.

[31] *Le Quadrilogue Invectif*, ed. R. Bouvier (Paris, 1944), *passim;* see especially pp. 74-76. For further treatment of this aspect of Chartier's thought, see F. J. Hoffman, *Alain Chartier. His Work and Reputation* (New York, 1942), pp. 90-121, 145-168, 204-205.

[32] See Kilgour, *passim,* for examples of decadence in French chivalric literature of the period.

[33] In addition to the distinctly disciplinarian and moral bent of the *Ordre of Chyualry* itself, see, for examples, Upton, *De Studio Militari*, pp. 7-8; *Boke of Noblesse*, pp. 61-62. See also Kilgour, pp. 183-184, 204, 209, 213, for examples in French literature of discipline to some extent modeled on ancient example.

It was not that the doctrine of courtly love was entirely alien to the military-political aspect of the chivalric ideal. Although to our prosaic way of thinking it seems more than a little frivolous, the idea that the knight increased in prowess, and hence in social usefulness, as a result of the love he bore his lady was stated by chivalric writers with the utmost solemnity.[34] In a day when government was customarily thought of in personal terms this was an attitude by no means ridiculous. Yet the connection between love and prowess, and even more so the connection between love and good government, although a perfectly logical expression of the courtly principle, was an artificial one even in the fourteenth century. Serious observers of the social scene in those days, Gower and Langland for example, looked to other qualities, equally personal, but more nearly associated with Christian than with chivalric values, for the stuff of good government. In any case it was a connection which did not necessarily have to be preserved. Nor was it preserved, except in the most poetic of senses, in Renaissance thought.

The ideal of *Frauendienst* did not, I am convinced, play a decisive part in the decline and transformation of chivalric idealism. It had been introduced as a graft on the parent stock of an essentially feudal chivalry. Like the Christian element so important in the later chivalric tradition, it unquestionably exercised a civilizing influence on a semibarbarous, almost exclusively military, aristocracy. But like that element it could always be separated from the original stem. Long after the chivalric ideal had ceased to serve as a system of values sufficient for the secular activity of the governing class, long after

---

[34] Sidney Painter quotes from Froissart a passage which merits repetition here. Relating the thoughts of Edward III about the beautiful but unco-operative Countess of Salisbury, the chronicler of chivalry has this to say: "And also if he should be amorous it would be entirely good for him, for his realm, and for all his knights and esquires, for he would hold more jousts, more tourneys, more feasts, and more revels than he had before; and he would be more able and more vigorous in his wars, more amiable and more trusting toward his friends and harsher toward his foes." *French Chivalry*, p. 141.

the knight had ceased to think of himself as the sole custodian of justice and order and had broadened his intellectual horizons to include the complex workings of Renaissance society, he was still capable of enjoying, perhaps also deriving spiritual benefit from, the conventions of courtly love. Those conventions blended readily with the Renaissance ideal of the courtier for which, indeed, they no doubt did much to prepare the way.[35] They were able to bridge the gap between medieval and modern thought more easily than most other aspects of the chivalric tradition because they were a response, not merely to peculiarly medieval conditions, but to feelings that have since the Middle Ages become universal in the Western World; and, of course, they in turn conditioned and gave direction to those feelings. The idea of romantic love, as C. S. Lewis has pointed out, was an original contribution of chivalric culture.[36] It was by no means taken for granted in earlier ages; and even during the medieval period it was tolerated by the custodians of morality, if at all, only very grudgingly.

Even during that period, however, it was possible for the serious-minded observer of society to separate the harmless romance of courtly love from that aspect of chivalry which bore an immediate relevance to the world of affairs. The very term "chivalry" they reserved more often than not for the military-political activities of the knight. It is the modern historian rather than the medieval writer who employs the term in such a way as to include all of the values normally linked to the secular life of the knightly class. To use an example—the aptness of which makes up for the fact that it is outside the time and space limits of this study—Alain Chartier saw no incompatibility between his criticism of French chivalry in the *Quadrilogue Invectif* and his own composition of such poems as the popular *Belle dame sans merci*. "In fact," wrote R. L. Kilgour, "he apparently considered chivalry

[35] Painter, p. 148.
[36] C. S. Lewis, *The Allegory of Love* (Oxford, 1936), chap. i.

as the military branch of the nation, with duties strictly war-like and practical, while courtly love was only a literary diversion which might charm knightly ears but which had no definite value for the order."[37]   Stephen Hawes, almost a century later, implied a similar distinction in his *Pastime of Pleasure* and one perhaps more characteristic of English than of French thought.   In that allegory of the knightly life he not only restricts the term "chivalry" to the military side of the knight's education, but subordinates both it and the courtly love element of his story to the demands of a liberal education.   But with him we are on the verge of a new social ideal, basically non-chivalric in its emphasis.

. . .

It is, then, in its political aspect that chivalric idealism maintained the kind of contact with reality which made it acceptable as a more or less complete scheme of secular values for a governing class that was no longer composed exclusively of knights and hence not literally chivalric.   It is undoubtedly true that even the military ideal could exert a profound influence on later generations and provide them with many of the forms in which the soldierly life could find suitable and decorous clothing.   Yet it is equally true that chivalry was the product of certain historical conditions, political in their bearing, and that as a characteristic and complete attitude toward secular life it proved incapable of surviving those conditions indefinitely.

That chivalric idealism outlived as long as it did the conditions that gave it birth remains, then, a fact requiring explanation.   At the risk of anticlimax, I must admit that I can offer no completely satisfactory answer—satisfactory, that is, in the sense that it can be placed by documentary evidence beyond the range of reasonable doubt.   I can, I believe, indicate cer-

[37] Kilgour, pp. 194-195.

tain approaches to the problem which should lead to something more than a possible solution. At an earlier point in this study I suggested that the ability of Englishmen in the late fifteenth and even the early sixteenth centuries to cling to a patently outdated code of values could be considered as part of the tendency generally discernible in the thought of the period to separate the ideal from the actual, and to allow ideas, once they had found in concrete symbols a local habitation and a name, to lead virtually a life of their own, tied to actuality only by the slenderest of threads. Perhaps this in turn represented a residual deposit in the popular mind from the school of realism once dominant in English philosophical thought, though long since superseded by the more particularizing habits, in the modern sense of the word the greater realism, of the nominalist school. Through this same process the Christian tradition had been rendered tangible, and also inflexible to the point of ossification, in the form of images and those external observances more or less related to the act of worship. Stated in such popular forms, doctrine had achieved an orthodoxy more rigid and unquestioned than that of the theologians. The tradition of chivalry, which was the secular counterpart of the Christian tradition in the scheme of medieval values, suffered similarly. From the modern point of view its formulas may be said to have degenerated into verbal stereotypes, and its ideals to have received the kind of expression in the literature of romance and in the external forms of courtly pageantry which can only be termed decadent. Yet to contemporary eyes they retained the stature of great truths rendered simply more understandable, more worthy of note, by their continual embodiment in familiar symbols. Thus the knight, although no longer the military and administrative factotum of the feudal monarchy, could nevertheless serve as the symbol of a government still considered protective in its primary purpose. Every part of his equipment and training, his sword, his armor, his spurs, the scheme of virtues and vices he was taught to consider peculiar to his estate, were capable of retaining much of the significance Lull had given them two centuries earlier. Nor had the mystical element so prevalent in the thirteenth-century manual been dissipated by the passage of time. The tournament, hollow show that it is to eyes unaccustomed to its symbolic meaning, could still evoke in the minds of specator and participant alike the feelings proper to the ideal of knighthood-in-action. And the chivalric romances, like the lives of the saints, were rich in concrete examples that reached well beyond the limits of time and place.

Of this coin, to be sure, the reverse and equally important side is the fact that in secular as in spiritual life no new formula had as yet achieved sufficient currency and sufficient prestige to challenge those still deeply embedded in the mythology of an earlier society.

But it is not necessary to look for an answer quite so far back in the dim reaches of the medieval mind. Chivalric thought in England had matured under conditions that greatly facilitated the retention of its basic ideals and that were in many respects peculiar to England. In one way or another those conditions may, as we have seen, all be traced to the early and effective centralization of royal authority. Owing to the nature of the Norman Conquest and the genius of a surprising proportion of the subsequently reigning monarchs, English feudalism became at an unusually early date oriented toward the king himself. Long before it could be called a national monarchy, England was a centralized one, its local elements pulled by a constantly centripetal force toward the king as the supreme feudal lord, the source of justice, the preserver of the peace, the defender of the realm. Even the king's dynastic policy, though not necessarily national in its implications, could command the allegiance of the English barons, and eventually in the Hundred Years' War became in a real if limited sense a national policy. During the wars of the fourteenth century English knights served more directly under the banner of the king than they had ever done before. The campaigns of the French wars were conducted in what most English knights were beginning to consider a foreign country. At home, the English knight became at an early date the valued agent of the royal administration in an increasing number of duties in local government. It has been said that English government in the Middle Ages was to a preponderant extent local. Who then should be more suited to conduct its business than the knights who knew the localities so intimately?[38] Eventually, too, the knights served as representatives of their districts in the king's parliaments, thus adding to their local responsibilities a share in the central government of the realm.

But, as we have seen, the public duties of knights had become so multifarious that their dwindling numbers were soon insufficient to provide the necessary manpower, with the result that those duties devolved upon men of comparable substance in the community who for one reason or another had not sought admittance to the order of knighthood. The actual function of the knight thus ceased to have any necessary connection with that order and tended to merge with that of the governing class as a whole. Logically considered, this should have had a profound effect on the mythology of chivalry. Originally an idealization of the belted knight and of those who aspired legitimately to the order of knighthood, chivalry might be expected to have lost much of its meaning as the knight lost his exclusive claim to be the protector of civil society.

And so it undoubtedly did. Just as the knight was absorbed into the texture of the centralized monarchy, so chivalric idealism eventually merged into a new awareness of citizenship in the national state and there lost its primitive political significance in the more sophisticated relationships of Renais-

[38] Treharne, p. 11.

sance government. In doing so it retained, of course, considerable relevance as a scheme of purely personal ethics and manners still capable of serving the purposes of aristocratic private life. Always at bottom a personal code, chivalry could not, however, maintain indefinitely its claim to be a code sufficient for the secular life of the governing class as the complexities of Renaissance society called attention with ever growing insistence to the distinction so basic to modern thought between private and public considerations.

Nevertheless, it is possible to see how chivalric idealism could follow the absorption of feudal loyalties into a rudimentary sense of patriotism expressed in loyalty to the person and the dynastic policies of the king. A highly significant peculiarity of English chivalry is its early and close relation to a burgeoning sense of patriotism. In England more than elsewhere the military loyalty of the knight had been transferred from the feudal lord to the king. It remained to a large extent a personal loyalty, but it could hardly escape the national implications, elementary as they were, of royal policy. Chivalric objectives could be, and doubtless were, habitually equated with those of the ruling dynasty. The king himself had taken some initiative in this process. His early control over the feudal system in England made it more than ordinarily feasible for him to do so. By the fourteenth century he found it both possible and useful to appeal to the sense of national interest among the governing class in order to enlist their support in his recruiting campaign.[39] Throughout the Hundred Year's War the English knight sought renown for feats of arms performed clearly and necessarily in the king's service. Indeed Edward III strove to embody in himself much of the chivalric idealism that hovered—at a genteel distance—above those often quite sordid episodes. Like the first Edward he deliberately fostered chivalric sentiment; and he encouraged it to find its center in the royal court by creating new orders of knighthood

[39] Keeney.

and by re-creating as nearly as possible the conditions of King Arthur's court.[40] At least in its more successful phases, the war itself seems to have had for him something of the quality of chivalric romance, with himself in the role of *preux chevalier*.

Even the critics of the war policy tended to examine it within a chivalric frame of reference. It is possible to see *The Vows of the Heron* as a bitterly satirical comment on the opening of hostilities, and one not a little tinged with disillusionment concerning chivalric motives.[41] In his propagandist poem entitled *In Praise of Peace,* John Gower attempted to dissuade Henry IV from continuing the war on the ground, equally chivalric in its terminology, yet equally alien to the more pugnacious aspect of the chivalric ideal, that the true knight will always prefer peace to war if there is any honorable choice.[42]

In Henry V the chivalric hero blends most effectively with the hero of patriotic tradition. Although the chroniclers by no means ignored his personal prowess, the noble feats of arms for which they find him most memorable are those of the general—siege operations, the tactics of pitched battle, ultimately, of course, the successful campaign which brought English power closer to its continental objectives than ever before or since. For nearly a hundred years patriotic English writers returned to him for the inspiration they could not hope to find in the dreary decades of defeat that followed his passing.[43]

The context of civil affairs was by no means so conducive to the retention of chivalric idealism as was that of military and dynastic policy. As long as fighting involved hand-to-

[40] R. S. Loomis, "Chivalric and Dramatic Imitations of Arthurian Romance," *Medieval Studies in Memory of A. K. Porter* (Cambridge, Mass., 1939), I, 79-97; and "Edward I, Arthurian Enthusiast," *Spec.,* XXVIII (Jan., 1953), 114-127; Cline, pp. 208-209.

[41] B. J. Whiting, "The Vows of the Heron," *Spec.,* XX (July, 1945), 261-278.

[42] *The Complete Works of John Gower,* ed. G. C. Macaulay (Oxford, 1899-1902), III, 480-492, especially lines 67-70, 115-161.

[43] E.g., *Boke of Noblesse,* pp. 2-20; C. L. Kingsford, ed., *The First English Life of Henry the Fifth.*

hand combat, the soldier, whether knight or squire or gentle-
man-adventurer, could feel a personal kinship with the men of
Agincourt. And as long as foreign policy was determined to
any large extent by dynastic considerations chivalric objectives
could readily enough be identified with those of the ruling
house, symbolized by the person of the king. It was far more
difficult for the ideals that had grown up around the institution of knighthood to survive the absorption of the knight's
function into that of the ruling class as a whole, ultimately in
fact into that of a national government. Nevertheless, it is
also possible to see how chivalric values could be made to
follow the absorption of the knight into a class of civil "governors" no longer necessarily based on the institution of knighthood and to retain some ideal significance for that much less
clearly defined group.

This absorption of the ideal of the knight into one em-
bracing the entire governing class was a gradual process which
had its origins in the feudal era. Although evidence of any
conscious awareness of its significance is scarce, a few items of
considerable value may be found in the literature of the latter
fourteenth century. Still orthodox in their approach to the
problems of society, the writers of that period were more aware
of those problems and of the national context within which
they presented themselves than any earlier group of writers.
Langland's references to the institution of knighthood are
especially interesting. They are also surprisingly few considering the vast sweep of the canvas upon which he painted,
a fact in itself not without significance in this era of rapid
change. Such as he makes are ordinary enough, but in their
emphasis tend rather to treat the knight as a member of the
landed governing class than as one who has been initiated into
a special, exclusive, and primarily military order. He is the
right hand of the king, the administrator and enforcer of the
king's decrees. More accurately he is the enforcer and/or the
administrator of the king's justice, for most legislation could

be said to serve the purpose of protecting legal rights. Government to Langland is essentially a matter of determining that each order in society performs its appointed duty in the interest of the community as a whole. It is the agency that set the plowman to "till and toil" for the "profit of all the people . . . as true life asketh." It establishes "law and loyalty . . . each man to know his own." In that process the knightly class occupies in Langland's poem a position not without ambiguity, but one which may for most purposes be safely equated with that of the governing class as a whole.

If we recognize that he used the terms "comune" and "comunes" with some freedom, at times approaching the modern meaning of the word "commons," sometimes that of the "commonalty," more often approximating the term "community" which, as in the "community of the realm," held an important place in the political language of Langland's own England, we shall be able to see in the following famous lines what was probably an orthodox description of a social order in which knighthood is the senior partner, unspecific in its function, but in general the active element in a royal government depending in the long run on the latent strength of the entire community.

Then came there a king . knighthood him led,
Might of the comunes . made him to reign,
And then came kind wit [common sense] . and clerks he made,
For to counsel the king . and the comune save.
　The king and knighthood . and clergy both
Cast [contrived] that the comune . should themselves find [provide for]
　The comune contrived . of kind wit's crafts,
And for profit of all the people . plowmen ordained,
To till and toil . as true life asketh.
The king and the comune . and kind wit the third
Shaped law and loyalty . each man to know his own.[44]

[44] B. Prol., Lines 112-122; See also B, VIII, lines 9-12; B, XI, lines 285-288; C, VI, lines 72-75. To my mind the most effective treatment of the Langland's handling of the lines quoted and of the problem of the "comune" in particular is F. Donaldson, *Piers Plowman: The C-Text and Its Poet* (New Haven, 1949), pp. 94 ff.

In the C-text, these lines for some reason become vaguer and less confident in their description of the political organism, yet perhaps nonetheless accurate in their reflection of contemporary thought: precision in constitutional concepts is not a virtue to be found in the more informal political literature of this period.

> Then came there a king . knighthood his led,
> The much might of the men . made his to reign;
> And then came kind wit . and clerks he made,
> And conscience and kind wit . and knighthood together
> Cast that the comune . should her comunes find.
> Kind wit and the comune . contrived all crafts,
> And for most profit to the people . a plough they began to make,
> With leel [true] labor to live . while life and land lasteth.[45]

The knight appears in a more specific and more recognizable context as the local "justicier," the ancestor of the Justice of the Peace on whose shoulders were to fall the multiple burden of Tudor administration and who already had come to assume the chief responsibility for preserving order and justice in the local district. He is appealed to by Piers against Wastour as the only agency capable of dealing with such an antisocial character. That he appealed in vain is a commentary on the effectiveness of the system, not on its structure, which Langland accepts.[46]

Langland it would seem had in his mind already stretched the term "knighthood" to encompass the broadening functions of the landed gentry in the actual affairs of civil society. The author of *Mum and the Sothsegger,* written around the turn of the century, found it unnecessary to speak of knighthood at all. In his shrewd commentary on English government he follows political reality in separating the governing class into the "lords," who, with the king, constitute the executive center of government, and the shire-knights who come to parlia-

---

[45] C, I, lines 139-146.
[46] B, VII, lines 161-172. Cf. B, VI, lines 21-24.

ment to represent their constitutents in a governmental system that was dependent upon their information and counsel.[47]

John Gower, on the other hand, reflects the changing status of knighthood much less vividly than did Langland. Though as concerned over the state of England as his more obscure contemporary and capable at times of a certain insight into the problems of English society, his thought remained in the realm of traditional theory and his expression in that of familiar formula. To him society was still a tripartite, functional organism:

> Sunt Clerus, Miles, Cultos, tres trina gerentes;
> Hic docet, hic pugnat, alter et arua colit.[48]

Into this simple pattern he fitted the more variegated aspects of contemporary life with honest insistence but with some difficulty.[49] The aristocracy bore in its various branches the same responsibility generally assigned to knighthood of providing that fundamentally protective government so essential to the common welfare. Knighthood remains in Gower's eyes still the sword arm of the body politic, its function primarily military, only secondarily civil.[50] Curiously enough, Gower has more to say about knighthood and makes more use of the chivalric formulas in the course of his comprehensive commentary on the social scene than Langland in his similarly universal critique. This fact would, I suppose, suggest that Gower was more familiar than Langland with the jargon of the class to which he belonged, more given by nature to stereotyped thought, possibly less vividly aware of the realities of contemporary life.

[47] See Ferguson, "The Problem of Counsel in Mum and the Sothsegger" (Studies in the Renaissance, II, 1955, 67-83) for detailed references to this curious fragment.

[48] Vox Clamantis, Lib. III, lines 1-2.

[49] See for example his treatment of the merchants and the legal profession in both the Mirour and Vox Clamantis.

[50] In Mirour, pp. 256-267, Gower distinguishes, but not at all clearly, between the duty of the greater lords and that of the knights and men-at-arms; nor is his treatment of the aristocracy significantly different from that of emperors and kings which precedes it. In Vox Clamantis he makes fewer distinctions, being, no doubt, by that time more concerned about the estate of the peasantry.

The fifteenth century provides us with additional examples both of confusion and, most significant, of an intermittent appreciation of social and political reality.

In the parliament of 1433 the chancellor, Bishop Stafford of Bath and Wells, delivered a sermon remarkable for its adherence to actuality. In surveying the "estates of the realm" he abandoned the traditional threefold division of society and, with his eye on the facts of the emerging English representative system, he grouped together the *"praelati, proceres et magnates,"* placed the knights, esquires, and merchants in the second of the three *"status regni,"* and left the *cultores, artifices et vulgares* to the third.[51] On the other hand, his contemporary, John Lydgate, though by no means unaware of the way the world wagged, habitually lapsed into the more traditional interpretation of the social order and treated knighthood more often than not as a military caste.[52] And even Bishop Stafford seems not to have been able to hold theory and fact so closely together as he did in his speech of 1433. Nine years later he, also, reverted to a description of the estates that differed little from the traditional tripartite form since it failed to separate the greater and lesser aristocracy, as he had done on the earlier occasion, and since it failed to demonstrate the close relation that had existed for some time between the knights and the merchants in their parliamentary capacity as the "commons."[53]

The habit of dividing society into three estates, a habit basic to the concepts of chivalry, died very hard. Indeed it seems to have been strengthened considerably in the literature of the latter fifteenth century. The appearance of *The Boke of Saint Albans* in 1486, although a compilation of stock items, is an instance of what may well have been a conscious attempt to restore the traditional theory in this Indian Summer of

---

[51] *Rotuli Parliamentorum*, IV, 419. Cf. J. S. Roskell, "The Social Composition of the Commons in a Fifteenth-Century Parliament," *Bull. Inst. Hist. Res.*, XXIV (1951), 152-172, 171 n. 8.

[52] See, for examples, *Minor Poems*, Part II, pp. 627, 549, 716, 776-777, 784, 811.

[53] *Rot. Parl.*, V, 35.

English chivalry. Perhaps Bishop Stafford's second recorded sermon to parliament may also have reflected this same desire of an increasingly insecure aristocracy to meet the challenge of the increasingly mobile society under cover of a deliberately reactionary social theory. Yet, alongside the apparently increased emphasis on the estate theory in the latter fifteenth century, and the apparent resurgence of general interest in chivalric idealism, must be set that genial old lawyer, Sir John Fortescue, who analyzed the problem of English government in an astonishingly empirical frame of mind and without the slightest reference to the language or concepts peculiar to the chivalric tradition.[54] Perhaps George Ashby might be a better illustration because he expressed himself in a more traditional medium. He turned the "mirror of princes," which had absorbed much of the chivalric idealism of the earlier era,[55] but which had little to do with actual conditions, into a canny and instinctively empirical study of English conditions. *The Active Policy of a Prince* (1470?) becomes accordingly a document bearing few of the characteristics of chivalric thought. The old civil servant, his long career spent at the center of a government too often paralyzed by the machinations of "over-mighty subjects," strongly urged the king to adopt the quite nonchivalric policy of appointing as his administrative officials men notable for their ability rather than for their social background.[56]

It would seem, then, that chivalric idealism could by the fifteenth century live only when separated from reality, and that its unquestionable appeal for Englishmen of the era was for that very reason truly romantic. It would seem that it lived in the clichés of a decadent literary tradition, in manuals of knighthood inspired by conditions existing two centuries earlier, in the artificial atmosphere of allegory and romance, or in the more or less deliberate reaction of books on the origins

[54] See especially *The Governance of England.*
[55] See below, chap. vi.
[56] *Active Policy,* p. 38.

and structure of the social estates. Chronicles alone among the widely circulated secular literature could be said to have expressed the chivalric tradition in the context of actual conditions because they treated chivalry mainly in the context of war where it retained a not too tenuous validity. The rest of these literary forms in which the tradition lingered harked back stubbornly to an earlier day. The one thing they all stressed in one way or another is that the knight, the embodiment of that tradition, had a political role to play, if only by virtue of the fact that he was a man of war, the protector of the community. It would, in short, seem that we have merely illustrated the peculiar faculty of the medieval mind for separating the ideal from the actual rather than explaining how it was possible for it to do so or why so many people in the late fifteenth century could take chivalry very seriously as a system of values sufficient for the secular life of the governing class.

Now one possible explanation is that the problem is to some extent a false one, that the dichotomy it presents is more apparent than real. Langland and Gower, if I may be permitted to return for a moment to those unrivaled interpreters of late fourteenth-century life, had more in common in their conception of knighthood than they had at issue. Neither one was at all preoccupied with chivalric idealism: the moral system to which they exhorted their readers to conform was that of Christian ethics in the broadest sense. But they both accepted the functional concept of knighthood upon which all that linked chivalry with practical affairs depended. Knighthood to both is roughly synonymous with the governing class. The difference between them was simply that between the insight of genius and the conventionality of the modestly endowed moralist. In a sense it was a verbal difference. Gower adhered to formula; Langland fitted his words to the world of reality in which he lived and from which even the mysticism of his message emanated. By Caxton's day this tendency to identify knighthood, if only symbolically, with the governing class seems to have proceeded so far that, instead of rendering chivalric idealism obsolete as a guide to the world of secular affairs, it had made possible the application of chivalric ideals to the entire politically active element in the commonwealth. Such, at any rate, seems to me the only plausible explanation for Caxton's decision to translate and publish for the English gentry Lull's book of knighthood. That he took his task seriously, in the nature of a public service, is demonstrated by his epilogue. It was, after all, a book of serious moral teaching, by no means to be confused with the mere courtesy-book or guide to the social amenities. It is built solidly on the function of the knight in a social order conceived as a hierarchy of functioning classes. Certainly its antiquarian value could have had small appeal to a generation not yet accustomed to reflect on the past as an age different in essentials from their own.

That men of affairs in Caxton's England should have conceived the function of the gentry to be even roughly co-extensive with that of the twelfth-century knight remains, however, a troublesome matter. Again we find that the problem seems more knotty than it really is. For it is difficult to exaggerate the conservatism of English thought in the late medieval period; and it is correspondingly easy to exaggerate the degree to which that thought anticipated the greater political awareness and sophistication of the Renaissance mind. The more we know of actual institutions, of parliament especially, and the processes of medieval legislation, the more prone we are to assume that the men of the period were as aware as we of the constitutional precedents then being set. It seems inconceivable that the men of Lancastrian England were significantly less conscious of the positive function of government and of the potentialities latent in it for the invention of constructive policies than were the men who grappled in their minds with the revolutionary problems of the mid-sixteenth century, and

reflected in their writings the positive quality of Tudor government. Surely a man of Caxton's experience must have seen
that government had long outgrown the role of a merely protective agency and that the governing class had likewise outgrown the simple function of bearing the sword in defense of
justice and peace.

To assume any such thing is, however, to miss one of the
most significant facts concerning the political outlook of the
late medieval period. In his more reflective moments, when,
that is, he is not embroiled in the actual detail of government,
the Englishman of the fifteenth century, like that of the fourteenth, thought of society as an organism ordained by the
Creator in a particular form, static in the sense that it could not
alter that form, subject to change only in the sense that it could
enjoy health or suffer illness. Change, he felt, was most likely
to manifest itself, as in the past, by a progressive illness of the
spirit, the result of the morbid viruses of sin. Since virtue
and vice are the determinants of health and sickness in his
society, he tended to view the problems of public life, like
those of private, in the light of personal morality. Improve-
ment, he felt, was unlikely in the long run to stem from anything else than a return to virtue on the part of all men, but
especially those who have the care of the whole community
as their primary responsibility. Such a regeneration, unlikely
in any event, is much less likely to follow governmental action
than it is the exhortation of preachers and moralists. And so
the task of those to whom the duty of secular government is
entrusted becomes the external and largely negative one of
preventing evil doers from trespassing upon the rights of
others.

Detailed demonstration of this habit of mind will have to
await another time and another context.[57] But a few examples
may at this point be helpful. The very essence of those com-

---

[57] The author has for some time been at work on a study of the political literature of the period with just such an end in view.

prehensive commentaries of Langland and Gower on late fourteenth-century England, this attitude toward government con-
tinues to crop up here and there in the writings of the succeeding century. A verse writer of the early fifteenth century
summed up the role of parliament, in which the knightly
class still enjoyed a preponderance, as that of a righter of
wrongs.

> When all a kingdom gathered is
> In God's law, by one assent,
> For to amend that was amiss,
> Therefore is ordained a parliament.[58]

In the sermon delivered by Bishop Stafford before the parliament of 1433, to which reference has already been made, that
discerning prelate declared the duty of the politically active
estates to be simply that of promoting peace and justice. True,
he sees this function as one involving a broader segment of
society than was customary in the "estate" literature: the prel-
ates and magnates bear the chief responsibility for peace,
unity, and concord; the knights share with the *"mediocribus,"*
that is, the merchants, and squires, the duty of working for
"equitas et mera justicia."[59] The governing class is expanding; but its social function remains ideally the same. Speaking
to parliament in 1468, the chancellor reiterated the profound
commonplace that government existed to preserve the peace
and security of the realm, which meant ultimately the maintenance of justice.[60] In a letter to the Bishop of Enachden intended for circulation among the men responsible for the
government of Ireland, Richard III expressed an ideal of local
government which was no doubt as representative of the political outlook of his day as it was dear to his own unsophisticated
and chivalrous heart.

... the king's grace in no wise will cure [permit] holy mother church
to be wronged . . . but that his said cousin [the Earl of Desmond]

---

[58] *Twenty-six Political and other Poems*, ed. J. Kail, E.E.T.S., O.S., No. 124
(1904), poem xiii, lines 1-4.
[59] *Rot. Parl.*, IV, 419.   [60] *Ibid.*, V, 622.

shall maintain, assist, and support it in every behalf, as justice and right requireth.   And, over that, to see that no manner robberies, spoliations, oppressions, or extortions be suffered to be committed amongst any of the king's subjects of those parts, of what estate, degree, or condition soever they be; and in case any happen to be, to see them so offending utterly to be punished according with the king's laws.   And that the said earl shall, by all ways and means of policy, see and provide that by the passage of the common highways there the subjects may be assured to go and pass without robbing and unlawful letting [hindrance]: . . ."

All this to the immediate end that the said earl "may appear and be named a very [true] justicier, as well for his proper honor and weal, as for the common weal of those parts, etc."[61] Here is the pattern of "good and abundant governance" for which all Englishmen of good will longed in those troubled years.   And it is by no means of negligible importance that this concept of government is linked with the "honor" of the local administrator.   Knightly reputation, even in the era of the Wars of the Roses, could be won in other ways than by military exploit.   Richard was, in fact, merely spelling out in this letter the ideal of the knight's political responsibility which Lull and his English adapters had set forth in more or less elliptical form.

Such an attitude, based as it was upon assumptions formed to fit the needs of a relatively uncomplicated era, could not of course be maintained indefinitely.   Even in his own day Richard III no doubt sensed the presence of a new spirit in public life, and one which was as alien to his temper as it was congenial to that of his rival and successor Henry Tudor.[62] The political literature of the fifteenth century also reveals in isolated flashes the still obscure growth of a new attitude, realistic and gropingly empirical, which under the jolting impact of events in the following century was to harden into a new sense of citizenship.   But the change was by no means sudden.   Most public-spirited Englishmen of the late fifteenth century

[61] *Original Letters Illustrative of English History,* ed. H. Ellis, 2nd Series (London, 1827), I, 123-124.
[62] This is a point of view presented by Kendall in his recent life of Richard III.

would have found the words of Richard, like Caxton's *Ordre of Chyualry,* the expression of a universal truth, sufficient for all normal purposes. These men could still accept the chivalric tradition because it idealized a way of life they felt still existed in all essential respects, no matter how bedeviled it might have become.

To maintain such an attitude required nonetheless an ability to separate the ideal and the actual in a way that seems deliberately romantic to persons accustomed to a more rapidly moving society. That separation accounts, however, for both the weakening and the preservation of the chivalric tradition in England. The political literature of fifteenth-century England, while not in any sense antichivalric, is frequently nonchivalric in tone. Its more realistic contributors, the author of the *Libelle of Englyshe Polycye,* for example, or Sir John Fortescue, thought along lines which were not likely to impinge on the chivalric tradition. That tradition by the Tudor era had become a source of ethical inspiration rather than a guide to the conduct of actual affairs. On the other hand, its separation from actual conditions allowed it to escape the contaminating influence of those conditions and to survive especially the disillusionment that followed war and rebellion. It is perhaps for this reason that chivalry was apparently in better repute, though less frequently written about, in England than in France where it was more closely identified with the actual life of the governing class and where it came during the fifteenth century to be the object of criticism and more than the normal amount of satire.[63] England produced a Fortescue to whom the ideal of chivalry was irrelevant; but she produced no Chartier to castigate with the bitterness of an outraged idealist the failure of the aristocracy to live up to its protestations, nor a Commines to demonstrate the absurdity of chivalric idealism as the inspiration for political action.

[63] Kilgour, *passim.*

V

CHIVALRY AND CHAUVINISM

AS THE PRECEDING CHAPTERS HAVE DEMON-
strated, chivalric idealism, though divorced from political
reality, continued during the fifteenth century to inspire the
attitudes of Englishmen, especially of those Englishmen who
breathed the artificially conditioned air of the royal court.
And nowhere is this tendency more apparent than in the discussion of what today would be called "foreign policy." In
the course of England's dealings with her neighbors war became a factor always to be reckoned with. The relatively
crude nature of interstate relations during the period of emerging territorial states made war or the threat of war a constant
and indispensable instrument of policy. Yet war, more than
any other aspect of medieval life, had become identified with
the values of chivalry. Chivalry was, I repeat, primarily an
idealization of the knight considered as the protector of the
community. As the duty of protection became enlarged to
include the support of dynastic claims, the protection of the
interests of the supreme feudal lord, chivalric values, properly
tinctured with Christian principles, were made to fit the purposes of dynastic policy, if only because they were the only
ones at hand; and chivalric terminology long continued to
color, and perhaps also to shape, any discussion of peace and
war. As the nation began to assume recognizable shape—
recognizable, that is, to contemporaries—it became increasingly difficult to make either the values or the terminology of
chivalry fit the realities of national policy or even the conduct
of war on an international scale. Under the combined impact
of events and of the newly reappraised example of classical

antiquity there emerged gradually during the sixteenth century something resembling a modern discussion of those subjects. Such discussion came more and more to be characterized by a realistic attitude in which pragmatic considerations tended to outweigh the values of knight-errantry and so to remove the obfuscating screen of both thought and language which too often in the medieval period had obscured, perhaps even to himself, the colder calculations of the statesman or general. At the same time a similar realism began to pervade the military life in its lesser, tactical aspects. An emphasis on prudence and the importance of success regardless of the means employed, though by no means unheard of in chivalric literature, tended with rapidly mounting insistence to replace the idealism with which a partially Christianized chivalry had decorously endeavored to clothe the stark figure of Mars.

. . .

Fortunately for our purposes one document has come down to us from the latter fifteenth century which, by its unequivocally chivalric treatment of England's foreign policy, affords us the kind of insight into the mind of the period seldom to be had in that sparsely documented era. If both Caxton and Malory, and perhaps Hawes as well, were concerned primarily with the rehabilitation of chivalry as a moral and intellectual system for the regeneration of the ruling class and through them of their sadly disturbed country, the author of *The Boke of Noblesse* seems to have been primarily moved by the argument of dynastic ambition and an aggressive foreign policy. It is now nearly a century since J. G. Nichols edited that curious pamphlet for the Roxburghe Club. Since then our knowledge of it and its literary context has been significantly enlarged.[1] It remains, however, a sadly neglected work; and

---

[1] Warner, ed., *Epistle of Othea to Hector*, pp. xliii-xlviii; C. F. Bühler, ed., *The Dicts and Sayings of the Philosophers*, E.E.T.S., O.S., No. 211 (1941), pp. xxxix-xlvi; K. B. McFarlane, "William Worcester: a Preliminary Survey," in *Studies Presented to Sir Hilary Jenkinson*, ed. J. C. Davies (London, 1957), pp. 196-221.

that fact helps in some degree to explain why English chivalric thought of the latter fifteenth century has so often been seen out of focus. Although scarcely an influential document (it exists in a unique manuscript and seems never to have been copied or adapted in an age much given to that sort of thing) nor one likely to appeal to students of letters, it nevertheless reveals the chivalric mind at work in ways seldom so clearly indicated in the more familiar literature of the period.

It was apparently written by William Worcester some time before the change of dynasty in 1461, in an effort to persuade Henry VI to emulate his father's bellicose policy toward France. It was then revised to attract Yorkist patronage when, in 1475, Edward IV was preparing actually to renew the war.[2] Worcester borrowed much of the more traditional material contained in it from the well known French books of knighthood by Honoré Bonet and Christine de Pisan, and he owed something to Alain Chartier. But, even in its earliest form, it was much more than a mere compilation of standard references on the subject of *noblesse*. What looks at first glance like just another manual of knighthood turns out, surprisingly enough, to be a piece of propaganda for a specific foreign policy. Indeed it is an excellent example of the late fifteenth century Englishman's ability to comment vigorously, sometimes shrewdly, on the contemporary political scene. In this respect it may be placed in the same category as Fortescue's *Governance of England,* if at a considerably lower level of sophistication.

What Worcester had in mind when he wrote the *Boke of Noblesse* becomes clearer when it is viewed in connection with a collection of documents he appears to have compiled as

[2] K. B. McFarlane, in the paper mentioned in the preceding note, has reviewed the problem of authorship in the light of much fresh manuscript evidence and concludes that Worcester was in all probability the sole author. This runs counter to Bühler's theory that the *Boke* was compiled originally by Stephen Scrope, another secretary to Fastolf, at some time around the middle of the century, and revised by Worcester in 1475.

"pièces justicatives" to the pamphlet itself.[3] These papers were derived from those which Sir John Fastolf gathered in the course of his career as military administrator for the Duke of Bedford in France. That illustrious old knight had maintained (and over-worked) William Worcester in the capacity of a sort of gentleman-secretary, "a member of that large and highly trained profession whose duty it was to manage the estates and households of the great."[4] By his personal example and by the records of his proconsulate, Fastolf provided Worcester with both the inspiration for a re-statement of foreign policy in terms of a chivalric chauvinism and the materials for relating the argument directly to the national experience.

In a prologue to this collection, recast after Worcester's death by his son, and rededicated to Richard III, the younger man throwns a good deal of light on his father's mind. Like his father, he combines foreign policy with chivalric idealism, quite unaware of any possible incongruity. He refers to the duty of the king to look to the defense and conservation of his "both realms" by practicing the cardinal virtues of "Justice, Prudence, Force and Temperance." But he must especially be capable of using Force so as to "vanquish through the might of God . . . your great adversary of France, and to make upon him a new conquest" or by a final peace to accomplish "the recovery of your rightful title of inheritance."[5] It was, he says, for this reason, that his father had prepared "this book" (apparently referring to *The Boke of Noblesse,* not the collection of documents to follow) drawing from the philosophers their wisdom concerning the use of force.[6] But, he adds, "the experience of men in chivalrous deeds exercised in arms . . . prevaileth most" and is therefore more useful than such theorizing. Hence the collection of records of "the right noble

[3] Warner, ed., *Epistle,* p. xliv.
[4] McFarlane, "Worcester," p. 198.
[5] *Collection,* pp. 521-522.
[6] *Ibid.,* p. 522. The *Collection* contains no material from the "philosophers."

chivalry" of the one-time regent of France, John, Duke of Bedford.[7]

They are a record of defeat, but in the eyes of the patriotic compiler and his son by no means cause for despair. The memory of Agincourt remained very much alive in the reign of Edward IV and the dynastic ambitions implanted by Henry V's brief ascendency in France died very slowly.[8] The policy that emerges from Worcester's documents retained a place in English foreign policy for a long time and found concrete, if somewhat equivocal, expression in the actual invasion of France in 1475.

It is, then, in the light of this strange collection of documents and its even stranger preface that *The Boke of Noblesse* itself should be examined. For it was the king's foreign policy which gave to the latter the consistency and practicality of purpose and the sense of urgency which set it aside from other contemporary books of knighthood. The reader is not, indeed, left long in doubt as to the immediate purpose underlying this ostensibly conventional study of *noblesse*. After somewhat perfunctorily imploring the grace of God and paying the briefest of respects to the subject of true nobility, the authors pass on to an impassioned statement of the disgrace and damage suffered by England as a result of losing her French provinces.[9] There is, to be sure, a connection between this subject and the problem of *"Noblesse."* Nobility is defined chiefly in terms of illustrious deeds done by the aristocracy in behalf of the commonwealth; and it is by recalling to the mind of the English "noble men in arms" the noble deeds of their predecessors that the author hopes to stimulate a sort of crusade to restore the lost territories. Accordingly much of the

---

[7] *Ibid.*, pp. 522-523.

[8] See, for example, the chancellor's speech to Parliament 17 May 1468, *Rotuli Parliamentorum*, V, 622-623.

[9] *Boke of Noblesse*, p. 2. The only serious treatment of this work as an example of chivalric thought may be found in W. Kleineke, *Englische Fürstenspiegel vom Policraticus Johanns von Salisbury bis zum Basilikon Doron König Jakobs I* (Halle, 1937), pp. 145-151.

book, much more than would be expected of a book of knightly virtue, becomes a history of the "acts in arms" performed by the "English nation" from its legendary beginning in the "noble ancient blood of Troy" through the more successful phases of the Hundred Years' War.[10] Much also is made of the knavery of the "French party" in breaking of truces;[11] and there is a good deal of talk about the true title of the English in the French lands.[12] Again in this book history provides the inspiration and the precedent for a renewed chivalry. In this instance, however, it is a chivalry that finds expression in national policy rather than in individual actions performed in the interest of a more or less abstract common weal.

Although remarkable enough, this tendency to express national policy in chivalric terms, or to expand the chivalric terminology to encompass the discussion of national issues, should not occasion too much surprise. As we have seen, chivalry in England, like the feudal system it idealized, had become oriented at a comparatively early date toward the king himself. The wars against the Scots, the Welsh, and, of course, the French had provided a protracted lesson in common action which, if it was often imperfectly learned, tended always to emphasize the royal policy—we might even say the national interest if we are careful to remember that the national interest was habitually interpreted in terms of dynastic and military policy. England, moreover, had found her patrons of chivalry and even in certain instances her chivalric heroes in her kings. Henry V, in particular, became for fifteenth-century writers a symbol, at once patriotic and chivalric.

In that era of national humiliation, it was possible for Englishmen to see in the chivalric tradition an inspiration not only for personal conduct but for patriotic action. Renown, the secular objective toward which all true knights must strive,

[10] *Ibid.*, pp. 2-5, 9-10.
[11] *Ibid.*, pp. 5-6.
[12] *Ibid.*, pp. 22-26.

could easily be equated with national prestige, and feudal loyalty with duty to the king. Englishmen of chivalric temper were thus able to escape the disillusionment that overtook so many French writers of the period who at times found in chivalry the expression of an anarchistic and selfish feudalism.[13] The chivalric scale of values remained, of course, exceedingly limited, leaving little room for the discussion of the political complexities of which such more realistic observers as Commines were already keenly aware. Chivalry could provide the language of chauvinism, but not of national policy.

I do not mean to imply that, in centering their attention on dynastic issues, the author of *The Boke of Noblesse* ignored the problem of personal conduct. Indeed it is doubtful if he made any clear distinction between the areas of public and private activity. That was, after all, a distinction even the most sophisticated of English writers seldom made in the fifteenth century. To the medieval mind public welfare resulted from the virtuous actions of individual men. Human life was a seamless web of ethical relationships. So, like the Christian moralists of popular tradition, Worcester finds the reason for the decay of England's interests in the moral decay of Englishmen. He would not even allow the stars a place in explaining the reverses recently suffered by England.[14] He emphasized, however, those ethical factors most closely related to the chivalric ideal, especially the element of physical discipline which derived from the original military function of the knight. In a period noted for the decadence of chivalric ideals and forms and for the predominance of social over military considerations, it is interesting to see this English writer stressing above all others, certainly above the courtly virtues, those qualities that make a good soldier. In doing so he gave expression to the tradition of Spartanism that runs so strongly through the

[13] See treatment of Gerson and Chartier, especially, in Kilgour, pp. 177-225. See also Perroy, p. 48.
[14] *Boke of Noblesse*, pp. 50-51.

literature of chivalry and gives to that literature much of its relevance to the actual life of the medieval knight.[15]

The man of true nobility will always keep himself fit for his primary assignment as protector of the community. In peace he will emulate the Romans (pictured not as the custodians of a peculiar culture, but as "chivalrous paynim" knights) and in war "the condition of a lion."[16] Conversely he must avoid sensuality, the love of ease and of the flesh which saps the physical as well as the moral stamina of the knight.[17] He must also avoid covetousness, and an addiction to those private interests which do not contribute to the common welfare. The knight should be capable, especially, of rising above the niggardly considerations of property and litigation and be able to dwell on the more appropriate level of noble deeds of arms.[18]

Perhaps it is in his treatment of the study of law and the conduct of local administration that Worcester reveals most clearly his chivalric bias and the limited view he had of the evolving function of the knightly class. He was seriously disturbed by the tendency of such studies to capture the mind of the English knighthood and to seduce it from its primary duty. The king, he urges, should see to it that, "for the greater defense of your realms, . . . also the advancement and increase of chivalry and worship in arms," the sons of the nobility and "for the most part of all those that be come and descended of noble blood, as of ancient knights, esquires, and other ancient gentle men," be instructed intensively in "disciplines, doctrine, and usage of school of arms." This, he says, was the custom in the days of the king's royal predecessors.

But now of late days, the greater pity is, many one that be descended of noble blood and born to arms . . . set himself to singular practice, . . . as to learn the practice of law or customs of land, or of civil matter, and so waste greatly their time in such needless business as to hold

---

[15] This ideal of Spartan discipline also colors Caxton's epilogue to *The Ordre of Chyualry*. See also Upton, *De Studio Militari*, pp. 7-8, 47.

[16] *Boke of Noblesse*, pp. 4, 75.

[17] *Ibid.*, pp. 22, 33, 79.

[18] *Ibid.*, pp. 57, 66, 75.

courts, to keep and bear out a proud countenance at the holding of
sessions and shires, also there to embrace and rule among your poor and
simple commons of bestial countenance that lust to live in rest.[19]

Few sentences in fifteenth-century English pamphlet literature tell more. On the one hand it bears unconscious witness
to the deep concern of the English landowner for the status of
his property in an increasingly litigious, yet basically insecure,
society—a concern which left small room for thoughts of
knightly exploits or the consideration of problems other than
domestic. It is a concern that gives to the Paston letters a
theme of grim consistency; and it is one with which Worcester
himself, as Fastolf's business agent, was only too familiar. On
the other hand it reveals the oddly anachronistic quality of the
chivalric tradition when applied, as Worcester consistently
applies it, to practical affairs. He is, to be sure, willing enough
to concede an important place to the law. In fact, he specifies
that the practice of law should be committed "to such persons
of demure countenance that were held virtuous and well dis-
posed," adding significantly "though he were descended but
of easy birth," and that such officers of the law be protected by
"lords and noble men of birth"[20] who would thus be perform-
ing their traditional knightly function as befitted their honorable status. But it is also true that to him, even more than
to such standard earlier authorities as Lull, the ruling class is
primarily a military class; and, although he in no way differs
from other fifteenth-century observers in considering government essentially protective in its function, he would distinguish
clearly between the honorable function of military protection
(always easily confused with aggression) and the protective
function exercised by the courts of law. The latter, though
good and necessary, cannot be considered honorable in the
knightly sense since it is maintained chiefly for those common
people who cannot protect themselves and whose main object

---

[19] *Ibid.*, p. 77. Cf. the similar complaint in Lydgate, *Minor Poems*, II, 845,
lines 25-32.
[20] *Boke of Noblesse*, p. 78. Cf. Caxton-Lull, *Ordre of Chyualry*, p. 30.

is to "live in rest"—a desire by definition alien to the chivalric ideal.

Yet throughout this discussion of a limited and, to the historian, anachronistic ideal we must not lose sight of the fact that *The Boke of Noblesse* was meant to be a practical application of chivalric values to the problems of contemporary England. There is in it a strong tincture of realism which links it to one of the most significant developments of the period, namely a tendency to treat the issues of public life in terms of political and economic reality. Like his master, Sir John Fastolf, Worcester was able to see the relationship between such considerations and the wars upon which he believed the honor and worship of England depended. It is more than probable that the touches of realism in *The Boke of Noblesse* were taken either in substance or spirit from the reports of that most practical of knights. In the collection of documents made by Worcester, consisting primarily of Fastolf's reports and proposals, the spirit of chivalry is all but extinguished in an effusion of facts and figures. There his faithful secretaries could find, for example, an abundance of inventories and accounts, including "mention of a part of the worshipful chivalry, [under his command] with a declaration of the costs and charges for one year."[21]

Logistical considerations bulk much larger in *The Boke of Noblesse* than the modern reader would expect in a book of chivalry. Funds for the projected invasion of France have, we are told, been hard to raise. The reason is found rather naïvely in the covetousness of the wealthy and in the unfortunate penchant of the English for extravagant clothing.[22] The remedy is equally simple: restrain the English people by sumptuary legislation and urge the well-to-do citizens to give voluntarily to the common cause.[23] This latter policy might, it

[21] *Collection*, p. 526; cf. p. 529.
[22] *Boke of Noblesse*, pp. 79-80.
[23] *Ibid.*, pp. 81-83.

is admitted, encounter some difficulty; for previous creditors, especially those of Henry VI, had not been duly paid for loans already given. In order to make up for the suffering caused by this situation the suggestion is made that the king let his own treasure "both jewels [and] vessels of gold and silver" be spread among his subjects "to the help and advancement of your conquest, and to the relief of your indigent and needy people."[24] Writing in the shadow of the Yorkist benevolences, the author is trying hard to find a more equitable alternative; and he is clever enough to realize that money over and above ordinary taxation could never be secured unless the commons, and especially the townsmen, were taken care of by the king. He urges Edward to show favor to the cities and towns; but his concern for the burgesses is strictly dependent on the necessity of securing the support of that class for the war policy. "And if the adversaries will work against the honor of your person, and the welfare of your realm, your said citizens and burgesses and good commons if they be tended shall be of power and of good courage, and will with their bodies and goods largely depart to be given for to resist them."[25] In that day, as in later times, the aggressive party must needs picture itself—even to itself—as the resister of aggression.

Another proposal echoes with an accuracy more than coincidental a bill of advice given in 1448 by Fastolf to the Duke of Somerset for administering the military occupation of France. The army, it is urged, should be promptly and regularly paid by honest officers not merely in order to secure a more efficient administration but to make it unnecessary for soldiers to live off the land, a practice which, in the late campaigns in Normandy, turned the inhabitants from loyalty toward their English lord to bitter hatred of the foreign invader.[26]

[24] *Ibid.*, p. 80.
[25] *Ibid.*, p. 81.
[26] *Ibid.*, pp. 71-72, 30-31; Cf. *Collection*, p. 593.

Despite the not inconsiderable resources of common sense revealed in this document and especially the willingness of its author to draw heavily on the actual experience of English administrators in France during the Hundred Years' War, despite the distinct evidence of a practical, largely instinctive empiricism in his treatment of foreign policy, the fact remains that *The Boke of Noblesse* appeals to the English gentry in the spirit of a chivalric idealism quite unrelated to the kind of realism that animates the pages of Commines or of Machiavelli, and that inspired the policies of Louis XI or Henry VII, or even of Edward IV. Once again we are faced with the curious penchant of the fifteenth-century mind to think on two separate levels and to separate the ideal and the actual whenever it seemed a good thing at the time to do so. The author of *The Boke of Noblesse* hoped to revive among the English gentry the spirit of chivalry without which he undoubtedly felt the objectives of dynastic policy would be meaningless. Yet the idealism of its message stands in the sharpest contrast to the frank realism that seems to have prompted the king's actual decisions.

In 1472 Edward decided to raise the issue of an invasion of France in good earnest.[27] It had been adumbrated in 1468, before the recurrence of civil discord. Now once more in charge of things, however precarious was his position as ruler, Edward saw fit for a number of reasons to alert parliament to the advisability of war. Someone, probably the Archbishop of Canterbury, spoke at length for the king and stated those reasons with remarkable candor. Paying only the briefest of respects to the chivalric forms, to the "knightly courage" of the king and to his natural desire to restore England to its "old fame, honor, and renown," the speaker emphasized the

---

[27] The fullest contemporary account of the invasion and the diplomacy leading up to it is in *Memoires de Philip de Commynes,* ed. B. de Mandrot (Paris, 1901-3), I, 286-326 and the several chapters preceding. See C. L. Scofield, *The Life and Reign of Edward IV* (London, 1923), Vol. II, Book IV, for the most extensive analysis of the sources.

element of expediency. The civil wars, he said, have left in
their wake a "multitude of riotous people" who have kept alive
the "great division" among the English people and have
plagued the land with all sorts of "extortions, oppressions, robberies, and other great mischiefs" to such an extent that it
threatens the wealth and prosperity of the king's subjects.
The "rigor of the law" cannot be used as a remedy, for if
everyone guilty were punished with death as he deserves there
would soon be too few people left in the realm to protect it
against external foes which, thanks to the "subtle and crafty
enterprises of Louis the king's adversary in France," beset the
land on all sides. And so, in order to "set in occupation of
the war outward the said idle and riotous people, under the
conduct of our sovereign lord, the lords, and gentles of this
land," and to frustrate the knavish tricks of King Louis, and
to restore England to her former prestige, the king is resolved
to press his rightful claim to the crown of France and to re-
cover in particular the duchies of Normandy and Gascony. To
this same end certain diplomatic and strategic considerations
point with compelling logic. The Dukes of Burgundy and
Brittany are in agreement and alliance with the English king,
a fact that leaves the King of France in a vulnerable position
in his own territories and places the King of England in some
sort of obligation (which he will ignore at his own peril, by
the way) to these confederates. Moreover, it is "not unknown
how there be there [in France] right wealthy and necessary
ports for the weal of merchandise and the maintaining of the
navy of this land." In French hands they will be a constant
source of weakness to England, whereas under English control
they would make it impossible for the French king to maintain any navy at all in those waters, and so would give England a predominant position in the trade of northeastern
Europe.

Yet he must also justify the war as one basically defensive.
In a sense it is to be a "preventive" war. Rather than wait to

be attacked and to "abide the defense of the war at home" the king should "prevent" his adversaries like Scipio, who defeated Hannibal in Carthage rather than in Rome.

Strong as these considerations were in the speaker's mind, he seems to have been especially preoccupied with the problem of domestic unrest, for he returns to the subject of the unruly elements at home. If, he suggests, the French provinces could be regained, "Many gentlemen, as well younger brothers as other, might there be worshipfully rewarded, and inhabit that land for the sure guard of the same; the men of war, that had none other purveyance [livelihood], to be set in garrisons and live by their wages, which else were like to continue the mischief in this land that they do now." He then adds the astonishing *obiter dictum,* drawn from what he considers an accurate reading of English history, "that it is not well possible, nor hath been since the Conquest, that justice, peace, and prosperity [the primary objectives of government, that is] hath continued any while in this land in any king's days but in such as have made war outward."[28]

Whether he is right or wrong in his analysis of English experience, he is here speaking the language of Machiavellian realism. In his reference to England's strategic position he is speaking in the similarly realistic tone of *The Libelle of Englyshe Polycye.* There is in his speech nothing whatever of the chivalric spirit that breathes so lustily in the pages of *The Boke of Noblesse.*

Very probably this speech reflected rather accurately the thinking of Edward IV himself in that year. Before he got around to the invasion itself, three years had elapsed, and his motives had no doubt changed; but it is a safe bet that they had about them no more of chivalric idealism than they had in 1472. Edward had a taste for chivalric pomp. He seems to have admired in that one respect the court of his brother-in-law

[28] *Literae Cantuarienses,* ed. J. B. Sheppard, Rolls Series (London, 1889), III, 274-285. See Scofield, p. 44 n. 1, on the question of the date of this document, listed by Sheppard as 1474.

of Burgundy. But he shared with Charles none of the temer-
ity, the rashness, that gave to that eccentric prince the name he
bears in history and caused Commines to picture him as the
archetype of chivalric folly. His motives, like his personality,
have languished under a cloud of unknowing caused by the
paucity and the cryptic character of the records. Only the
memoirs of shrewd old Philippe de Commines are much help,
and they are too unfriendly to Edward to be taken always at
face value. Perhaps, however, his explicit suggestion that
Edward hoped to get money from his subjects by proclaiming
war, and from his enemies by making peace, is not too far
from the truth.[29] This, in the event, was exactly what he did.
Beginning in 1472 he asked for money for the proposed invasion, but it was not until 1475 that the expedition set sail.
And after alarming Louis XI into negotiating rather than
taking to the field he accepted the generous terms offered
with what many on both sides felt to be a readiness unbe-
coming a chivalrous prince. By that time, of course, Charles
the Bold had virtually deserted him and he was left in a position from which he could expect to do little more than seriously embarrass his enemy. In return for giving up territorial
ambitions he may never have nourished seriously, Edward
received by the Treaty of Piquigny an outright payment in
cash, an annual pension of 50,000 gold crowns, and a favorable
marriage for his eldest daughter.

He may have been acting in response to much the same
mixture of indolence and practical intelligence that conditioned
the policy of Charles II in not too dissimilar circumstances.
Like his Stuart successor Edward had been through a restoration to a throne still not firmly established. Like him he had
no wish to be again on his travels. Like him he hoped to
enjoy his kingdom in as much ease as was consistent with his
dignity and the prosperity of England. Like him also he was
willing to accept the substance in the form of a French pension

[29] *Memoires*, I, 325-326.

which would free him from parliamentary interference in place of the shadow that might be cast by a more heroic policy.

If this estimate of Edward's motives is anywhere near the truth it places him among the ignoble army of those who, like Commines himself, believed that he who has the profit in war has the glory.[30] It ranges him with the inglorious company of those whom the author of *The Boke of Noblesse* held to be not true Englishmen because they preferred to live at rest rather than seek combat for the honor of England. It separates him in particular from his conservative brother, Richard of Gloucester, who by training and temperament belonged to the old order and who, in fact, bitterly denounced the shameful negotiations at Piquigny—though, we are told, he brought himself after the event to accept from Louis a handsome present as his share of the influence Louis dispensed with such unchivalrous prodigality among the chivalry of England, and with such devastating effect.[31]

Many Englishmen, however, agreed with Richard that it was a shoddy treaty and a defeat rather than a victory for English arms. While still in France, Edward had trouble with some of his captains. Morbidly afraid that the Frenchmen were laughing at them for their unheroic conduct, they put their leader to some pains to interpret the expedition as a diplomatic triumph, and the pensions as tribute.[32] Back in England Edward continued to hear criticism from men who had willingly or unwillingly put hand in pocket to finance a war in which they generally believed. Many an old knight could recall with the fondness of romantic memory his service long ago in France; and many more viewed the possibilities for profit and adventure that a foreign conquest promised with an enthusiasm born of ignorance. Nor was the popular chau-

[30] *Ibid.*, I, 286-390.
[31] *Ibid.*, I, 319. See also Schofield, II, 147. Richard's most recent biographer, P. M. Kendall, chooses to gloss over this episode. *Richard III* (Chicago, 1955).
[32] Schofield, II, 145-146; Commines, I, 321-322, 328.

vinism confined to the gentry. Edward had leaned heavily on the burghers of London for support in his war policy; and there is no reason to believe that they took more kindly than their country cousins to the news of a bloodless victory.[33]

It was to this aggressive and naïvely patriotic public that *The Boke of Noblesse* had apparently been addressed—through channels. Possibly it was intended to become part of a more general appeal: it is hard to say, since no other evidence of such propaganda has been preserved. The *Boke* helps nonetheless to explain something that has always been just a little puzzling, namely how a renewal of war with France, a war one would think had been pretty well discredited by its dismal failure, came to be so popular among a people still plagued at home with disorder, misgovernment, and economic insecurity. Edward's mixed motives are more understandable. If those motives were communicated to parliament as candidly as the speech of 1472, quoted above, would indicate (it is not at all certain that the speech was actually delivered) they probably struck a responsive chord in many a practical mind. But then, as now, the climate of opinion in which policies of any sort thrive is composed in large part of the vapors that arise from cherished ideals; and it was possible, nay necessary, even for practical men to justify a policy of aggression on the most idealistic of grounds. In fifteenth-century England those grounds were chivalric—transmuted, it is true, into patriotic terms but still basically chivalric; the honor and renown of England, the right of a dynastic claim, in general the maintenance of peace and justice against the mischievous workings of an external enemy.

· · ·

Many years were to pass before another such effort to place the issues of foreign policy in the context of chivalric values

[33] Commines, I, 325-326.

made its appearance. After the abortive invasion of 1475, English kings abstained from continental adventure for some time. Both Edward IV and Henry VII found much to be done at home. The first Tudor monarch was content to work with the unglamorous tools of diplomacy rather than with the weapons of war; and when he resorted to war he did it briefly, reluctantly, and with little fanfare. Not until Henry VIII felt it necessary to cut a figure in European politics did England again become seriously embroiled in foreign war. After a few ineffective gestures which brought neither fame to him nor advantage to England, he set out in good earnest to exercise his military arm. In 1513 he sent an expedition to France. The motives were to modern eyes flimsy, a tissue of dynastic rivalry, political ambition, and a typically chivalric search for renown through military adventure. The pattern of modern power politics was already in the process of emerging, with its impersonal balance of competing states. Henry's policy, indeed, soon became entangled with, and dominated by, the more mature policies of Pope Julius II, the Emperor Maximilian, and Ferdinand of Aragon. Yet the true nature of the situation was very probably less apparent to the young and romantic Tudor than to seasoned realists like Machiavelli; and in any case it was still possible for Henry to consider military action, in the light of chivalric values, as an end sufficient unto itself. In the mind of the young monarch medieval and Renaissance elements blended in a general feeling for the dramatic, for the magnificent, for, in other words, those characteristics of Renaissance life that lay nearest the surface and could most readily become confused with the romance and glitter of chivalry still apparent in much of the courtly life of the day. Even Polydore Vergil, a man more than ordinarily aware of political reality and as little given to the stereotypes of chivalry as any other humanist scholar of his generation,[34]

[34] See *The Anglica Historia of Polydore Vergil,* ed. Denys Hay, with translation, Camden Society, LXXIV (London, 1950). See also below, notes 43-44.

admits that Henry entered into the game of continental politics at least in part because he was "not unmindful that it was his duty to seek fame by military skill."[35]   He tells us also that Henry was at one point determined to lead the army himself, partly because Englishmen fight more fiercely under the personal command of their kings, but also in order to "create such a fine opinion about his valor among all men that they could clearly understand that his ambition was not merely to equal but indeed to excel the glorious deeds of his ancestors."[36]

If Vergil wrote these words with his tongue in his cheek (he consistently refused to give Henry's pomp and ceremony the full treatment of conventional chivalric language) there were those around Henry in the days of his youth who were quite capable of more forthright expression.[37]   Hall's chronicle, in its treatment of these episodes, breathes the atmosphere rather of Froissart than of Renaissance historiography.   It dwells lovingly on all the chivalric spectacles that occupied the time of Henry's court.   And it stresses the crusading piety with which, the year before his invasion of France, Henry agreed to assist his shifty father-in-law in a campaign against the infidel Moors—a campaign which, to the disgust of the gartered knight who begged to lead it, ended in anticlimax of humiliating and costly proportions.[38]

It was clearly in an effort to push him toward a war of conquest that one anonymous historian undertook to translate, with editorial comment, Tito Livio da Forli's life of Henry V.[39]   The latter had been able to combine the scholarship of

---

[35] Hay, trans., p. 161.

[36] *Ibid.*, pp. 197-199.

[37] Perhaps Henry may have found in Lord Berners a spokesman for a policy of military adventure.   See above, chap. ii.   It has been suggested that John Skelton used the opportunity of his position as Prince Henry's tutor and later as court poet to advocate a strong policy toward France.   H. L. R. Edwards, *Skelton, the Life and Times of an Early Tudor Poet* (London, 1949), p. 133; but cf. W. Nelson, *John Skelton, Laureate*, p. 137.

[38] Hall, pp. 516-522.   See above, chap. i.

[39] C. L. Kingsford, ed., *The First English Life of Henry the Fifth* (Oxford, 1911).   On the "translator" and his relation to his original see Kingsford's editorial introduction and his *Historical Literature in Fifteenth Century England*, pp. 64-68.

the early *Quattrocento* and a personal background of Italian Renaissance culture with the still strong tradition of chivalry prevailing in England. That tradition he apparently shared with his patron Duke Humphrey who retained many of the habits of medieval England despite a familiarity with Italian learning rare in the Northern society of his day. Livio's work was therefore well suited to a court still open to chivalric appeal, yet sophisticated enough to demand thoughtful and readable history. His translator—and glossator—made it available to that audience in a vigorous and basically faithful version, keeping his comments within reasonable bounds and adding material from other histories and sources with some discretion.

Like William Worcester and Caxton and, perhaps, Malory also, the "Translator of Livius" sought to draw inspiration for the present from the experience of the past, an experience already interpreted in terms of chivalric values. Like Worcester, too, he was immediately concerned with an impending invasion of France. Ironically, the war he hoped to support by his propagandist use of history dissolved into an equally facile peace before he was able to present his finished product to the king. But he proceeded with his project, simply altering the dedication, his original purpose and prejudice left clearly showing. In this *proheme* he justifies his labors somewhat lamely as the duty of a true subject to his sovereign under the conditions existing at the time of the invasion. He had hoped, he says, that Henry, seeing "the virtuous manners, the victorious conquests, and the excellent . . . wisdoms" of his renowned predecessor, might "in all things concerning his person and the regiment of his people, conform himself to his life and manners." In addition he had hoped that, in the specific situation of war then impending, the king might "by the knowledge and sight of this pamphlet" be "provoked in his said war to ensue the noble and chivalrous acts of this so noble, so virtuous, and so excellent prince, which so followed he might the rather attain to the like honor, fame, and victory."[40]

But the "Translator of Livius" belongs to a different generation from William Worcester. In his pages, full as they are of Henry's knightly example, there is a freshness which indicates that the Indian Summer of English chivalry is almost over. He is as didactic as any medieval moralist, but the virtues he finds outstanding in Henry V and which he hopes to find in Henry VIII are the virtues common to the broader Christian tradition, not those peculiar to chivalry. He is impressed by Henry V's humility, his continence, his piety, and his freedom from avarice. He cherishes the story of Henry's refusal of all booty from a captured town except "a goodly french book, of what history I have not heard."[41] Above all he approved of Henry's sense of duty to the commonwealth. His "constant love of the public weale" should be a salutory example to any princes who "court more their singular pleasure, honor, and profit than the universal advantage and wealth of his people."[42] Although there is nothing new in the words used to express this sense of public service—similar formulas crop up again and again in the standard textbooks of knightly and kingly conduct—[43]the reader becomes gradually aware that the context has changed. It is no longer the context of pure chivalry. Rather it is that of English humanism.[44] The desire of the "Translator" to bring the example of the past, albeit a chivalric example, to the aid of the present foreshadows the Tudor humanists as distinctly as the stereotypes of a chivalric chauvinism recall the chivalric apologists of the preceding generation.

. . .

The early years of the Tudor regime witnessed, indeed, not only these somewhat exotic expressions of conventional chival-

[40] *First English Life*, p. 4.   [41] *Ibid.*, pp. 5, 92-93; cf. p. 45.
[42] *Ibid.*, p. 18.   [43] See above, chap. ii.
[44] On the "Translator's" relation to humanist historiography, see Kingsford, *First English Life*, pp. xi-xiii.

ric thought, but the continual and apparently accelerated growth of a nonchivalric, if not consciously antichivalric, point of view. It stemmed from two trends in late medieval thought, neither of them new or necessarily antichivalric, but both capable of growing rapidly away from the chivalric attitude toward war and the military life. One of these, the Christian tradition, had become so closely identified with the chivalric that a new influence was required to separate the two, the influence of Christian humanism. The other, the tendency toward political realism inherent in much of late medieval English thought, was taking shape quite outside the accepted forms and could be as little related to the Christian as to the chivalric traditions. It belongs to the same tendency in European thinking as was expressed by Commines and Machiavelli —the former consciously antichivalric, the latter deliberately non-Christian. It was not, of course, recognized then as anything so radical in its separation from the traditional habits of thought. It was not always expressed in terms of *Realpolitik.* For the most part it appears unobtrusively in the literature of public discussion as an intuitive reaching out after the tangible, the practical, the analyzable elements in political life. It was all but untouched by the more mature realism of Renaissance culture and for the most part innocent of the New Learning. It was simply the reaction of practical men to situations in which experience alone seemed likely to provide a practical answer.

Even in the late years of the fourteenth century, John Gower had been able to look upon the English monarchy with a shrewdness surprising in a person of his conventional turn of mind. He was especially sensitive to the effect of war upon the economic well-being of the country. War brings taxes and poverty and is bad for the business life of the "Great City."[45] He nourished the highest regard for chivalric ideals, criticizing

[45] "In Praise of Peace," *Works,* III, 481-492; *Vox Clamantis,* Liber VII, line 283; Liber V, lines 485-486.

the knightly order only for its failure to live up to them. But it is hard to read his English poem "In Praise of Peace," the product of his last and most politically minded period, without sensing that the old moralist had lost some of his faith in chivalric idealism as a framework for national policy. In the apparent hope of restraining Henry IV from renewing the war he wrote:

> O King fulfilled of grace and of knighthood, . . .
> If peace be proffered unto thy manhood,
> Thine honor save, let it not be forsaken.
> Though thou the wars durst well undertake,
> After reason yet temper thy courage,
> For like to peace there is no advantage.[46]

The latter stages of the Hundred Years' War brought some English observers to a remarkably realistic appraisal of England's strategic position—one in which the language of chivalric idealism played little or no part. We have seen already something of the practical statesmanship reflected in the papers of Sir John Fastolf, who knew more than most English knights the cost of war and the value of power. Even more significant in this respect is the verse treatise, entitled *The Libelle of Englyshe Polycye,* on England's strategic position, written in the light of the siege of Calais in 1436.[47] The author writes more nearly in the idiom of Renaissance power politics than most English writers prior to the sixteenth century. England's power and prosperity depend on her ability to "keep the narrow seas" and to use to its utmost her natural ability to produce good wool and cloth for the purpose of striking advantageous bargains with the countries of northwestern Europe. There is in this poem no trace whatever of the chivalric language, none of the quest for glory. The assumptions made by its author are strictly materialistic, devoid alike of chivalric and, except in the most formal sense, of religious sentiment.

---

[46] Lines 155-161.
[47] *The Libelle of Englyshe Polycye,* ed. G. Warner (Oxford, 1926). Cf. Schirmer, *Lydgate,* p. 202.

In that day when the vocabulary of chivalry, and more than we always appreciate of its spirit, still found their way into statements of foreign policy, it stands virtually alone, reflecting the realities of England's position, not the mythology of sentiment.

There are, nevertheless, evidences in the literature of the latter fifteenth century that the author of the *Libelle,* however advanced he was in his political awareness, was by no means without successors. The reader may recall how a London chronicler set the Earl of Warwick's "knightly" feats of arms within a context of national defense to which Calais and control of the narrow seas were held to be essential.[48] A lesser "libel" appeared, probably in Edward IV's reign, in which the author again took as his text the economic and naval power of England: *"Anglia, propter tuas naves et lanas, omnia regna te salutare deberent."*[49] George Ashby in his *Active Policy of a Prince* warns his courtly readers (the pamphlet was addressed to Prince Edward about 1470) not to begin war lightly, whether for gain or to satisfy a whim, or out of sheer stupidity. Don't, he says, be cowardly, but beware of entering into war in a spirit of "wilfulness"; for once begun, no one can tell how it will end.[50] This is a counsel, not so much of Christian idealism as of political expendiency. A mature appreciation of the strategic position of England in relation to the other powers of Western Europe, as well as surprisingly frank admission of ulterior political motives, characterized the speech (quoted earlier in this chapter) which was prepared for delivery to parliament in 1472 in connection with the proposed invasion of France. In this same spirit Edmund Dudley composed his *Tree of Commonwealth (ca.* 1509), drawing upon his experience in the calculating counsel of his erstwhile master, Henry VII. In one of the least conventional passages in this gen-

[48] See above, chap. ii.
[49] Wright, II, 282-287.
[50] *The Poems of George Ashby,* ed. Mary Bateson, E.E.T.S., E.S., No. 76 (1899), pp. 12-41 *passim,* especially stanzas 97-98.

erally conventional tract, he issued a sober warning against the sort of bootless war upon which the new king was about to embark and of which the veteran public servant may already have suspected him capable.

> I suppose right great treasure is soon spent in a sharp war, therefore let every man beware what counsel he giveth to his sovereign to enter or to begin war. There are many ways to enter into it, and the beginning seemeth a great pleasure, but the way is very narrow to come honorably out thereof, and then oftentimes full painful, besides that it is very dangerous for the soul and body. This root of peace must needs be rooted in the person of our prince and by this means, that is to say, by such good and sure liege [faith?] and amities and noble alliances as his grace by the advice of his honorable council will have with outward princes.[51]

These words reflect that unglamorous but intelligent statesmanship which, as the chronicler Fabyan recognized, made it possible for Henry VII to secure peace and to subdue his external enemies "by his great policy and wisdom, more than by shedding of Christian blood or cruel war."[52] It is the language of Renaissance politics, not of chivalric chauvinism. It contains none of the naïvely conventional mixture of nationalism and knight-errantry that animates *The Boke of Noblesse.*

As good an illustration as any of this tendency to look beyond chivalric idealism for the true measure of statesmanship may be found in the *Annales Henrici VII,* written as court history by Bernard André. The author goes out of his way to praise his master for his shrewd monetary and commercial policies and to suggest that in these things, rather than in the exercising of force, is true cause for praise. Through his handling of the thorny problem of the coinage Henry improved England's position among the nations and demonstrated how one-sided was the reputation of those princes whose fame rested

---

[51] *The Tree of Commonwealth,* ed. D. M. Brodie (Cambridge 1948), p. 50. Skelton, whose native shrewdness overshadowed the sparse growth of humanism in his mind, turned in his later years from jingoistic praise of military adventure to a sober statement of this same view that wars are expensive and inconclusive. William Nelson, *John Skelton, Laureate* (New York, 1939), p. 137.

[52] Fabyan, p. 690.

solely upon their military prowess.[53] Especially praiseworthy, André feels, was his commercial treaty with Flanders, as a result of which he "by the acts of peace alone, without sword or bloodshed," provided so well for his kingdom that he deserves to be called *"pater patriae,"* and to be known throughout the world as *"rex pacificus."*[54] Nor need he suffer in this respect by comparison with the great names of classical antiquity. This is more than the praise of peace common to all medieval literature. It is a consciously comparative judgment of value recording a specific policy of economic diplomacy.

Now André, it is true, was in a difficult position. His job was to praise Henry and he does it with all the fulsomeness and with not a little of the rhetorical elegance and exaggeration customary among court writers of the Renaissance. He might be expected to bear down most heavily on those things which were indeed to Henry's credit and to slip tactfully over that monarch's undeniable backwardness in martial accomplishment and even in the striking of conventionally chivalric attitudes. Writing after Henry's death and looking at another and less creditable side of his financial policy, Polydore Vergil labeled it sheer avarice; and this opinion seems to have been widely held.[55] André could hardly say as much to the king's face even if he had wanted to. And anyway, flattery is always couched in terms of those values most likely to be respected by the persons flattered. Although Henry's policies were not so novel as was at one time believed, they reflect nonetheless a quality of calculation and pragmatism in his statecraft which Machiavelli himself would have found thoroughly acceptable. It is reasonable, therefore, to suppose that Henry encouraged a similar judgment of values in those around him. He seems to have been willing enough to employ men of humanist

[53] *Annales*, pp. 81-82. Cf. pp. 88 and 94.
[54] *Ibid.*, p. 84.
[55] *Vergil*, pp. 129, 147. Stephen Hawes, in *A Joyfull Medytacyon to All Englande* (1509) (S.T.C. 12953) speaks of it being a common opinion and seeks to apologize for it by suggesting the unlikely theory that the money was probably being stored up to finance war against the Turk.

learning like André; and humanistic studies tended to demonstrate, through the medium of classical example, the complexity of the *respublica* and the need for a more than protective, sword-bearing capability in its government. Antiquity
bequeathed to its Renaissance admirers plenty of warlike
examples—they had, as we have seen, even been incorporated
into the chivalric mythology. But the examples that became
increasingly popular among humanist writers were those involving the arts of peace in which the wisdom of the statesman
and of the citizen active in public affairs found special embodiment. In praising Henry's prudence rather than his military capabilities André was, I believe, making a reasonably
honest evaluation.

Prudence had always been considered part of the knight's
moral armament. One of the cardinal virtues, it could scarcely
be ignored in the traditional manual of knighthood. Lull, as
rendered by Caxton, interpreted it primarily in military
terms.[56] It is the virtue of profiting by experience both in
things material and things spiritual, which is a definition broad
enough to cover most contingencies. But he develops it
strictly as the virtue of using one's head in battle and of over-
coming one's adversary by strategy rather than by main force.
Even so stated it is a virtue too frequently wanting in medieval
armies; but it does not extend to the function, also, though
dimly, recognized by Lull, of the knight acting as governor.
To André, prudence was the very essence of civil government.[57] A few years later, young Thomas More used the idea
in a similarly nonchivalric way in referring to Edward IV,
who, incidentally, he pictured almost as a bourgeois monarch
in contrast to the militarily impeccable but otherwise repre-
hensible Richard III. Edward was successful enough and bold
in warfare, but "no farther than wisdom would, adventurous."
Anyone who examines the record will, he says, "no less com-

---

[56] *Ordre of Chyualry*, pp. 95-97. This point is discussed with useful references
by Gist, pp. 177-178. See also above, chap. ii.
[57] *Annales*, p. 84.

mend his wisdom where he avoided than his manhood where he vanquished."[58]

· · ·

It was the generation of More and the Erasmian humanists that made the sharpest break with the chivalric tradition concerning the virtues of military activity. At the very moment when the "Translator of Livius" was engaged in his abortive attempt to inspire the young king to seek "worship and renown" in a war with France, when, according to Polydore Vergil, Henry himself was already thinking in some such terms, the English humanists were taking a long look at the emerging problems of international relations from the vantage point of their new learning. It was a point of view as much Christian as classical in its inspiration, and conditioned to a very considerable extent by the practical, common-sense attitude toward the affairs of men that we have seen expressed in much of the earlier political literature. Warham and Colet both preached against the war, the latter in the spring of 1513 with a vigor few of Henry's other subjects would have dared to display.[59] Erasmus, then an uneasy guest in England, was saddened by the deterioration in the temper of English life resulting, he felt, from the war preparations; and he soon left those isles which he had once thought so fortunate and in which he had hoped to find a truly congenial home. The spectacle of Christian people incited by the pope himself to make war on other Christian peoples Erasmus found increasingly repellent and contrary both to the spirit of Christianity and to the dictates of reason. Several of his most pacifistic utterances stem from these years when power politics seemed

[58] *The History of Richard III*, in *The English Works of Sir Thomas More*, ed. E. W. Campbell (London, 1931), I, 400; cf. 401-402. A not dissimilar position is taken in one of the late medieval English versions of the *Secreta Secretorum*. *Three Prose Versions of the Secreta Secretorum*, ed. R. Steele, E.E.T.S., E.S., LXXIV (1898), pp. 37-38.

[59] R. W. Chambers, *Thomas More* (New York, 1935), pp. 113-114. On Colet's influence upon Erasmus, see R. P. Adams, "Erasmus' Ideas of his Rôle as a Social Critic *ca.* 1480-1500," *Renaissance News*, XI (Spring, 1958), 11-16.

likely to preoccupy European statesmen and inhibit the prom-
ising beginnings of humane learning in England. In his
Institutio Principis Christiani he attacked the Machiavellian
statecraft in which war had become a normal instrument. In
the *Adagia* he embroidered on the laconic saying, *"dulce bellum inexpertis"*—sweet is war to those who have never been
in one—drawn perhaps with deliberate irony from that favorite
of the fifteenth-century aristocracy, Vegetius' *De re militari.*
In the longer and even more passionate *Querela Pacis,* completed in 1517, he made his most systematic statement on the
subject.[60]

In both books of *Utopia* More also expressed a settled aver-
sion to war as an instrument of international politics. Thoroughly patriotic (unlike the cosmopolitan Erasmus who
claimed citizenship only in the republic of letters), capable of
answering French invective with appropriately warlike epi-
grams, More agreed with Erasmus to this extent at least that
he saw nothing inherently noble in war and considered it
something to be engaged in only for just cause and as a last
resort and then (if we may consider the policies of the Utopians to have reflected in any way More's own sentiments)
preferably by hired armies.[61] Nothing could have been more
antithetical to the spirit of chivalric idealism still discernible
in the prologue of the "Translator of Livius" or in the attitudes
of the young Henry VIII than this spirit of Erasmian humanism. Both Erasmus and More were conservative in their vision
of a Christian world order, yet their conservatism had its roots

[60] An extensive and informative, if rather excited and inadequately documented
account of Erasmus' pacifistic writings may be found in J. Chapiro, *Erasmus and
our Struggle for Peace* (Boston, 1950). This book also contains a translation of
the *Querela Pacis. Dulce Bellum Inexpertis* has been recently edited and translated
into French by Yvonne Remy and R. Dumil-Marquebreucq, Collection Hatomus,
Vol. VIII (Brussels, 1953). Important work is being done on the early Tudor
humanists by R. P. Adams—see his "Literary Thought on War and Peace in English
Literature of the Renaissance," *Year Book of the American Philosophical Society,*
1955 (Philadelphia, 1956), pp. 272-277.

[61] *Utopia,* ed. H. Osborne (London, n.d.) Book I, paragraphs 31, 42, 62, 80-87;
Book II, paragraphs 231-250. See also F. Caspari, "Sir Thomas More and *Justum
Bellum," Ethics,* LVI (1946), 303-308.

in a most realistic appraisal of the Europe of competing dynastic states, the fundamentally anarchic world order which was in fact taking shape and which jeopardized their humane ideal of a life lived in conformity with the dignity and rational nature of man.[62]

For both men the issues transcended the antagonism between humanistic and chivalric values. Knight-errantry, whether on an individual or on a national scale, had as little to do with the Erasmian ideal of a Christian and rational world order as it did with the world of Machiavellian realism that More analyzed with such insight in Book I of *Utopia*. Its values could not, of course, be completely ignored; and there are times when an antichivalric bias clearly colors the classically inspired sentiments expressed by More. As C. S. Lewis recently wrote, "The military methods of More's Utopians are mischievously devised to flout the chivalric code at every turn."[63] For the most common sense of reasons they prefer to proceed against their enemies by guile rather than directly by force of arms; and they prefer, for similar reasons, to employ mercenary troops rather than to risk the lives of their own citizens in what is at best but a sordid necessity.[64] Master Raphael, the world traveler, points with admiration to the people of Persia whose "life is commodious rather than gallant, and may better be called happy or wealthy than notable or famous"—the fame he refers to being as closely related to the chivalric quality of gallantry as the happiness is with the commodious and wealthy life.[65] More even seems to identify explicitly, as many of his day did without thinking about it at all, the values of chivalry with an aggressive foreign policy.[66] But the enemies he fought in the new world of competing sovereign states were armed with new and larger weapons,

[62] Cf. R. P. Adams, "Designs by More and Erasmus for a new Social Order," *Studies in Philology*, XLII (April, 1945), 131-145.
[63] C. S. Lewis, *English Literature in the Sixteenth Century* (Oxford, 1954), p. 29.
[64] *Utopia*, ed. H. Osborne, pp. 96-106.
[65] *Ibid.*, p. 25-26.
[66] *Ibid.*, p. 14.

infinitely more deadly than the rusty lance of a decadent chivalry.

English humanism tended, in fact, to be nonchivalric rather than antichivalric. Despite an antichivalric bias that is more apparent the closer they were to the Continental, especially the Erasmian, influence, the early Tudor humanists seldom came to grips with the chivalric tradition. Had that tradition been more clearly articulated, had chivalry become in reality more than an often frivolous adherence to conventional forms, had, in short, the serious apologists of the preceding generation been more successful in their efforts to revitalize chivalric ideals, a true contest might well have ensued. As it was, Polydore Vergil, close as he remained to the pageantry that still gave a superficially plausible veneer of chivalry to the court of the Tudor Henrys, virtually ignored chivalric forms in his account of that era and wrote with the least possible use of the chivalric vocabulary.[67] The episode of the "Field of the Cloth of Gold" he treats merely as an elaborate, perhaps an unnecessarily elaborate, diplomatic meeting, the social aspect of which was quite overshadowed by the political implications. The English women, he tells us, learned wanton styles in dress from the ladies of Francis I's court; and he records with the utmost brevity the official courtesies that took place. But it is the clash of dynastic powers that he places squarely in the foreground.[68] There may be just a hint of antichivalric prejudice in his comment on a disastrous and foolhardy attack pressed during the Anglo-French hostilities by two English naval captains on the French fleet, either vying with the other "in their desire for glory." It showed, he said, "more spirit than prudence," and cost the lives of six hundred Englishmen.[69] And he points out that Henry VIII went ahead with his invasion of France

[67] Tournaments are mentioned in connection with the marriage of Catherine to Prince Arthur in 1501, but only in passing, Hay trans., p. 123. See above, n. 35; J. S. Brewer, *The Reign of Henry VIII* (London, 1884), I, 44.

[68] Vergil, pp. 269-271.

[69] *Ibid.*, pp. 187-189.

in part at least because it was "his duty to seek fame by military skill"—and this in the face of the most rational advice to the contrary from his own magnates.[70] Perhaps he distrusted any repuation based solely on military accomplishments.[71] But the prevailing tone of his chronicle is nonchivalric rather than antichivalric.

Other English writers, the "Translator of Livius," for example, or Edward Hall, were quite capable of combining a predilection for things chivalric with the discipline and some of the spirit of humanism apparently unaware of any antagonism that might exist between them. Hall leaned heavily on Vergil's impeccably humanistic historiography in the compilation of his chronicle of the early Tudor reigns, yet loaded his narrative to excess with detailed accounts of jousts and tourneys and the chivalric trappings that accompanied diplomatic meetings.[72] Perhaps he appreciated more clearly than Vergil the real temper of the Henrician court, at least in its earlier phases. Perhaps, like the courtiers themselves, he was merely following by habit the lines of deeply engrained convention.

Difficult as it is to estimate exactly the degree to which humanism permeated English thought, there is no denying the fact that, in the days of its early enthusiasm and in the work of its most dedicated partisans, humanism brought to the discussion of war and peace a scheme of values that was, to say the least, radically nonchivalric.

. . .

It would be wrong, however, to assume that the humanists alone were capable of creating an atmosphere inimical to the aggressive propensities of the chivalric mind. The Christian tradition had always been against war. It was also deeply distrustful of the knight's eager quest for glory which, though

[70] *Ibid.*, p. 161.
[71] Koebner, p. 35.
[72] E.g., *Hall's Chronicle,* pp. 605-622.

harmless if properly channeled, drifted only too often into the cardinal sin of pride. The chivalric idealization of fighting as the highest form of secular activity could never be wholly reconciled with the Christian ideal of a world at peace. Yet chivalry itself had to a large extent been domesticated by the church, its ideals incorporated with some modifications into the accepted system of medieval thought. It had in consequence its peace-loving side.

But the expressions of peaceful sentiment that may frequently be found clinging to the reverse side of the military ideal should be scrutinized rather narrowly if the medieval attitude toward both war and peace is not to be seriously distorted; for to the medieval mind a regard for peace and a glorification of combat were not at all incompatible. The moralist liked to think of the sword as the weapon of justice, and the knight, whose function in society it was to bear the sword for the king, the enforcer of rights. Justice in turn brought peace. The true purpose of the knight, as of all civil lordship, could therefore be considered that of seeking peace and preserving it. Gower, maintaining as always a firm grasp on the obvious, gave explicit expression to this unquestioned point of view.

It is bidden that a brandished sword always be held, in order that judgment may strike down wrongdoers more promptly. When the sword is at rest, it cannot hold the world in check. Let he who wishes to rule protect justice with blood. Arms bring peace; arms curb the rapacious. A worthy king should bear arms so that the guilty man may fear them.[73]

. . . .

If knighthood were worthy, then peace, with which all prosperity would return, would not be slow in coming . . . The knight who is worthy knows well and demonstrates that the beginning of peace in the world comes from the ending of war.[74]

Now it is clear that these words must not be interpreted in

[73] *Vox Clamantis*, Liber VI, lines 709-714. I am using the excellent translation by E. W. Stockton (Harvard dis.. 1952).
[74] *Ibid.*, Liber V, lines 485-494

the context of the modern state or in that of the modern state system. Justice was to the medieval mind qualitatively the same whether applied to the private individual who has been wronged or to the monarch whose dynastic rights have been infringed upon. Peace became accordingly much the same thing as order in the body politic, the latter conceived either as the national community or the Christian world community. As the chancellor expressed it in his speech to parliament in 1468, the function of government is basically that of maintaining justice from which, if properly performed, will follow peace and security.[75] War, which could justifiably be undertaken only to right a wrong—and that would include the defensive act of repelling invasion as well as the aggressive act of recapturing territory wrongfully seized—could be thought of simply as the sword-arm of justice extended to encompass the relationships between peoples.[76] In the fifteenth century those relationships were becoming more clearly national and were acquiring strategic meaning. In the speech prepared for delivery to parliament in 1472 on the subject of the projected invasion of France the language of power politics becomes, we have seen, the dominant feature.[77] But the idea of war as exclusively an instrument of the foreign policy of a state followed the course of events with remarkable tardiness. And it is by the same token dangerous to look, even in late medieval thought, for anything so intimately bound up with the modern world as pacifism. It was therefore quite reasonable (and, as a matter of fact, quite orthodox) to glorify the military function of knighthood and at the same time to emphasize the ultimate desirability of peace as the ideal state of human society, to be preferred, if at all possible, to war.

Let us not, then, commit the error of attributing to the antiwar sentiments of the medieval moralist a pacifist bias that

[75] *Rot. Parl.*, V, 622-3.
[76] This is, I think, the philosophy implied in the speech referred to in the preceding note.
[77] *Literae Cantuarienses*, III, 274-285.

might be looked upon as the forerunner of humanistic pacifism; nor should we interpret the praise of peace as a denial
of chivalric values. Gower expressed himself without the
slightest inconsistency in favor of peace and of the fearless use
of the sword. He spoke in laudatory terms of Edward III's
campaigns in support of his dynastic claims[78] and urged Henry
IV to stop a war which was getting nowhere and costing a
lot.[79] Lydgate[80] and Hoccleve, whose close association with
the royal court at times outweighed their moralism, wrote with
equal facility about the military renown of their hero Henry
V and the justice of his cause and about the advantages of
peace and the cost of war. Hoccleve's ambivalent attitude is
especially revealing. In *The Regement of Princes* (*ca.* 1411-
1413), he followed the classic Christian argument against war.
War is permissible only for a just cause. At best it is costly
and cruel. If Christian princes must fight, let them unite
against the Infidel rather than fight amongst themselves.[81] A
couple of years later, when the royal policy had abandoned
negotiation, and Henry V was ready in good earnest to invade
France, Hoccleve sings a more warlike tune, exhorting the
notorious Lollard knight, Sir John Oldcastle, to cease dabbling
in theology like a clerk and tend to the profession of arms as
a true knight should. Why, he asks, is Sir John not now
standing at the side of his liege lord? Study Vegetius, he
urges him, and heed the example of Launcelot.[82] In the interests of an aggressive royal policy he reverted to the authentic
language of chivalry. But here again let us be cautious about

[78] *Ibid.*, Liber VI, chaps. xiii-xiv.

[79] *In Praise of Peace*, Works, III, 480-492. On the expense of the war see also
Vox Clamantis, Liber VII, chap. iv, lines 269 ff., and n. 49 above.

[80] *Troy Book*, Prologue, pp. 1-4, and Book V, lines 3366 to end. See Walter F.
Schirmer, *John Lydgate, ein Kulturbild aus dem 15. Jahrhundert* (Tübingen, 1952),
pp. 42-43. "On the Prospect of Peace," Wright, II, 209-215. See Schirmer, p. 75;
cf. p. 202. See also Lydgate's *Minor Poems*, II, 556.

[81] *Hoccleve's Works*, ed. F. J. Furnivall, III, E.E.T.S., E.S., No. 72 (1897), 188-
196, *passim*. On this and other points regarding fifteenth-century attitudes toward
peace, see R. P. Adams, "Pre-Renaissance Courtly Peace Propaganda," *Papers of the
Michigan Academy of Science, Arts and Letters*, XXXII (1946), 432-446.

[82] "Address to Sir John Oldcastle," *Works*, I, 8-24.

finding in the words of a fifteenth-century English propagandist distinctions that could only have meaning in a modern, or at the earliest a Renaissance, situation.

. . .

What proved in the long run fatal to chivalry, considered as a military ideal, was not so much a feeling against war as such, nor any scorn of the military profession (though the Erasmian humanists admitted both), but rather the gradually maturing realization that both war and the profession of arms must be set within the framework of national life and interests. By Elizabeth's day it was no longer possible to consider the governing class exclusively, or even primarily, a military class; nor could war be considered essentially dynastic, the expression of a sort of collective knight-errantry in support of the king's feudal rights. Just as in the field of administration the years of the break with Rome marked the change from a royal to a distinctly national government,[83] so the revolutionary decades of the midcentury witnessed the emergence of England as a nation among modern nations, her pamphleteers as well as her statesmen accustomed as a matter of course to think in terms of power politics. The chivalric apologists of the fifteenth century had made their appeal for national regeneration primarily to a class. Tudor pamphleteers appealed to all Englishmen in the interests of the commonwealth.[84]

Strictly subordinated to the requirements of state policy,

[83] G. R. Elton, *The Tudor Revolution in Government* (New York, 1953), Introd.

[84] The ideal of the "very and true commonweal" which flourished among the pamphleteers of the early Tudor period was an expression of this sense of national solidarity. There were those who insisted upon the duty of every citizen to make his voice heard in the airing of grievances and the discussion of policy. See, for example, Robert Crowley, *The Way to Wealthe*, ed. J. M. Cowper, E.E.T.S., E.S., No. 15 (1872), p. 132; Thomas Becon, *The Policy of War*, in *The Early Writings of Thomas Becon*, ed. J. Ayre, Parker Society (Cambridge, 1843), p. 235; *A Discourse of the Common Weal of this Realm of England*, ed. E. Lamond (Cambridge, 1893), pp. 10-11. Richard Morison, in *An Exhortation to Styrre all Englyshemen to the Defence of Theyr Countrye* (London, 1539), sig. Aiiii, stresses this duty of every subject with reference to defense, even envisaging the possibility of a nation in arms, each man equipped and ready to serve (sig. Bv). See also *ibid.*, conclusion.

the conduct of war, both in matters of strategy and tactics, had to be considered free from all but a moral or sentimental reference to the prowess and the "worship" of the individual soldier. As Richard Morison noticed in the dedicatory epistle he prefaced to his translation of Frontinus' *The Strategemes, sleyghtes and Policies of Warre* (1539), it is the commander, not the individual fighting man, who is the key figure in war; it is he who gets (and, Morison implies, deserves) both the praise and the blame for whatever happens on the field. And he must be equipped with more than courage or prowess, for "Many more fields have been lost for lack of policy than for want of strength, many towns won by slights which a long season easily were kept against greatest might, strength, and force."[85] It was indeed, a conclusion implicit in the development of warfare among major territorial states. It had already influenced the actions of fifteenth-century commanders such as Henry V and the Earl of Warwick, perhaps more than they themselves realized.[86] It was, if we allow for the peculiar bent of More's satire, the moving spirit of his Utopians when faced with the necessity of waging war. It was also a conclusion toward which the example of antiquity, as interpreted by such humanist scholars as Morison, was bound to lead the thought of literate Englishmen. More than contemporary Italian military doctrine (the most advanced in Europe, but, after the Henrician Reformation not too accessible to Englishmen), more than the example of Hebrew strategy (though that too had its students), the classical military writers "exerted a salubrious influence upon the nation at large. In them, citizens learned to respect strategy and discipline" and to trust less fondly in the "plain shock and even play of battle," innocent of "strategem," which Shakespeare still liked to think marked the tactics of his hero, Henry V.[87] The brave and accom-

[85] S.T.C. 11402, sig. Aiiii.
[86] See above, chap. ii.
[87] Paul A. Jorgensen, "Alien Military Doctrine in Renaissance England." *M.L.Q.* XVII (March, 1956), 43-49. On the whole subject of Elizabethan military life and

plished soldier, "seeking the bubble, reputation, even in the cannon's mouth," the modern successor of the medieval knight, continued, of course, to live. He found his most sublime expression in the military career—and reputation—of Sidney. He flourished even more mightily in the pages of romance, and in the historical drama. To an increasing extent, however, his existence became confined to just this realm of romantic idealization.

Seen in the longer perspective of military policy, the change from a medieval to a modern, or more specifically from a chivalric to a national point of view, will perhaps become clearer if we glance for a moment at some of those men of Elizabethan England who wrote about war and the military life and are therefore as nearly comparable to the authors of *The Boke of Noblesse* as any sixteenth-century writers can be. Let us take, for example, those who wrote in 1578 and 1579 under the influence of a renewed interest in the military life and with the crisis in the Netherlands and England's equivocal position among the European powers no doubt particularly in mind. Geoffrey Gates, Thomas Proctor, and Barnaby Rich[88] all express deep concern for the safety of England. They believe that the country has not taken pains to maintain a military force and has accordingly let down its guard at a time when all other nations have been forced to raise theirs. They are especially alarmed at the lack of respect paid to the military profession. They look upon all Englishmen as bound together by common interests and common dangers. The military profession, while peculiarly suited to the gentry and aristocracy (it is an "honorable" career and one to which the poor man, who cannot live of his own, can hardly be expected to devote

---

thought, see the same author's *Shakespeare's Military World* (Berkeley and Los Angeles, 1956).

[88] Thomas Proctor, *Of the knowledge and conducte of warres* (London, 1578), S.T.C. 20403; Barnaby Rich, *Allarme to England* (London, 1578), S.T.C. 20978; Geoffry Gates, *The defence of militarie profession* (London, 1579), S.T.C. 11683.

himself),[89] is by no means the preserve of the gentle born, nor is it able to compete with other vocations, such as the law, for the services of the governing class.[90] All "citizens," Gates argues, should be "furnished and practiced for the field" as in France, Italy, and Germany.[91]

Conversely, the soldier's duty to society is not confined to his professional capacity. Proctor insists that the general should be able in time of peace "to be as profitable unto the civil estate by his industry and policy as he was by his valor in the wars." And Rich insists that soldiers and learned men have much in common.[92] The knight must now be also a citizen, which is to say that he must be able to take his part in the civil life of the national state and lend his ear, perhaps also his active counsel, to the discussion of its vital concerns.

Strategically speaking (and it is worth noting that these writers are able and willing to speak strategically), all Englishmen are subject to the same conditioning factors. Gates dwells on England's island position, in which he finds both defensive strength and the source of a dangerous complacency.[93] Proctor even finds in climate and geography the explanation of the English temperament: the fertile land of England and its temperate climate should cause its sons to excel all nations in arms, were it not also for a tendency, presumably stemming from the same conditions, to "lack of endeavor, and discipline." The context is, in short, always that of the nation, and moreover, the nation considered as a power among powers. The language of chivalric tradition is totally absent. Proctor urges Englishmen to read Vegetius, the military textbook of late medieval chivalry, but recognizes explicitly, as few, if any, medieval writers could have done, that

[89] Proctor (n. pag.).
[90] See especially, Rich, sig. Hiii; Gates, pp. 9-11.
[91] Gates, p. 53.
[92] *A right exelent and pleasant dialogue, Betwene Mercury and an English souldier* (London, 1574), S.T.C. 20998. See also Jorgensen, *Shakespeare's Military World*, pp. 223-224.
[93] Gates, p. 18.

it refers to an earlier and different society[94] and is hence of limited value to his own day. He also (and possibly more significantly) recommends Machiavelli's treatise on the art of war as a useful authority, though likewise somewhat foreign and dated.

Any attempt to apply to the discussion of foreign policy or national defense the language and values of chivalry was bound to be a self-defeating project. Indeed, in expressing patriotic sentiment in such terms, the chivalric apologists of the fifteenth century were traveling a dead-end road. The trouble was not so much that chivalric thought and national consciousness were by nature incompatible, though it is true that, like the broader Christian synthesis of which it had become a part, the chivalric ideal tended strongly toward the universal. Rather it lay in the fact that the chivalric values were growing less and less relevant to the real issues of national life. Stimulating as they remained for a long time as a code of individual conduct, they were quite inadequate in the realm of public discussion. It is a measure of the ingrained medievalism of late fifteenth-century thought that an attempt could still be made, in apparent seriousness, to adapt chivalric concepts to the rapidly rising requirements of national policy. Equally significant is the fact that, under the combined influence of brute fact and ancient example, an increasing number of Englishmen began in the Tudor era to see how difficult it was becoming, and withal how unnecessary, to transfer chivalric values from private considerations to public.

[94] See above, chap. iii, n. 27.

VI

CHIVALRY AND THE EDUCATION
OF THE CITIZEN

BOTH THE CHIVALRIC IDEAL AND THE RENAIS-
sance ideal of the gentleman-governor involved a concept of
education. Both indeed, derived their peculiar quality in large
measure from that concept. It was in this respect that the
chivalric tradition proved itself most unsuited to the needs of
the changing society of late fifteenth- and early sixteenth-
century England. The orthodox educational ideal appears to
have remained throughout the latter fifteenth century pretty
much as it had been set forth in the standard manuals of
knighthood.[1] It was still common, if not the rule, to draw a
heavy line between the education proper for the knight and
the clerk, and for the aristocracy to hold in contempt the study
of the liberal arts.[2] Even the study of law, as we have seen,
was suspect to the authors of *The Boke of Noblesse,* although
it must be admitted their attack represents an even stricter
interpretation of the knightly career than was usual in chivalric tradition. There were learned noblemen in the period—
witness the scholarly interests of those professional soldiers,
Lord Rivers and the Earl of Worcester. And William Caxton,
at least, had the highest respect for their learning. But few
there were who would have valued such praise as Erasmus
gave to his patron, Lord Mountjoy: *"inter doctos nobilissimus,*

[1] Lull's treatise was standard, and may be considered typical. For a condensed
summary of the contents of the books of knighthood, see James D. Gordon, ed.,
The Epistle of Othea to Hector (U. of Penn. dis., Philadelphia, 1942), introd.

[2] As a Scottish poet of the early sixteenth century said, "Nobilite suld mell but
with nobilnes." *Buke of gude consale to the king* (Edinburgh, 1508). See also
Wright, II, 244-245, in which Oldcastle is taken to task for meddling with theology
which "is no gentil mannes game"; Kilgour, p. 105; Caspari, p. 80.

inter nobiles doctissimus." Yet it was becoming gradually apparent that the traditional chivalric ideal here, as elsewhere in the lives of the English ruling class, was an anachronism. At the same time, especially in the early decades of the Tudor era, it was in fact giving way before an ideal contributed by humanism, an ideal that needed no artificial stretching to make it encompass the needs and aspirations of that class. It is characteristic of a transitional age that the two ideals should for a time have existed side by side; and aristocratic education in England has never quite lost a certain tincture of chivalric idealism. But it was in the late fifteenth and, especially, the early sixteenth centuries that a revolutionary change took place in the educational ideal of the English nobility and gentry. It is that change that I hope to trace in this chapter.

. . .

The education normally specified in manuals of chivalry and described in the romances for the young gentleman who would, or could if he wished, become a knight was narrow in its scope. Generally speaking it was that received by Chaucer's Squire—seldom more, and no doubt frequently less, especially among those families whose lives lay remote from court. Although Chaucer does not mention it, the squire of good family was likely to have had some of the elements of a grammar-school education, if not exactly the equivalent of it. Even the writers of the medieval English chivalric romances on occasion took pains to include a certain amount of book-learning among the other training in polite accomplishments to which their heroes were subjected. In *The Lyfe of Ipomydon* (early fifteenth century) the young hero is taught "upon the book,/ Both to sing and to read."[3] The hero of *Floris and Blaunche-flur* (thirteenth century) learned as a child to read latin and

[3] In *Metrical Romances,* ed. H. Weber (Edinburgh, 1810), II, 281-365, lines 54-55. See also Mathew, "Ideals of Knighthood in Late Fourteenth-Century England," pp. 361-362.

"write on parchment."[4]   By far the greater emphasis seems, however, to have been placed on the courtly or military accomplishments: carving, hunting with hawk and hound, dancing, and, above all, fighting.[5]

An excellent example taken from the period with which we are most concerned is contained in a list of duties of the "Master of Henchmen" who had charge of the young gentlemen of Edward IV's court.   His task was "to show the schools of urbanity and nurture of England" and to see that his charges were able "to ride cleanly and surely; to draw them also to jousts; to learn them wear their harness; to have all courtesy in words, deeds, and degrees; diligently to keep them in rules of goings and sittings, after they be of honor.   Moreover to teach them sundry languages, and other learnings virtuous, to harping, to pipe, sing, dance, and with other honest and temperate behavior and patience," and, of course, to fear God and honor the Church.[6]   This is chivalric education to the very core. That it is also chivalric education at its best, we have the word of Sir John Fortescue who, although no apologist for the chivalric way of life—he insisted that his own princely charge, the young prince Edward, be instructed above all things in the law of the land—was in a position to know whereof he spoke. Referring to the education of orphans of noble families, he stops long enough to express his esteem for "the magnificence and grandeur of the king's household, for within it is the supreme academy for the nobles of the realm, and a school of vigour, probity, and manners by which the realm is honoured and will flourish, and be secured against invaders, and will be made formidable to the enemies and friends of the kingdom."[7]

[4] Ed. George H. McKnight, E.E.T.S., O.S., No. 14 (1866), lines 31-34.
[5] E. G. *Ipomydon*, lines 56 ff.   Cf. *The Geste of King Horn*, in *Metrical Romances*, ed. J. Ritson (London, 1802), II, 91-155, lines 234 ff.
[6] *A Collection of Ordinances and Regulations for the Government of the Royal Household* (London, 1790), p. 45.   Cf. *ibid.*, pp. 28-29.
[7] *De Laudibus Legum Angliae*, ed. S. B. Chrimes (Cambridge, 1942), chap. xlv. On his recommendation of law as a study for princes, see also chaps. iv, v, vi.   Cf. C. F. Arrowood, "Sir John Fortescue on the Education of Rulers," *Speculum*, X (October, 1935), 404-410.

At this point it might be enlightening to glance ahead approximately a century and examine very briefly a plan drawn up early in the reign of Elizabeth by Sir Humphrey Gilbert.[8] For between the two lies the story of the transformation of aristocratic learning in England. It is a project for setting up an academy in London for the training of "her Majesty's Wards, and others the youth of nobility and gentlemen." Thus it is roughly parallel in purpose to the rules set forth for the king's henchmen in the reign of Edward IV. The latter, to be sure, merely ordered what was apparently the general practice; Gilbert's project, on the other hand, is visionary to the extent that no such institution existed, or had much chance of being actually established in Elizabethan England. But it was meant to be considered seriously, it was almost philistine in its utilitarian bias, and it no doubt reflected with considerable accuracy the educational philosophy of those Englishmen who accepted the greatly expanded responsibilities of Renaissance citizenship. Although Gilbert repeats what had come to be a stock criticism of the English aristocracy for their neglect of education, it is obviously to a sophisticated group that he appeals, and one already well aware of the values of higher learning.[9] Indeed, one reason for the project, he admits, is that it would relieve the pressure on the universities and make it possible for "poor scholars" to receive "scholarships and fellowships" otherwise monopolized by the "youth of nobility and gentlemen."[10]

Gilbert would include in his proposed curriculum virtually everything the "Master of Henchmen" was under order to teach the young gentlemen of King Edward's court. Such training is, however, subordinated to, indeed all but lost in, a vastly broader discipline in all branches of learning, with special and constant emphasis on the role the young gentleman is presumably to play in the service of his country. It is basically

[8] *Queene Elizabethes Achademy,* ed. F. J. Furnivall, E.E.T.S., E.S., VIII (1869).

[9] On this point see J. H. Hexter, "The Education of the Aristocracy in the Renaissance," *Journal of Modern History,* XXII (March, 1950), 1-20.

[10] *Achademy,* p. 10.

a humanistic education; but Gilbert has already gone beyond the earlier generations of humanists in emphasizing the immediate and practical training for citizenship in a state uniquely dependent on its nobility and gentry for the actual administration of government, even for the counsel out of which policy must emerge. He would have his scholars well grounded in ancient language and "example"; but he no longer professes the faith in classical precept that the humanists held in the days of their first enthusiasm. He would leave purely book learning to the universities and the professional study of law to the Inns of Court. But he would have the young gentlemen learn enough philosophy and enough law to enable them to be conversant on the one hand with the theory of government and on the other with all but the technicalities of the Common Law. He would have them study—in English—the art of the orator, the learned art of persuasion, not only by the application of reason but also "with the examples and strategems both antique and modern" to be found in history and literature. He would in particular have them study—in English—the principles of "civil policy," drawn from a reading of contemporary history. Thus they would learn "the principal Cause concerning justice, or their revenues, whereby they [be] any way increased or diminished."[11] They would also learn heraldry and the graceful arts of the courtier.[12] And, of course, they would learn the art of war, to which Gilbert applies the word "chivalry" in its original, and perhaps most accurate meaning; but the warfare he has in mind is of a kind far removed from anything the medieval knight was used to, for it involved what to him would have been an appallingly confusing discipline in mathematics, engineering, ballistics, and military history and theory.[13]

This "Academy of Philosophy and Chivalry" would, Gilbert hoped, bring "this silly, frozen, island into such everlasting

[11] *Ibid.*, pp. 2-3.   [12] *Ibid.*, pp. 7-8.
[13] *Ibid.*, pp. 3-5.

honor that all the nations of the world shall know and say, when the face of an English gentleman appeareth, that he is either a soldier, a philosopher, or a gallant courtier."[14]   In these words is packed a century of as crucial change as any in the history of English culture.

To return to the young knight of the fifteenth century, he was still supposed to be primarily a soldier. It is for him that the many manuals of knighthood were written. Lydgate had said of Henry V that as a youth he used to "haunt his body in plays martial, . . . After the doctrine of Vegetius," then added, with a logic he no doubt believed impeccable, "Thus is he both manful and virtuous."[15]   Such social attainments as the knight might have (and they bulk large in the above-quoted document of Edward IV's reign) were those of the knight in his equally traditional function as the ornament of society, the custodian of courtesy. There may, however, be just the hint in these orders given the "Master of Henchmen" of that tendency to make a courtier of the knight which characterized the Burgundian court of the same period. There sixteen esquires of the best families were constantly in attendance on the prince providing him with entertainment in the form of songs, the reading aloud of romances, or conversation about such favorite topics of chivalric society as love and military renown.[16]   Nevertheless, increasingly the courtier though they tend to be, the young squires of the English court are still very far from the intellectually oriented courtier of the Italian Renaissance, and even farther from that reflection of Plato's philosopher-king which the humanists hoped to find in the English "governor."

Yet there is a high degree of sophistication in this traditional education; and the English aristocracy can hardly be blamed for accepting it as the last word. Was there not before

[14] *Ibid.,* p. 11.
[15] *Troy Book,* prol., lines 71-89.
[16] Cartellieri, p. 67.

their eyes the example of the Burgundian court, then at the height of its brilliance, the rallying ground not only for the finest jousters, but the best artists, poets, and chroniclers of Northern Europe?[17]   Although even there the chivalric tradition was in many respects wearing thin—Charles the Bold took a not strictly conventional delight in the histories of ancient conquerors, and his courtiers at times took refuge from the stereotypes of chivalry in an equally romantic taste for the bucolic—Burgundian society still moved, however theatrically and artificially, in the patterns of chivalry.   And as a result of their close commercial and political relation with the Low Countries, Englishmen had plenty of opportunity to see in it a model of cultural refinement for their own immeasurably less mature society.   It is worth remembering in this connection that Caxton began his career as a translator, and doubtless also as a printer, under the patronage of Margaret, Duchess of Burgundy.[18]

Sophistication is only to be expected of an old tradition.   It is, indeed, an element of that very decadence which was sapping the vitality of chivalric idealism.   The proliferation during the late Middle Ages of manuals on the duties and training of a knight may in itself be seen as the expression of a hardening process, a desire to define, to codify, and to elaborate what had at one time been more or less flexible and spontaneous.[19] Lull's treatise marks the beginning of this formalizing process; and it is interesting to notice that he sensed, even in the thirteenth century, the need for more formal methods of educating young aristocrats to supplement the "on-the-job" training usually obtained in the retinue of a noble household.   In place of this practical education he advocated the founding of schools in which the knight, like the clerk, could be taught the prin-

---

[17] See on this whole subject, Cartellieri; also Huizinga, *Waning of the Middle Ages.*
[18] Crotch, p. xcviii.
[19] A. T. P. Byles, "Medieval Courtesy Books and the Prose Romances of Chivalry," in *Chivalry,* ed. E. Prestage (New York, 1928), pp. 183-205, p. 186.

ciples of his order by means of books—his own doubtless included.[20]

. . .

Other books were, of course, available to the knightly class and were no doubt standard reading for any member of it who was literate enough and interested enough to make use of them. If we consider his education in the broadest terms, the squire or knight could condition his mind and sharpen his ideals on the entire body of history and romance we have discussed in a previous chapter.[21] It was, as we have seen, in part at least a desire to contribute to this broader aspect of the knight's training that led Caxton to translate and otherwise edit for publication in readable form the cream of late medieval English culture. His list of publications may well serve as a sample of the reading, recommended if not prescribed, for the instruction of the knight. What with its chivalric romances and histories, its medievalized classics, its treatises on arms and manners, it was comprehensive and suited well to the purpose.

But there were certain books that must have been given special consideration in this respect. There was, in particular, Vegetius's famous text on the art of war which Caxton printed in 1489 as a translation of Christine de Pisan's French version. This book, its original classical character suitably transposed into a contemporary key, continued throughout the fifteenth century to be the accepted authority on the profession the knight believed peculiarly his own. The bearing of this work on the education of the knight is obvious. The same cannot

[20] *Ordre of Chyualry,* pp. 22-23. See Painter's comment, *French Chivalry,* pp. 81-82.
[21] One of the very few references to the books actually owned by a fifteenth-century English knight may be found in the *Paston Letters.* See Bennett, *The Pastons and their England,* p. 111 and Appendix I. On the literacy and cultural interests of the gentry, see H. S. Bennett, "Science and Information in English Writings of the Fifteenth Century," *Mod. Lang. Rev.,* XXXIX (January, 1944), 1-8; J. W. Adamson, "The Extent of Literacy in the XV and XVI Centuries," *The Library,* X (1929-30), 162 ff.; Thrupp, p. 247; Bennett, *English Books and Readers,* chap. ii.

be said of another fairly large category which seems, nevertheless, to have commanded considerable respect among the more serious minded of the English aristocracy. I refer to those written ostensibly for the instruction of princes and following in the tradition of the pseudo-Aristotelian *Secreta Secretorum* and the *De Regimine Principum* of Aegidius Romanus. Supposedly a letter from Aristotle to Alexander the Great, written for the purpose of instructing the young conqueror not only in the art of ruling but in the ordering of his private life as well, the origins of the *Secreta* are obscure. It seems, however, to have come to Europe from Arabic sources. It first received wide circulation there in the twelfth or thirteenth centuries; and from that time on it served as the basis for a whole family of treatises, perhaps the most famous of which was Aegidius Romanus' *De Regimine Principum*. In the process of its translation—or, more accurately its adaptation, for few medieval translations were other than free renderings of the original, full of editorial comment and sometimes whimsical alteration—it was made to fit nicely the purposes and prejudices of the medieval mind.[22]

These treatises were undoubtedly meant for a wider public than that of royalty alone. Although the patronage of one prince was to the medieval writer worth as much as general popularity among the court aristocracy, his prestige and his ability to secure princely patronage depended somewhat on the universality of his appeal and on his acceptance by those who mattered at court. Fifteenth-century England produced little that could be called an original contribution to this "mir-

---

[22] On the "Mirror of Princes" literature in general and the *Secreta* tradition in particular, see Wilhelm Kleineke, *Englische Fürstenspiegel vom Policraticus Johanns von Salisbury bis zum Basilikon Doron König Jakobs I* (Halle, 1937); Alan H. Gilbert, *Machiavelli's Prince and its Forerunners* (Durham, N. C., 1938), and the same author's "Notes on the Influence of the *Secretum Secretorum*," *Speculum*, III (January 1928), 84-98; Robert Steele, ed., *Secrees of old Philosoffres*, E.E.T.S., E.S., No. 66 (1894), introd.; L. K. Born, ed., Erasmus' *The Education of a Christian Prince* (New York, 1936). Yonge's translation is reprinted in *Three Prose Versions of the "Secreta Secretorum,"* ed. R. Steele, E.E.T.S., E.S.. No. 74 (1898). See also Kingsford, *Henry V*, p. xviii. Useful references may be found throughout Cary's *The Medieval Alexander*.

ror of princes" literature. It was in fact ill suited to the limited monarchy so deeply rooted in the English tradition; and except in the hands of men like George Ashby and, in a later generation, Sir Thomas Elyot,[23] it had little if anything to do with specifically English conditions. It is perhaps a tribute to Caxton's practical sense and his awareness of English problems that he passed over this voluminous and respected, if thoroughly otiose, literature, though *The Game and Playe of Chesse* is closely related to it. But the century did witness several translations and adaptations, especially of the *Secreta*. That the latter appealed to the chivalric mentality is attested by the fact that James Butler, Earl of Ormonde (1392-1452), at one time a soldier of Henry V, in later years notable for his love of the kind of history that was essentially chivalry teaching by example, authority on the law of arms and benefactor of the College of Heralds, commanded James Yonge to do a translation of the *Secreta* in English prose.[24] If for no other reason than that reading matter having to do with secular affairs was scarce, the type seems to have enjoyed a steady popularity. It continued, indeed, to command enough of an audience in the following century to justify Erasmus in adding one more item, a highly sophisticated though not especially original one, to the already long list of books belonging to this genre. Replete as these books are with precepts for a man placed in a position of lordship in the community, they could be considered especially valuable as supplementary reading for the local lord, be he squire, knight, or magnate, who fulfilled

[23] See Ashby's *Active Policy of a Prince* and Elyot's *The Image of Governance* (1541), S.T.C. 7664. Fortescue also undertook to advise a prince, but he abandoned the tradition and wrote "in praise of the laws of England."

[24] The most original of the English adaptations were Hoccleve's *Regement of Princes*, deriving both from the *Secreta* and Egidius Romanus (See *Regement*, stanzas 292-294), and Ashby's *Active Policy*, which broke to a large extent from the domination of either. Examples of more or less faithful versions of the *Secreta* may be found in *Three Prose Versions*, ed. Steele; Gilbert of the Haye's *The Buke of the Governance of Princis*, ed. J. H. Stephenson, The Scottish Text Society (1914); *Secrees of old Philosoffres;* William Forrest, *Pleasaunt Poesie of Princelie Practise*, printed in extract in S. J. Herrtage, *England in the Reign of Henry VIII*, E.E. T.S., E.S., No. 32 (1878).

the obligation traditionally incumbent upon a knight to act not only as the sword-arm of the body politic but also as a "governor."[25] This was especially feasible in a day when, as we have seen, both duties tended to merge in the single, overriding duty of civil government to protect the rights of all persons in the community. Justice and peace in other words depended alike on the coercive power of the prince and the sword of the knight; and, as a matter of fact, the power of the prince to establish and enforce justice was in England normally delegated in the localities to the knight acting in the capacity of Justice of the Peace. The institution of a prince could therefore have a good deal of meaning for the man actively engaged as a member of the governing class in the business of local government.

This is not the place for an extended discussion of this literature. Only a few questions need answering, the chief among them being what, if any, bearing did these books *de regimine principum* have on the chivalric outlook? To begin with, they take chivalry largely for granted. There is in them little specific reference to the ideals and practices of chivalry. The original authors and most of their adapters and translators were clerks trained in scholastic and patristic learning, more accustomed to the language of the school and the pulpit than of the court, the field, or the tilt-yard. They emphasize the Christian virtues which, it is true, had become part also of the chivalric ethos, but which remained nevertheless a readily separable element. The result is a deceptively nonchivalric appearance which is likely to obscure the fact that the prince is himself a knight and that chivalric values are indeed taken for granted. Then, too, especially in those books that represented a more or less direct adaptation of the *Secreta Secretorum,* specifically chivalric concepts are often lost in a deluge of practical common sense as universally applicable as were

[25] Haye makes something of a point of broadening his version of the *Secreta* to include "lordis" as well as kings and princes. See, for example, p. 75, lines 24-25, and p. 89.

the Christian values themselves. In addition to the usual moral advice to be continent and to avoid avarice, to be merciful and just, prudent and pious—the prince is told, often at tiresome length, how to dress, how to exercise his body, what to eat, whence comes a stomach ache, and what is the nature of wine.

But the chivalric assumptions are usually there, if not always obvious. In Hoccleve's *Regement of Princes* (1412), one of the few English works of the century in which the hackneyed "mirror of princes" material is given at all original treatment, the chivalric element crops up with sufficient frequency to indicate that it underlay much of the classical lore and Christian moralism that dominates the surface.[26] Clerk that he was, his mind reflected something of the aura of chivalric idealism that already shone with renewed intensity from the person of the future Henry V for whom the book was written. The king is also a knight—so obviously so, indeed, that Hoccleve finds it unnecessary to labor the point. With the utmost ease and unconcern he shifts from the word *king* to the word *knight,* and after the custom of his day interprets the stories derived from ancient history in terms of knighthood. The king must be "true," so must the knight. The king is a soldier, so also is the knight; and they accordingly share the chivalric virtues pertaining particularly to the soldier. They both must be valorous, eager for renown, but magnanimous, not given to vainglory, and interested only in just causes. Both are concerned primarily with the preservation of peace through justice.

The relationship between the mirror of princes and the manual of knighthood will, I believe, become clearer if it is recognized that they both rested on the same assumption concerning the nature of government, namely that public life represents simply an extension of the moral life of the indi-

[26] See, for example, *Regement,* lines 2238-2240, 2297-2299, 2404-2408, 2451-2460, 2651-2653, 2948 ff., 3249 ff., 3263-3269, 3498 ff., 3429; see especially lines 3963-4004.

viduals concerned. That more than anything else is what separates the medieval attitude toward secular life from the modern. The king and his counsellors are persons, subject like all other men to the conflict between virtue and vice which is the essence of the divine tragedy. A society is healthy if all men in it behave as they should; unhealthy if they do not. The task of government is accordingly to check or if possible extirpate vice and by so doing to allow virtue to accomplish its beneficent work. To perform it properly the prince must above all have good counsel. But counsel is itself dependent on the moral qualities of the counselor. Its essence is simply truth, not policy in the modern sense of the word—what is wrong with the community, not what will lead to a better or more powerful one. Seen from this point of view the function of the governor, at whatever level of society he is situated, remains the comparatively simple one of protection, or to put it in a way more familiar to the medieval mind, the maintenance of justice and peace. There is little need in it for constructive intelligence or for the pooled ingenuity upon which the modern state depends for its characteristic dynamism. All of which leaves the knight exactly where the manuals of knighthood placed him. He is the sword-arm of the body politic, the maintainer of justice which is the means toward the higher good of peace. The treatise *de regimine principum* merely adds an element of Christian morality and pseudoclassical philosophy to the military and feudal tradition of chivalry. And, by the same token, the manual of knighthood remains in itself a sufficient guide for the military and feudal duties to which the knight was still confined—confined, that is, by virtue of his limited political horizon, not by any policy consciously formulated.

When, especially in the late fifteenth century, important exceptions to this general tendency begin to appear they lead in the direction of the Renaissance state and Renaissance realism rather than in that of an amplified chivalry. George

Ashby's *Active Policy of a Prince* (the title itself is significant) becomes, under cover of the traditional form of the mirror of princes, the vehicle for analysis of actual English conditions and for the discussion of practical policy. Himself a member of that class of intelligent and occasionally literary men who were drawn into public life by the Tudors, often from the middle ranks of society, Ashby clearly adumbrates the "active policies" by which both Edward IV and, more successfully, Henry VII strove to erect an efficient and centralized administration on the crumbling foundations of Lancastrian government. And it is interesting to see in passing that, among such policies, there begins to take shape in his mind that of employing in the royal administrative offices men of low estate and high personal ability in preference to those whose chief claim to recognition lay in their aristocratic status.[27] To Ashby this is largely a practical matter, dictated more by fear of the overmighty subject than by any belief in the creative potential inherent in the trained intellect. Nevertheless, there is here the emphasis on personal worth rather than status which was to become an increasingly obtrusive theme in the writings of early Tudor England. There is here also the tendency ever more apparent in English writings for chivalric assumptions to evaporate in the dry light of a practical, undoctrinaire, largely pragmatic realism.

. . .

The fifteenth-century knight was called upon to take some part in the administration of local government, especially in the capacity of Justice of the Peace. It was a duty by no means foreign to the letter of the chivalric tradition. Lull, it will be recalled, left specific room for the knight to act as governor. It was part of his broad function as one who protects those entrusted to his care. But it was a duty left quite vague by

[27] *Active Policy*, lines 807-813; cf. lines 639-642.

Lull, who obviously could not have foreseen the complex relationship that was to develop between central and local government in England. And Caxton, concerned principally with the values of chivalry rather than with the specific duties of the knight in the administrative system, saw no reason to elaborate. The local knight or squire had therefore to look beyond the traditional books of chivalric precept for the information he needed about the procedure and law relating to his office. He was apparently able to find this detail in a number of factual manuals written for the purpose, especially in the latter part of the century, which made no pretence to intellectual eminence or chivalry sublime.[28]   Such was the flexibility and practicality of the fifteenth-century Englishman that he was able to bridge in this way the ever-widening chasm between the ideal and the practice of knighthood. The knight was becoming a civil functionary as much as, if not a great deal more than, a man-at-arms.

He was also forced increasingly to use the courts of law for his own protection in a day when untold land-grabbing went on under the guise of litigation. A knowledge of the law was essential to many a beleaguered county family. Here again the young squire had to look beyond the boundaries of the traditional education of his class and read books on land law. Or, better still, he could obtain a legal education at the Inns of Court.

Fortescue bears witness—perhaps more enthusiastic than accurate, for he was drawing upon his memory in the latter years of his life—to this tendency on the part of the English aristocracy to seek in those most unchivalric of institutions the least chivalric of educations. Although he admits that noble families still customarily farmed their sons out with other families of their own class and maintains that the king's house-

[28] See B. H. Putnam, *Early Treatises on the Practice of the Justices of the Peace in the Fifteenth and Sixteenth Centuries* (Oxford, 1924). There was an important manuscript of this sort dating from 1422. The first printed manual bears the date 1506.

hold is "the supreme academy for nobles of the realm," he tells us also that the Inns of Court were patronized chiefly by the aristocracy.   The study of law is, he says, especially fitting for the gentleman.   And anyway, education at the Inns of Court costs too much for men of mean estate.

Because of this costliness, there are not many who learn the law in the Inns except the sons of nobles.   For poor and common people cannot bear so much cost for the maintenance of their sons.   And merchants rarely desire to reduce their stock by such annual burdens.   Hence it comes about that there is scarcely a man learned in the laws to be found in the realm who is not noble or sprung of noble lineage.

The Inns of Court provide also a general education in the aristocratic graces, and so knights, barons, and other magnates place their sons there "though they do not desire them to be trained in the science of the laws, nor to live by its practice, but only by their patrimonies."[29]   But these patrimonies, as *The Boke of Noblesse* emphasizes, tend to deflect the knight from his traditional military duties, for they embroil him constantly in civil concerns.   The Paston family, whom the author of *The Boke of Noblesse* must have known quite well through his attachment to their mutual patron, Fastolf, is for us, as no doubt for him, the perfect example of such preoccupation. Young Sir John, vastly impressed by the brilliant life of the court with its tournaments and chivalric trappings, stands in the sharpest contrast to his mother and brother at home, fighting for all they were worth (literally) in order to keep the hard-won lands of the family from the more or less legal aggressions of a greedy neighbor.[30]   Whether they liked it or not, the English knight and those of the gentry who aspired to his status and manners were committed to a life in which civil concerns and, for some, the business of government were to reduce their military function to a secondary, largely emer-

[29] *De Laudibus Legum Angliae,* trans. and ed. G. B. Chrimes (Cambridge, 1942), chaps. xlv and xlix.   See above, n. 7.

[30] Bennett, *Pastons and their England* pp. 22 and 105.   See also Thrupp, p. 318; Kelso, pp. 44-50.

gency role. And it is interesting in passing to notice that
gentlemen trained in the law were being returned in considerable numbers as members of parliament.[31]

. . .

Significant as was the study of law in the gradual transformation of aristocratic education, it was not until the virtues of
a still broader education were recognized that we are able to
discern the true shape of things to come. Supervision of justice had always been accepted as part of the knight's duties. A
formal knowledge of the law could without too much difficulty
be interpreted as a logical extension of that duty—*The Boke of
Noblesse* to the contrary notwithstanding. It was quite otherwise with the liberal studies traditionally prescribed for clerks,
to say nothing of those newfangled studies brought home from
Italy by a few earnest scholars who had followed in the footsteps of Duke Humphrey of Gloucester.[32] That one of these
scholars should have been among the first to foreshadow the
humanistic attitude toward the education of the aristocracy is
very appropriate. John Tiptoft brought back with him from
Italy a mind deeply impressed with the image of Roman
antiquity. On the other hand it is typical of this transitional era
that this young English nobleman whose Latin oration is said
to have brought tears of joy to the eyes of that ardent classicist,
Pius II, and who drank so deeply at the springs of humanistic
learning, should later have served with distinction in England
as president of the Court of Chivalry and have turned the keen
edge of his mind to the task of fashioning a series of ordinances
for "Jousts and Triumphs."[33]

[31] Roskell's study, already referred to, of the parliament of 1422 indicates that,
even at that date, lawyers constituted a considerable percentage of the members.
[32] On the early generations of English humanism see R. Weiss, *Humanism in
England during the Fifteenth Century* (Oxford, 1941). On Tiptoft in particular,
see pp. 112-122.
[33] Mitchell, chap. vii. See also, on the Court of Chivalry, F. P. Barnard, "Heraldry," in *Medieval England,* ed. H. W. C. Davis (Oxford, 1928), *pp.* 195-244,
pp. 232-237. It is possible that the famous oration was the work of a scholar in his
pay. Weiss, p. 119.

Tiptoft was, however, able to see chivalry from the vantage point of a nonchivalric culture. Familiar both with the conventions of a decadent chivalry and the vagaries of a factious nobility, he must have wondered many times what should be the mark and duty of the true knight. Some such question doubtless prompted him to translate, about 1460, the *Controuersia de Nobilitate* of Buonaccorso da Montemagno.[34] In that *novella* on the Fulgens and Lucresse theme (which Caxton, by the way, published some twenty years later as *The Declamacion of Noblesse*) the traditional view of nobility as stemming from riches and illustrious ancestry and expressed in military and courtly pursuits is contrasted with the Renaissance ideal of the man who achieves true nobility by personal virtue and inherent worth.

The novelty of this Italian import lies not so much in the preference of the author for knightly character over aristocratic descent and knightly deportment[35] as it does in a consistent emphasis on learning at the pathway to virtue which, in turn, must find expression in public service. Virtue had always occupied a primary place in the chivalric ideal, but it was virtue sought within the scope of the knight's traditional function.[36] It was the work of the Renaissance to link virtue with learning as well as with the innate character of man. It was to become something of a commonplace among the humanistically influenced social writers of the sixteenth century to find in both virtue and learning a main source of nobility despite an equally strong prejudice in favor of a society of hierarchical degree founded upon gentility of birth.[37] Early in the century it

---

[34] *The Declamacion of Noblesse,* ed. R. J. Mitchell, in that author's *John Tiptoft,* Appendix I.
[35] Cf. Mitchell, p. 182.
[36] See *The Boke of St. Albans* on this point; also G. M. Vogt, "Gleanings for the History of a Sentiment: *Generositas Virtus non Sanguis,*" *Journal of English and German Philology,* XXIV (1925), 102-124; Reed, "Chivalry and the Idea of a Gentleman."
[37] Kelso, pp. 29-30; Mason, p. 8.

found expression in a statement which Thomas More added to his translation of the Latin life of Pico della Mirandola.[38]   In it he insists, somewhat gratuitously considering the admitted aristocracy of Pico's lineage, that true nobility stems not from noble birth and inherited possessions but from learning and virtue.   Honor derives from those qualities only.   It is, of course, especially related to virtue.   Pico's colossal erudition was not an end but a means to the achievement of the higher objective.[39]

Tiptoft may well have visualized himself in the experience of Gayus Flammyneus, the more accomplished of the suitors competing for the hand of Lucresse.   Both were able soldiers, but military discipline had been a small part of their training. Both studied classical languages and steeped themselves in "eloquence and philosophy."   Both collected books—"first I shall show you my library" Gayus Flammyneus promises his newly won lady in one of the least chivalric passages in fifteenth-century literature.[40]   Both turned their learning and their labors to the service of the commonwealth.

It is in this sense of duty to serve the community through learning that *The Declamacion of Noblesse* foreshadows sixteenth-century English humanism most remarkably.   An ideal of public service was not in itself new.   The English knight in the late medieval period was groping his way toward a simple concept of duty to the community that was somewhat broader than that of the soldier.   Those, at any rate, who wrote of knighthood were coming to realize that the knight's protective function extended to civil government.[41]   But even considered as a governor, the medieval knight was still far from the Renaissance ideal of the soldier-scholar who not only protects society, but, by means of the wisdom and virtue to be had through learning, is capable also of giving assistance in

---

[38] *English Works*, I, 349.   See also *ibid.*, introd., p. 16.
[39] *Ibid.*, pp. 351-354.
[40] *Declamacion*, p. 240.   See also Weiss, p. 117.
[41] See above, chap. iv.

the shaping of policy, of sharing in the positive direction of the commonwealth. The following passage from *The Declamacion* might quite concievably have been taken from a dialogue by Thomas Starkey, so closely does it parallel the strong sense of citizenship, and the ideal of philosophic counsel that the Thomas Lupset of his actual dialogue set such store by.

But after that [his diligent study in philosophy and ancient languages] when I remembered me how every man which hath virtue or cunning is bound to serve therewith the estate public, I gave my self wholly and fully to the weal public of the city.[42]

To what extent Tiptoft made this book his own, how seriously he took it all, we shall, of course, never know for certain. We may assume, however, that he would hardly have chosen this among the many works of the Italian *Quattrocento* to translate had he not been in sympathy with the most prominent idea it contained. In any case, close study of such a book, with its emphasis on the importance of the soldier-scholar to the commonwealth, and its clear and reiterated distinction between "things public" and "things private,"[43] must have done much to create in Tiptoft's receptive mind a concept of citizenship quite different from that still held by most members of his class. Nor can the publication of the translation in 1481 be considered an event of minor importance in the history of English thought.

It is also more than likely that John Tiptoft, Earl of Worcester, knight, scholar, and governor, the transitional figure *par excellence* of this transitional era, made a deep impression on the mind of Caxton, who printed not only *The Declamacion of Noblesse* but also a translation of Cicero's *De Amicitia* which he attributes to Tiptoft. In his prologue to the latter work Caxton refers to the "noble famous earl, the Earl of Worcester

---

[42] P. 235. Cf. *A Dialogue between Cardinal Pole and Thomas Lupset, in England in the reign of King Henry the Eighth*, ed. J. M. Cowper, E.E.T.S., E.S., No. 12 (1871), p. 235.
[43] See, especially, p. 236.

. . . which in his time flowered in virtue, and cunning, to whom I knew none like among the lords of the temporality in science and moral virtue."[44]

Once again Caxton's editorial comments do us the service of a weather-cock in the shifting intellectual atmosphere of his day. Basically medieval in his assumptions and in his choice of books to print, thoroughly convinced of the importance of chivalric examples, he nevertheless recognized, if only dimly, the importance of a liberal education for men of affairs, an education in which the classical authors should have an important, if not a dominant, part. In his prologue to *Tullius of Olde Age* (translated perhaps by William Worcester at the request of the aging soldier-administrator, Sir John Fastolf, and printed in 1481) he shows considerable respect for the example of citizenship to be found in the history of Rome and suggests the components of the public for which his editions were intended. This book, he says, is "nor requisite nor convenient moreover for every rude and simple man, which understandeth not of science nor cunning, and for such as have not heard of the noble policy and prudence of the Romans, but for noble, wise, and great lords, gentlemen and merchants that have seen and daily been occupied in matters touching the public weal. . . ."[45] It is interesting to notice that Caxton here envisages a public broader than that for which he prepared the *Ordre of Chyualry*. Apparently the classics were good for all responsible and educated men, whereas the lore of chivalry was fit reading only for the aristocracy. Possibly Caxton was also beginning to see in the classics a necessary supplement to the standard chivalric education.

It would be unwise, however, to treat Caxton's *obiter dicta* as statements of a conscious social philosophy. He was not a

[44] Crotch, p. 44-45; cf. epilogue to *Declamacion, ibid.,* pp. 46-47. This attribution of the translation to Tiptoft has been questioned by K. B. McFarlane in his recent study of William Worcester, pp. 215-216.

[45] Crotch, pp. 42-43; cf. *ibid.,* pp. 108-109. On the question of authorship, see McFarlane, pp. 215-216.

systematic thinker. His attitude toward ideas is marked by an ambivalence typical of the practical man in a time of changing values. Instinctively and by training he adhered to the old order and the old values. His choice of texts includes little that was not the common stock of late medieval culture. The two orations of Cicero, alone among the products of his press, represent an unmedievalized antiquity; and the *Declamacion of Noblesse,* published, it might be noted, together with the works of Cicero, alone represents the influence, rather indirect, of the Italian Renaissance. But these remain items of considerable importance, and his comments on them reflect a high regard for scholarship, for the example of the ancients, and for a liberal education.[46] He was, moreover, on terms of respectful intimacy with John Skelton, a fact which if it does not link him directly with the New Learning, links him at least with a man to whom humanistic learning was by no means a closed book.[47] Yet his thought was very far removed from that of the later generation of humanists who, like Sir Thomas Elyot, found it possible to embrace in a broad scheme of humane education whatever chivalric values were by that time worth keeping. For Caxton the problem was, in fact, just the reverse. Whatever in the classical tradition could be turned to the common profit could readily and legitimately be absorbed in the traditional education. This order of priority was all the more natural to him because, to judge from his frequent acceptance of a medievalized antiquity, he tended habitually to interpret classical examples in chivalric terms. In the light of future developments, perhaps the most significant aspect of Caxton's thought becomes his willingness to see both the values of chivalry and the precepts of classical antiquity as parts of a fundamentally practical learning geared to the

[46] See prol. to *Tullius of Olde Age,* Crotch, p. 41; prol. to *Caton, ibid.,* pp. 77-78; prol. to *The Four Sonnes of Aymon, ibid.,* p. 106; prol. to *The Book of Good Manners, ibid.,* pp. 99-100.

[47] Prol. to *Eneydos,* Crotch, p. 109; H. L. R. Edwards, *Skelton* (London, 1949), introd.; I. A. Gordon, *John Skelton, Poet Laureate* (Melbourne, 1943), pp. 99-100.

"governance of the common profit . . . named in latin *Res Publica.*"[48]

. . .

It was, indeed, the increasing demands made by the commonwealth upon the services of the English gentleman that led some enlightened observers in the early years of the following century to criticize the chivalric concept of education. As the Renaissance state emerged from the feudal monarchy, as France and England in particular emerged from the conflict and confusion of the fifteenth century, it was becoming ever clearer that the business of governing required wise and resourceful counsel. Although few as yet recognized the fact, the medieval concept of the "commonwealth" served only to camouflage the dynamic state, the ends of which demanded of government not only a will to redress wrongs but the ability to shape policy to meet the exigencies of a new and secular society and of a competitive system. Political theory in its more formal aspects reflected this change very slowly. Almost to the end of the sixteenth century its basic structure remained medieval. Many of the early Tudor humanists, however, reveal in their attitude toward public issues a new awareness of the need for creative intelligence in the councils of state.[49] They saw, therefore, that the English gentleman, on whose shoulders the responsibility for government in what they mostly believed to be an aristocratic social order necessarily rested, must train himself for service in this secular and troubled England. He must be able to perform new tasks as well as those at one time left largely to clerks. He must above all be able to give constructive counsel. For these new and enlarged duties the traditional chivalric education could provide but a partial preparation. Should he fail to meet the test

[48] Crotch, p. 41.
[49] Ferguson, "Realism in the 'Commonwealth' Literature." See also Caspari, p. 101.

he must accept the elevation of those of humbler origin who could.[50]

The new state would be served by new men if necessary, by the old only if possible. Henry VIII, in fact, paid scant attention to birth or status in choosing his most trusted advisers. Neither Wolsey nor Cromwell nor More could claim aristocratic origin. And when, during the Pilgrimage of Grace, the men of the still feudal North expressed their resentment at the power exercised by the low-born Cromwell, Henry was at pains to justify a policy in many respects contrary to the chivalric ideals for which he still retained a strong emotional attachment. Through the writings of such humanistic pamphleteers as Richard Morison, he appealed for a brief time to enlightened opinion in the interests of something periously close to the doctrine of careers open to talent. It was, indeed, during the revolutionary events of the 1530's that public minded Englishmen came generally to recognize that their government had less use for the armed knight than for an educated gentry.[51]

The direction in which the world was moving had not, however, gone unnoticed. At the courts of Henry VI and the Yorkist kings, classically trained men had from about 1440 been employed with enough frequency to argue something approaching policy on the part of the royal administration.[52] Henry VII, as we have seen, appears especially to have appreciated the value of learning in public life. If he failed to see in it the source of statecraft and constructive counsel upon which the Renaissance state came eventually to depend, and which later generations of humanists strove earnestly to provide, at least he recognized the prestige value of the lettered man.[53] The new diplomacy in particular required the services of the graceful rhetorician rather than the lance of the cham-

[50] Caspari, pp. 137-138.
[51] *Ibid.*, p. 9. For the propagandist offensive against the rebels of 1536, see Zeeveld, chap. viii.
[52] Weiss, p. 181.
[53] See above, chap. iv.

pion. If, as Professor Mattingly reasonably suggests, the remark of a contemporary—and an opponent—to the effect that an oration by Coluccio Salutati fell into the scales of political decision with the weight of a thousand horse is an exaggeration, it is one that reflects rhetorically the high regard in which rhetoric was held as an instrument of practical affairs.[54] Moreover, to record the accomplishment of the monarchy called for the services of a Polydore Vergil rather than those of the traditional chronicler or court minstrel. Accordingly Henry attracted scholars from Italy and encouraged those at home who where able to speak the language of the New Learning. The transitional character of Henry VII's court is quaintly symbolized by his conferring of the highest honor in English chivalry, the Order of the Garter, on Guido, Duke of Urbino, who was, according to Polydore Vergil, "of all princes in our day the most versed in both Lation and Greek literature and the science of war," and by the fact that the envoy sent to England to accept the dignity for his master was none other than Count Baldassare Castiglione.[55]

. . .

It is very easy to underestimate the importance of Henry VII's court as a factor in the transition from a medieval to a Renaissance society. Of recent years the tendency has been for historians to stress the continuity of medieval concepts and habits in the first generation or two of the Tudor regime. In an understandable reaction against the older interpretation of English history that made the year 1485 one of climactic significance and the "New Monarchy" a sudden apparition upon the political scene, we are told that the methods employed by Henry VII, and his objectives as well, differed little from those of his immediate predecessors of the House of York and that the ideas of his subjects, including the humanists, were still

[54] *Renaissance Diplomacy*, pp. 62-63.
[55] Vergil, pp. 140-143.

basically medieval. It is during the revolutionary events of the 1530's that the balance begins perceptibly to shift from the old to the new order.[56] Now there is much to be said for this point of view—so much in fact that I have no desire to adopt another. But it is still very possible by accepting it uncritically to miss some of the real meaning of the period before 1520. For our purposes in this study it is worth pausing to notice that, despite the chivalric forms still characteristic of the court of Henry VII, there are unmistakable signs of a new and non-chivalric spirit in its intellectual life.

In the last chapter we saw how one of Henry's laureates, Bernard André, could evaluate his foreign policy in terms of a political realism quite outside the comprehension of the truly chivalric mentality. A similar freshness of mind may be detected in André's references to the education of young Prince Arthur. At the age of sixteen, the lad was plunged into a thoroughly classical curriculum in which the studies dear to the heart of the humanists hold a prominent place. After a list of authorities in grammar in which the names of Guarino and Valla appear among the more traditional classical ones, come the "poets"—Homer, Virgil, Lucan, Ovid, Plautus, and Terence. In *"oratoria"* we find the twin supports of humanistic study, Cicero and Quintilian. History rounds off the list with such names as Thucydides, Livy, Caesar, Suetonius, and Tacitus.[57] All in all it is an impressive list. If the boy really went through it with the precocious intellect André ascribes to him, it must have given him a frame of reference in which chivalric ideas and attitudes could have had little but the most artificially contrived position.

Of even greater importance is the fact that in the writings of these men drawn for their learning and literary ability to Henry's court there is more than a hint of the utilitarian atti-

[56] An excellent statement of this general position is made by A. R. Myers in *England in the Later Middle Ages* (Penguin Books, 1952), pp. 181 ff.
[57] *Vita Henrici* VII, p. 43.

tude toward education which became a prime characteristic of English humanism and which led most sharply away from traditional notions of how the young gentleman should be trained. Like the medieval moralists, the humanists insisted that a healthy society and good government in particular depended on the virtue of those in charge of it. Unlike them, however, the humanists looked for virtue not solely in Christian precept and the moral life, but in learning, including the quite secular learning involved in the study of ancient Rome. Like the chivalric apologists of the fifteenth century, the humanists looked to history for the "example" so necessary as a guide to the governing class in its secular activity. Unlike them, however, they turned not to the examples of chivalric deeds but to that of ancient history, now to an increasing extent interpreted in nonchivalric terms, in terms, that is, which the humanist in his simplicity believed to be those peculiar to antiquity itself. In ancient history they found, above all, the example of a statecraft which they believed depended on the persuasive power of eloquence, which in turn was the end product, for all practical, worldly purposes, of learning. By means of learning, speaking with the tongue of eloquence, peace and a virtuous life might the sooner be achieved in the society of men. History and rhetoric became therefore essential to the education of anyone who would aspire to a place of responsibility in the commonwealth—which, to an increasing extent, meant the aristocracy and gentry acting as members of the secular community.

This attitude is apparent, though by no means dominant, in the work of Skelton. Though too original—or too cross-grained—to fit neatly into the humanistic pattern, he owed his own position at court to his learning, and he understood the practical value of learning, virtuously acquired.[58] In a Latin piece, rare for this stubborn adherent to the English tongue,

---

[58] In this discussion of Skelton I am indebted especially to Nelson's treatment. See especially chaps. ii and iii.

entitled *Speculum principis* (1501),[59] he pays special tribute to learning as an essential part of the training of the young prince. Breaking away to some extent from the form crystallized in medieval tradition by the *Secreta Secretorum,* he fulfils his obligation as tutor to Prince Henry by concentrating on the example of classical antiquity and by indicating that, in one who would rule, virtue is more to be prized than ancestry and that it may be had through study of the ancient authorities. It is the same faith in classical learning as a preparation for public responsibility which we have seen reflected in André's account of Prince Arthur's studies.

.   .   .

The best evidence comes, curiously enough, from Stephen Hawes. Not apparently so formally engaged in the business of education as either André or Skelton, retained at court for his value as an entertainer more than for any other reason that may be seen at this distance, Hawes nevertheless made the problem of education a main theme of his allegory, *The Pastime of Pleasure.* Although written ostensibly as light reading for a gentle public, it was in the best tradition of medieval didactic literature. Hawes despised "ballads" and "trifles without fruitfulness."[60] But he wore his didacticism with a difference. It is necessary to remember[61] that his unusual combination of love allegory and chivalric romance was set within the larger pattern of the "pilgrimage of the life of man," and that his representative man is a member of the knightly class. So it is really an allegory of chivalric life. Considered in this context Hawes's opinions on education become very valuable to anyone seeking among the sparse and equivocal documents of the period a clue to the chivalric mind in transition.

I should like to emphasize the medievalism of this context.

[59] Ed. F. M. Salter, *Speculum,* IX (1934), 25-37.
[60] *Pastime,* lines 1390-1393.
[61] See above, chap. iv.

Not only did Hawes draw the principal ingredients of his poem—the allegory of love, the chivalric romance, and the pilgrimage theme—from the most familiar of literary traditions, the education he prescribes for the man aspiring to the status of knighthood is essentially scholastic. It is the well-worn formula of *trivium* and *quadrivium*.[62] Moreover, the final end of the seven sciences is to lead the soul to heaven.[63] Before he is finished, Hawes has rung in the seven deadly sins,[64] an echo of the Dance of Death,[65] and the admonitory commonplace that earthly fame is soon dissipated in the spiritual vastness of eternity.[66] His single-minded admiration for "his master," John Lydgate, "flower of eloquence," "the chief original of my learning,"[67] may or may not indicate an equally strong link with the culture of medieval England, depending on how one interprets the mind of that tedious, but erudite, genius. It is, I think, fair enough to say that, but for a more comprehensive familiarity with classical authors and themes than was common among fifteenth-century English poets, and a sensible, though not at all necessarily humanistic, regard for the English language, Lydgate was likely to have bequeathed to his younger admirer little that would help him cross the threshold of Renaissance culture.[68]

Even that legacy of familiarity with classical authors is, however, important. If it failed to make a humanist of Hawes in the way that More, for example, was a humanist, it gave him the raw materials of humanism to work with, and may well have accounted for his undeniably fresh handling of old themes. It also made it possible for him to enter the circle of classicists employed at court. It was from that group, more probably than from his legacy of medieval classicism, that he

---

[62] For an analysis of his treatment of both in relation to his medieval sources, see Mead, *Pastime*, pp. xlvii-lxiv.

[63] *Ibid.*, lines 1574-1575.   [64] *Ibid.*, lines 5411-5494.

[65] *Ibid.*, pp. 205-206.   [66] *Ibid.*, lines 5607-5795.

[67] *Ibid.*, lines 27 and 1373-1375.

[68] See *ibid.*, pp. 55-57, for a detailed survey by Hawes of Lydgate's work. Cf. Murison, p. 231.

derived the high regard for rhetoric as a practical instrument for life in the world of affairs that constitutes the most extensive as well as the least medieval part of an otherwise quite traditional treatment of education.[69]

"Cunning" is for Hawes a thing not only pleasant but fruitful; and rhetoric is the discipline through which it achieves its fruitfulness. It is the instrument through which "poets," who are the custodians of practical wisdom as well as artists in words, must make their contribution to society. It is through them and their study of the "fatal problems of old antiquity" that justice was established. To use a term not yet current, it was they who led mankind from the state of nature into civil society and the rule of law.

> Before the law, in a tumbling barge
> The people sailed, without perfection,
> Through the world all about at large.
> They had no order nor no steadfastness
> Till rhetoricians found justice doubtless
> Ordaining kings of right high dignity,
> Of all commons to have the sovereignty.
>
> The barge to steer with law and justice
> Over the waves of this life transitory,
> To direct [correct] wrongs and also prejudice;
> And those that will resist a contrary [wrongfully]
> Against their king, by justice openly
> For their rebellion and evil treason
> Shall suffer death by right and reason.
>
> O what laud, glory and great honor
> Unto these poets shall be notified.
> The which distilled, aromatic liqueur
> Cleansing our sight with order purified,
> Whose famous draughts, so exemplified,
> Set us in order, grace and governance
> To live directly [in orderly manner],
>   without encumbrance.
>
> But many one, the which is rude and dull,
> Will despise their work for lack of cunning.

[69] *The Education of a Christian Prince*, trans. and ed. L. K. Born (New York, 1936), p. 200.

> All in vain they do so hayle and pull [harass and criticize]
> When they thereof lack understanding.
> They grope over where is no feeling;
> So dull they are that they cannot find
> This royal art for to perceive in mind.[70]

In short, poets, by the discipline of rhetoric, are able to point their fellows "the ways of virtue, wealth and stableness."[71] And the matter they interpret for the rest of their society is the history and literature of ancient Rome, where the "noble paynims" labored disinterestedly for the profit of "the comyn welthe."[72]

Thus spoke Stephen Hawes. And if the words have a medieval ring, the spirit is that of Tudor humanism, pure and simple. It falls far short of the realistic discussion of public issues that marks so much of the work of the humanists in the third and fourth decades of the century. *The Pastime of Pleasure* had, indeed, scarcely received its first printing before Thomas More had followed the New Learning far beyond the naïve faith of Hawes in the "fruitfulness" of rhetoric to a newly realistic appraisal of contemporary England. But it represents nonetheless a development in the history of chivalric thought of considerably greater import than its contribution to the history of *belles lettres*. For it must always be borne in mind that Hawes addressed the English aristocracy and gentry ("O ye estates surmounting in nobleness"),[73] that the education he described in such detail was clearly and specifically a prelude to knighthood,[74] and, as for the successful suitor in Tiptoft's dialogue, the way to advancement.

Hawes's treatment of book learning indeed quite overshadows his description of the hero's training in the military skills and the chivalric principles that were the very essence of the traditional manuals of knighthood.[75] Unless we read into the word "rebels" a hint of the seditious risings that so fre-

---

[70] *Pastime*, lines 876-896.   [71] *Ibid.*, line 1119.
[72] *Ibid.*, lines 246-252.   [73] *Ibid.*, line 245.
[74] *Ibid.*, lines 428-431. See also pp. 126-127.
[75] *Ibid.*, pp. 128-130.

quently had challenged Henry VII's title to the crown, and therefore find Hawes enlarging the protective function of knighthood to include support of the "new monarchy,"[76] there is nothing new in it at all. The novelty arises rather from the interlocking assumptions underlying the whole allegory, namely, that the knight is a soldier in only one aspect of his activity, that he is a person who owes a primary duty to the whole commonwealth simply as a member of the governing class, and that learning, even of the most traditional kind, is essential to the proper fulfilment of that duty. He even recognizes as a fact—not a very praiseworthy one, but a fact nonetheless—that the knight is also a person with economic interests.[77] It was a fact few apologists for the chivalric ideal cared to contemplate and some, the authors of *The Boke of Noblesse* for example, heartily deplored. The hero's anticlimactic decision in his less passionate years to devote himself to making money is as accurate sociologically as it was contrary to all the prejudices of medieval knighthood.[78]

. . .

Although not one of the scholar-poets who gave something more than a veneer of humanism to the still largely chivalric court of Henry VII, Edmund Dudley was if anything in a better position to estimate the value of education in the life of the knightly class. The reader will recall that, at the beginning of the succeeding reign, Dudley drew upon his experience in the counsels of Henry VII to offer some realistic advice to the English aristocracy. In his *Tree of Commonwealth,* otherwise a thoroughly traditional survey of the estates, he admonished the governing class of England to look to the education of its sons so that they might be able, like good "christian knights," to serve not only the church but the prince

[76] *Ibid.,* lines 3361-3388.
[77] *Ibid.,* lines 3364-3367. Cf. lines 886-889, 2299.
[78] *Ibid.,* lines 5370-5382.

and to labor for the "wealth of our commons and the prosperity of our selves."[79]   For this already enlarged sphere of knightly activity the English gentry were, he maintained, very ill equipped. "For verily I fear me, the noblemen and gentlemen of England be the worst brought up for the most part of any realm of Christendom." For that reason, he adds, the children of mean folk are promoted to places of authority.[80] He is a bit vague as to the kind of education that would be suitable. He stresses "cunning" in addition to virtue as its general aim. But he fails to show how learning may be brought to fruition in virtue. He contented himself with referring the propagation of "cunning" to the clergy in the universities.

Those institutions, still strongholds of traditionalism in Dudley's generation, and still meant primarily for men entering the church, seem an unlikely place for the layman to go for the kind of education he sought. But they were the only source of higher learning available, with the partial exception of the Inns of Court; and, if gentlemen sent their sons more frequently to the latter, there is some reason to believe that a few young gentlemen went to the universities for a general education during the middle and latter years of the fifteenth century.[81]   Dudley himself attended Oxford, probably for a brief training in the arts before going on to the Inns of Court.[82]   It was not until well on in the reign of Henry VIII that the English gentry began that systematic infiltration into Oxford and Cambridge which by the end of the century amounted to a conquest. By then the principle had become generally accepted that the broadest bookish education possible was not too broad for the men who would assume a position of responsibility in secular society. University education might even con-

[79] *Tree*, p. 98.
[80] *Ibid.*, p. 45.
[81] Chambers, *More*, pp. 66-67; Hexter, "The Education of the Aristocracy in the Renaissance," deals briefly with this early problem in the course of an excellent general discussion.
[82] Brodie, ed., *Tree*, introd.

stitute in itself a claim to gentility in the shifting social order of Elizabethan England.[83]

. . .

Meanwhile criticism of the English aristocracy for adherence to an obsolete ideal of education continued to mount. Stephen Hawes repeatedly refers to the rude and unlettered who in their ignorance fail to appreciate the pearls of wisdom cast before them by the practitioners of the "royal art" of rhetoric; and, since his concern was first and always with the governing class, it is fair to assume that it was they on whom especially he vented his bitterness.[84] Before long it came to be a commonplace, almost a stereotype, for the enlightened writer to lay a rod to the back of the gentry who scorned the education of "clerks."

Though there no doubt remained many who were incapable of appreciating a humane education and who failed even to see in it a practical means of self-preservation in a society no longer dependent upon the protective function of the knight, such criticisms are, as Hexter has pointed out,[85] to an increasing extent belied by the facts. Anyone who writes about the reform of education is naturally prone to build up his product by exaggerating the need for it. But in the early years of the century it is more than likely that such criticisms were well enough founded. The frequency with which Hawes refers to the ignorance around him and the feeling with which he makes them suggest real provocation. There is also something very convincing in the circumstantial detail with which Richard Pace in 1517 told his now famous story about the gentleman who, during a discussion of a humanistic education, exploded with the vehemence of a true barbarian:

All learned men are beggars . . . even Erasmus, the most learned of them all . . . . I swear by God's body I'd rather that my son should

[83] Smith, *De Rep. Angl.* Book I, chap. xx.
[84] *Pastime*, lines 792-819; 897-903; 925-931.
[85] "Education of the Aristocracy in the Renaissance."

hang than study letters. For it becomes the sons of gentlemen to blow the horn nicely, to hunt skillfully, and elegantly carry and train a hawk. But the study of letters should be left to the sons of rustics.

Whereupon Pace answered that, should a foreign ambassador come to the king, the learned sons of rustics would be called upon to answer him, the gentleman's son being able only to blow his horn.[86]

. . .

The story of the new education has been well told. Only a few references need here be made to the greatest of those who refashioned the educational ideal of the English gentry. It is in the early work of Erasmus and More that the new educational ideal achieves a certain precocious maturity of expression. In his *Enchiridion Militis Christiani* (1501-1503) and in his otherwise far from noteworthy *Institutio Principis Christiani* (1516), Erasmus placed the stamp of his immense influence on the ideal of a humane education for the prince and the governing class, and education that had as its primary objective such knowledge as would make possible a life of virtue led in the service of the community.[87] It was an ideal possibly more optimistically nourished in those years when heaven still laughed and the earth still rejoiced at the prospect of the enlightened patronage of Henry VIII than it could after Europe had become involved in chronic warfare and the realism of Machiavelli seemed more likely to prevail than the *philosophia Christi*. Yet it was an ideal quite practical in its objectives and one which did in fact exert a marked influence on the education of the English gentlemen for the rest of the century.

In *Utopia* (which, incidentally, appeared in the same year as the *Institutio*) More likewise endorsed a humanistic educa-

[86] In Furnivall, ed., *Early Eng. Meals and Manners*, E.E.T.S., O.S., No. 32 (London, 1868), pp. xii-xiii. See also Skelton's "Colin Clout," in *The Poetical Works of John Skelton*, ed. A. Dyce (London, 1843), I, 334; Caspari, pp. 92-93; Paul N. Siegel, "English Humanism and the New Tudor Aristocracy," *J. H. I.*, XIII (October, 1952), 450-468.

[87] For a recent analysis of Erasmus' educational theory, see Caspari, chap. ii. See also L. K. Born, trans. and ed., *The Education of a Christian Prince* (New York, 1936).

tion. His discussion in Book I of the wise and learned man's obligation to place his wisdom and learning at the disposal of the commonwealth is especially significant, for it demonstrates how completely the medieval commonplace that good government requires good counsel had been placed in the fresh context of secular learning and Renaissance culture. More faced the issue squarely in the light of his own personal predicament as the man of affairs, trained in humane letters, the "philosopher" about to be drawn into the discriminating but thankless service of the new monarchy.[88]

It is a context in which the questions characteristic of the chivalric tradition are no longer relevant. More has, in fact, little to say about chivalry as such. That both he and Erasmus looked upon chivalric values with some degree of contempt seems incontestable. Erasmus is explicit in his scorn of this relic of the "barbarous" Middle Ages. He laments in the *Institutio* that "today we see many a [boy] taking delight in tales of Arthur and Lancelot."[89] And More has devised the educational theories of the Utopians to coincide with humanistic learning in perhaps deliberate contradistinction to chivalric training. But here, as in the matter of war and the military life, both men are remarkable for their ability to ignore chivalry rather than for their antagonism to it, however instinctive the latter might have been. Erasmus' objection to the Arthurian legends stems primarily from his feeling that, in addition to providing an example of government no more edifying in substance than that of the ancient tyrants, they are "very poorly done, stupid, and fit to be 'old wives' tales,' so that it would be more advisable to read the comedies or the legends of the [ancient] poets instead of nonsense of that sort." As for More, he forces us to find his anti-chivalric bias almost wholly between his lines.

It may be argued, and with some plausibility, that More

[88] See Hexter, *More's "Utopia": The Biography of an Idea* (Princeton, 1952), pp. 103 ff.

[89] Erasmus, *Education of a Christian Prince*, p. 200.

brought to his discussion of education for citizenship not only the values to be derived from the New Learning, but also an outlook typical of the middle-class Londoner who could scarcely be expected to think in terms of chivalry.[90]   But Caxton, the most devoted spokesman for the chivalric way of life in the generation only slightly older than More's own, came from the same burgher background and was, if anything, closer to the mercantile activities of the great city.   Few, it is true, of More's contemporaries could free themselves so completely from traditional habits of thought.   Yet the *Utopia* marks nonetheless the beginning of a new era, for it grew in an intellectual climate quite different from that of the deceptively chivalric fifteenth century.

Sir Thomas Elyot is perhaps an even better example than More.[91]   He shared More's strongly humanistic bias and his concern for the commonweal and his belief in the possibility of achieving an intellectual aristocracy.   He was probably influenced personally by More and by Erasmus indirectly.   He inherited as it were the mantle of Erasmian humanism.   But he belonged to a slightly younger generation of English humanists.   He is closer than More to the "commonwealth men" who, by turning their Platonically conditioned minds to the investigation of specific English problems, made the common characteristic of a large group of commentators what had in More been exceptional and confined largely to his early *Utopia* period.   It is in his application of humanistic principles to actual conditions that he, like Starkey, Morison, and Hales, made his greatest contribution.   And he was probably in a better position than More to appreciate the particular conditions that affected the sons of the country gentry.   He was born into the landed class, the lesser aristocracy, and knew at first hand the duties and headaches likely to fall to the lot of the

[90] More's class background has been stressed by Russell Ames, *Citizen Thomas More and his Utopia* (Princeton, 1948).

[91] The most recent and most thorough treatment of Elyot and Elyot scholarship is in Caspari, chap. iv.

young gentleman in local government. He had himself been Justice of the Peace and sheriff, as well as active in the king's central administration. He knew what it was for a knight to be called upon to serve as "governor." He therefore faced perhaps in a more practical way than did More the problem of the education best suited to the sons of the English country families. Both men had received the order of knighthood, and both, such was now more than ever the nonmilitary, nonfeudal, in the stricter sense nonchivalric meaning of the honor, earned it in the civil service of the national state. But Elyot was born to a class for whom the memory of the chivalric past was still green and the chivalric discipline and the chivalric amenities still retained a certain value. He strove accordingly in his *Boke named the Gouernour* (1531) to outline for the sons of the gentry an educational ideal that would combine whatever of value there remained in the chivalric tradition with the values of humanism.

Elyot will accordingly serve very well as valedictorian for this chapter—indeed for this entire study. He reflected with peculiar clarity the influences that were in the process of shaping a new social ideal. He was himself an excellent specimen of the new knight whose strength lay in his mind rather than in his arms, whose pen was at least as mighty as his sword and of considerably more service to the community, and who owed his knightly dignity to public service performed in a civil capacity rather than as a soldier or captain. In one of his lesser pamphlets, in the course of an argument against some who still felt that a concern for things spiritual "doth not pertain to a knight, much less to a sheriff," he stated the new concept of knighthood with admirable specificity:

A knight hath received that honor not only to defend with the sword Christ's faith and his proper country, against them which impugneth the one or invadeth the other: but also, and that most chiefly, by the mean of his dignity (if that be employed where it should be and esteemed as it ought to be) he should more effectually with his learning and wit assail vice and error, most pernicious enemies to Christian men, having thereunto for his sword and spear his tongue and his pen.[92]

He is cousin-german to the Knight in Hales's *Discourse of the Commonweal.* He is a convinced believer in the aristocratic principle. Yet he has a touchingly profound faith in the virtues of humanistic learning as the "knowledge which maketh a wise man" and in the wise man himself as the true counsellor of princes and executor of civil authority. He preached, and in himself effected, that union of the *vita activa* and the *vita contemplativa* which was the ideal of the platonically inspired humanists of England. Above all he was a servant of his "proper country." The new learning and the new wisdom he hoped it would make possible are such as to make of England "a public weal equivalent to the Greeks or Romans."[93] The education he prescribes for young gentlemen is such as to insure that "throughout all the world should be found in no common weal more noble counselors."[94]

It is this more than anything else, that separates the new social ideal from the old. Elyot would have his young gentleman trained in the practice of arms and in the courtly graces—though he preferred the humanistically conditioned courtliness already made popular on the Continent by Castiglione, to the more jejune accomplishments of the medieval knight. But it is as a trained mind, capable of placing its wisdom at the disposal of the national state and desirous of so doing, that he must excel. Elyot thus combined all that was worth saving of the chivalric training with that of the Italian "courtier" and subordinated both to an ideal of education in which virtue and wisdom could be derived from a study of the ancient writers and turned toward the service of the national community as their principal objective. After his generation it was impossible to revive the medieval knight—the man-at-

---

[92] *A Preservative agaynste Deth* (1545), S.T.C. 7674., sigs. Aii-Aiii.
[93] *Governor,* I, 162.
[94] *Ibid.,* I, 143-144.

arms whose primary duty was the simple protection of society, the *preux chevalier* in the service of holy church, of his lord, and of his lady, the debonair adulterer, the "errant" in search of adventure and renown, the landowner who left all but the lighter forms of learning to clerks—without the exercise of a conscious and historically deceptive archaism.   In Elyot's "governor" social theory is once more brought into a workable relationship with social reality.   In him medieval chivalry disappeared as such, its still active trace elements absorbed in a new and much more powerful compound.

VII

CONCLUSION

IT IS HARD TO ESCAPE THE CONCLUSION THAT, with all its apparent completeness, its apparent vitality, there was something exotic and decadent about the chivalric thought of the late fifteenth century. Like all Indian Summers it was an illusion, bearing little relationship to the actual procession of the seasons. An illusion is, to be sure, an historical reality; and an illusion at all widely nourished can become an historical force of more than incidental importance. There is no gainsaying the sincerity with which many people in that day looked to a reaffirmed chivalry for a badly needed guide to personal conduct and an inspiration in public life. Yet to an increasing degree these men were seeking reassurance in a stereotype. Until classical learning had been reinterpreted under conditions different from those of feudal society and to a large extent free from the assumptions common to medieval thought, until the example of classical antiquity had been studied in an historical perspective more accurate than the medieval mind was usually capable of, there existed no other scheme of values, no other source of inspiration, no other "example" than that of chivalry. Even the changing facts of society itself, although they contributed in the long run to the decline and transformation of chivalric idealism, were for the purpose of thought placed within an intellectual pattern they no longer fitted.

Few, it is true, seem to have appreciated how inadequate the traditional values had become. Few at any rate attacked the system directly. Preachers had for generations castigated the failure of the knight to live up to the ideals of his order;

but they seldom criticized the ideals themselves provided the worldly element in those ideals, the search for personal renown, for example, did not degenerate into sin. Like Chaucer, who in Sir Thopas satirized a decadent chivalry, yet in his Knight portrayed the very model of chivalric virtue, the late medieval Englishman was quick to attack the perverted form but content to retain the ideal itself.

The most effective intellectual force operating against the chivalric ideal in the latter fifteenth century was the spirit of undoctrinaire realism, of practicality and good sense, that becomes increasingly apparent in the political literature of that era—including, paradoxically enough, the work of such apologists for the chivalric way of life as Caxton. It is the spirit of *The Libelle of Englyshe Polycye* with its shrewd analysis of England's potential greatness in terms, not of a chivalric chauvinism, but of economic policy. It is the spirit of Fortescue, and to some extent of George Ashby, both of whom undertook in the wake of the civil wars to analyze England's plight in terms, not of knightly values, but of reformed administrative machinery. These men ignored the chivalric system, and gave only tacit evidence of its failure to satisfy their minds. Their French contemporary, Commines, on the other hand, a man even more penetrating in his capacity for realistic analysis, found it necessary at times to recognize the existence of the chivalric mentality and to make an oblique attack upon it. His antichivalric *obiter dictum*, "qui a le prouffict de la guerre, il en a l'honneur," would have been just as applicable to the policy urged in *The Boke of Noblesse* as to the vagaries of Franco-Burgundian politics to which it was in fact applied; yet no Englishman in the late fifteenth century felt called upon to pass so Machiavellian a judgment.

We must always remember, in evaluating these later expressions of English chivalric thought, that chivalric idealism remained respectable in England longer than it did in France even though the chivalric forms lasted longer in France than

in England. It had, in England, become identified with a
crude, semifeudal patriotism. It was allowed to feed on the
memory of Edward III's successful campaigns and, especially,
on the brilliant conquests of Henry V. It did not suffer, as in
France, from too close a connection with an era of national
humiliation or with the reckless actions of an undisciplined
and factious nobility. The defeat of English arms in the latter
stages of the Hundred Years' War and the specter of domestic
anarchy that presented itself during the Wars of the Roses both
came at a time when chivalric idealism had in England become
sufficiently isolated from practical affairs to enable it to maintain an air of respectability no matter what its supposed dev-
otees could do to discredit it. Knighthood had in England
ceased at a comparatively early date to be a prerequisite to
public service, whether military or civil, and the chivalric
values in which it found ideal expression had by the mid-
fifteenth century receded with it to a respectable distance from
the rough-and-tumble world.

Here is another paradox, and not the least of those that dog
the would-be interpreter of this transitional era. Chivalry could
be taken seriously as a system of abstract ideals long after the
facts of English life would to modern eyes have rendered them
obsolete because it had at so early a period ceased to be intimately related to those facts. Perhaps Englishmen have always
been able to maintain the characteristic continuity of their
traditions by just such an unconscious separation of the ideal
and the actual. At any rate, the chivalric apologists of the
fifteenth century were able to approach their subject in a spirit
of practical citizenship, quite free from the cynicism and conscious realism of their French neighbors. And those, like
Fortescue, who shared to some extent that realism, if not the
cynicism that went with it, seem to have felt no need to recognize the existence of chivalry at all.

By the early years of Henry VIII's reign it is clear that the
climate of English opinion has undergone a seasonal change.

Despite occasional gusts blowing in from the preceding era, the Indian Summer of English chivalry is over. Its passing was marked by no storms. Except in the matter of education, where no doubt a few reactionaries like Richard Pace's old barbarian appear to have resisted an intellectuality they could neither understand nor respect, the English governing class seems to have relinquished without struggle and with few regrets the attempt to preserve the ideals of late medieval chivalry as an organic scheme of values. With a practical adaptability that characterizes much of what happened in these early phases of the English Renaissance, the English gentleman retained those elements of chivalric idealism that served to lend dignity and meaning to his life and to command his emotional response—those aspects, in other words, that have since the Middle Ages enjoyed universal respect among Western peoples: the ideal of honor, for example, the desire for glory, whether personal or national, the idealization of women, the romantic addiction to legends of the "age of chivalry." With equal adaptability he accepted the fact that chivalry no longer sufficed as a scale of values for the governing class. He accepted as his duty a career in the civil affairs of the state, not merely in its armed service; and he accepted book learning as a prerequisite. He also (by no means a negligible feat) managed for the most part to overcome the habit of interposing between his eye and the society in which he labored the distorting screen of chivalric language.

Much of the credit for this subtle but significant change of attitude must go to the humanists who provided an intellectual context more suited to the needs of a new society and at the same time one in which the chivalric ideal had little practical meaning. The humanism of Henry VIII's reign and that of his son represented an especially sharp break with the chivalric tradition; or, more accurately, these fundamentally Erasmian humanists attempted a radical restatement of the Christian tradition in the light of a pre-feudal, classical, largely Platonic culture to which the values of chivalry were utterly irrelevant. English society and thought stood for a brief while starkly revealed in this new light, and it was never again possible for the cultivated Englishman to forget what he saw. Events, however, also contributed. For half a century Englishmen were preoccupied with rebellions and depressions at home and distracted by wars, heresies, and wonders abroad. Their world was, in fact, a new world, in which the medieval knight was himself quite out of place. Events, too, accentuated the tendency already marked in the preceding era to apply to English affairs an analysis based on experience and common sense and on a respect for the complexities of civil government. And so the comment even of the Tudor "martialist" is placed squarely in a national context, all but free from the chivalric assumption that the aristocracy constituted an exclusively military class.

When, with the restoration under Elizabeth of national pride and public order, men of letters again sought inspiration (and a touch of political propaganda) in the legends of Arthur's court, and when the Elizabethan aristocracy sought in the chivalric code an ethical form for life in a new and swashbuckling society, theirs was a really nostalgic, truly romantic, at times even a frivolous attempt to re-create the spirit of an irretrievable past.

Works Cited

Adams, R. P. "Designs by More and Erasmus for a New Social Order," *Studies in Philology*, XLII (April, 1945), 131-145.

——. "Erasmus' Ideas of his Rôle as a Social Critic ca. 1480-1500," *Renaissance News*, XI (Spring, 1958), 11-16.

——. "Literary Thought on War and Peace in English Literature of the Renaissance," *Year Book of the American Philosophical Society, 1955* (Philadelphia, 1956), pp. 272-277.

——. "Pre-Renaissance Courtly Peace Propaganda," *Papers of the Michigan Academy of Science, Arts and Letters*, XXXII (1946), 432-446.

Adamson, J. W. "The Extent of Literacy in the XV and XVI Centuries," *The Library*, X (1929/30), 162-193.

Allen, J. W. *A History of Political Thought in the Sixteenth Century.* London, 1928.

Ames, Russell. *Citizen Thomas More and his Utopia.* Princeton, 1948.

Arrowood, C. F. "Sir John Fortescue on the Education of Rulers," *Speculum*, X (October, 1935), 404-410.

Ascham, Roger. *English Works,* ed. W. A. Wright. Cambridge, 1904.

Ashby, George. *The Poems of George Ashby,* ed. Mary Bateson. (E.E.T.S., E.S., No. 76.) 1899.

Aurner, Nellie S. "Sir Thomas Malory—Historian?," *PMLA*, XLVIII (March, 1933), 362-391.

Barnard, F. P. "Heraldry," in *Medieval England,* ed. H. W. C. Davis. Oxford, 1928. Pp. 195-244.

Baugh, A. C. "Documenting Sir Thomas Malory," *Speculum*, VII (January, 1933), 3-29.

Becon, Thomas. *The Policy of War,* in *The Early Writings of Thomas Becon,* ed. J. Ayre. (Parker Society.) 1843. Pp. 230-261.

Bennett, H. S. *Chaucer and the Fifteenth Century.* Oxford, 1947.

——. *English Books and Their Readers, 1475-1557.* Cambridge, 1952.

——. *The Pastons and Their England.* Cambridge, 1932.

——. "Science and Information in English Writings of the Fifteenth Century," *Modern Language Review*, XXXIX (January, 1944), 1-8.

Bennett, Josephine W. *The Evolution of "The Faerie Queene."* Chicago, 1942.

Bentley, S. *Excerpta Historica.* London, 1831.

Berdan, J. M. *Early Tudor Poetry, 1485-1547.* New York, 1920.

Berners, John Bourchier, Lord (trans.). *The Chronicle of Froissart,* ed. W. P. Ker. London, 1901-03.

Blair, Claude. *European Amour 1066 to 1700.* London, 1959.

The Boke of Duke Huon of Burdeux, ed. S. L. Lee. (E.E.T.S., E.S., No. 40.) 1882.

Buke of gude consale to the king. Edinburgh, 1508?

The Boke of the Ordre of Chyualry, ed. A. T. P. Byles. (E.E.T.S., O.S., No. 168.) 1926.

The Boke of Noblesse, ed. J. G. Nichols. London, 1860.

The Boke of St. Albans, ed. W. Blades. London, 1881.

Bonet, Honoré. *L'Arbre des Batailles,* trans. and ed. G. W. Coopland as *The Tree of Battles.* Cambridge, Mass., 1949.

Bouwsma, W. J. "The Politics of Commynes," *Journal of Modern History,* XXIII (December, 1951), 315-328.

Bradner, L. *Edmund Spenser and "The Faerie Queene,"* Chicago, 1948.

Brende, John (trans.). Quintus Curtius, *Historie of . . . the actes of the greate Alexander.* London, 1553.

Brewer, D. S. "Form in the *Morte Darthur," Medium Aevum,* XXI (1952), 14-24.

Brewer, J. S. *The Reign of Henry VIII.* London, 1884.

Brinkelow, Henry. *The Complaynt of Roderyck Mors,* ed. J. M. Cowper. (E.E.T.S., E.S., No. 22.) 1874.

The Brut, ed. F. W. D. Brie. (E.E.T.S., O.S., No. 136, Part II.) 1908.

Burkart, E. A. *Stephen Hawes's "The Pastime of Pleasure."* London, 1899.

Bush, D. *The Renaissance and English Humanism.* Toronto, 1939.

Byles, A. T. P. "Medieval Courtesy Books and the Prose Romances of Chivalry," in *Chivalry,* ed. E. Prestage. New York, 1928, pp. 183-205.

Cartellieri, O. *The Court of Burgandy.* New York, 1929.

Cary, George. *The Medieval Alexander.* Cambridge, 1956.

Caspari, Fritz. *Humanism and the Social Order in Tudor England.* Chicago, 1954.

———. "Sir Thomas More and *Justum Bellum," Ethics,* LVI (1946), 303-308.

The Castell of Love. London, 1540.

The Castell of Plesure, ed. Roberta D. Cornelius. (E.E.T.S., O.S., No. 179.) 1930.

Caxton, William. *The Prologues and Epilogues of William Caxton,* ed. W J. B. Crotch. (E.E.T.S., O.S., No. 176.) 1928.

Chambers, E. K. *Arthur of Britain.* London, 1927.

————. *English Literature at the Close of the Middle Ages.* Oxford, 1947.

————. *Sir Thomas Malory.* (The English Association Pamphlet No. 51, January, 1922).

————. *Sir Thomas Wyatt and Some Collected Studies.* London, 1933.

Chambers, R. W. *Thomas More.* New York, 1935.

Chapiro, J. *Erasmus and our Struggle for Peace.* Boston, 1950.

Chartier, Alain. *Le Quadrilogue Invectif,* ed. R. Bouvier. Paris, 1944.

Chaucer, Geoffrey. *Works,* ed. W. W. Skeat. 6 vols. and suppl. Oxford, 1894-1900.

Cheke, Sir John. *The hurt of sedition.* London, 1549.

Chrimes, S. B. *English Constitutional Ideas in the Fifteenth Century.* Cambridge, 1936.

————. "'House of Lords' and 'House of Commons' in the Fifteenth Century," *English Historical Review,* XLIX (July, 1934), 494-497.

Clapham, R. C. *The Tournament, Its Periods and Phases.* London, 1919.

Cline, Ruth H. "The Influence of Romances on Tournaments of the Middle Ages," *Speculum,* XX (January, 1945), 204-211.

Cohen, Gustave. *Histoire de la Chevalerie en France au Moyen Age.* Paris, 1949.

A Collection of Ordinances and Regulations for the Government of the Royal Household. London, 1790.

Commynes, Phillipe de. *Memoires de Phillipe de Commynes,* ed. B. de Mandrot. 3 vols. Paris, 1901-03.

Cope, Sir Anthony. *Historie of . . . Anniball and Scipio.* London, 1544.

Cornish, F. Warre. *Chivalry.* London, 1901.

The Court of Love, in W. W. Skeat, ed., *Chaucerian and Other Pieces* (Suppl. to Skeat, ed., *Works of Geoffrey Chaucer*). Oxford, 1897. Pp. 409-447.

Courthope, W. J. *A History of English Poetry.* New York, 1920.

Cripps-Day, F. H. *The History of the Tournament in England and in France.* London, 1918.

Crowley, Robert. *The Way to Wealthe,* ed. J. M. Cowper. (E.E.T.S., E.S., No. 15.) 1872.

Cursor Mundi, Part I, ed. R. Morris. (E.E.T.S., O.S., No. 57.) 1874.

The Dance of Death, ed. Florence Warren. (E.E.T.S., O.S., No. 181.) 1931.

Davies, R. T. "Malory's Launcelot and the Noble Way of the World," *Review of English Studies,* N.S., VI (October, 1955), 356-364.

————. "Malory's 'Vertuouse Love,'" *Studies in Philology,* LIII (July, 1956), 459-469.

Davis, H. W. C. (ed.). *Medieval England.* Oxford, 1928.

Denholm-Young, N. "Feudal Society in the Thirteenth Century: The Knights," *History,* XXIX (September, 1944), 107-119.

Dickmann, Mary E. "Characterization in Malory's Tale of Arthur and Lucius," *PMLA*, XLV (September, 1950), 877-895.

The Dicts and Sayings of the Philosophers, ed. C. F. Bühler. (E.E.T.S., O.S., No. 211.) 1941.

A Discourse of the Common Weal of this Realm of England, ed. E. Lamond. Cambridge, 1929.

Donaldson, F. *Piers Plowman: The C-Text and Its Poet*. New Haven, 1949.

Douglas, Gavin. *The Palice of Honour*, in *Works*, ed. J. Small. Edinburgh, 1874.

Les Douze Triomphes de Henry VII. Memorials of King Henry the Seventh, ed. J. Gairdner. (Rolls Series.) 1858.

Dudley, Edmund. *The Tree of Commonwealth*, ed. D. M. Brodie. Cambridge, 1948.

Dunbar, William. *Poems*, ed. J. Small. Edinburgh, 1893.

Duncan, E. *The Story of Minstrelsy*. London, 1907.

Early English Meals and Manners, ed. F. J. Furnivall. (E.E.T.S., O.S., No. 32.) 1868.

Edwards, H. L. R. *Skelton, the Life and Times of an Early Tudor Poet*. London, 1949.

Ellis, H. (ed.) *Original Letters Illustrative of English History*, 2nd Series. London, 1827.

Elton, G. R. *The Tudor Revolution in Government*. New York, 1953.

Elyot, Sir Thomas. *The Boke named the Gouernour*, ed. H. H. S. Croft. London, 1880.

———. *The Image of Governance*. London, 1541.

———. *A Preservative agaynste Deth*. London, 1545.

An English Chronicle, ed. J. S. Davies. (Camden Society, 1st Series, LXIV.) 1856.

The Epistle of Othea to Hector (or *The Boke of Knyghthode*), ed. G. F. Warner, London, 1904. See also edition by J. D. Gordon, University of Pennsylvania Dissertation. Philadelphia, 1942.

Erasmus, Desiderius. *Dulce Bellum Inexpertis*, ed. and trans. into French, Yvonne Remy and R. Dumil-Marquebreucq. (Collection Hatomus, Vol. VIII.) Brussels, 1953.

———. *The Education of a Christian Prince*, ed. L. K. Born. New York, 1936.

———. *Querela Pacis*, trans. in J. Chapiro, *Erasmus and our Struggle for Peace*. Boston, 1950.

Fabyan, Robert. *The New Chronicles of England and France*, ed. H. Ellis. London, 1811.

Fayttes of Armes and of Chyualrye, ed. A. T. P. Byles. (E.E.T.S., O.S., No. 189.) 1932.

Ferguson, A. B. "The Problem of Counsel in *Mum and the Soth-segger*," *Studies in the Renaissance,* II (1955), 67-83.

———. "Renaissance Realism in the 'Commonwealth' Literature of Early Tudor England," *Journal of the History of Ideas*, XVI (June, 1955), 287-305.

Feylde, Thomas. *Conversation between a Lover and a Jay,* ed. T. F. Dibdin. London, 1818.

Flenley, R. (ed.). *Six Town Chronicles.* Oxford, 1911.

Fletcher, R. H. *The Arthurian Material in the Chronicles.* Boston, 1906.

Forest, William. *Pleasaunt Poesie of Princelie Practise,* printed in extract in S. J. Herrtage, *England in the Reign of Henry VIII.* (E.E.T.S., E.S., No. 32.) 1878.

Fortescue, Sir John. *Governance of England,* ed. C. Plummer. Oxford, 1885.

———. *De Laudibus Legum Angliae,* ed. and trans. S. B. Chrimes. Cambridge, 1942.

Froissart, John. *Oeuvres de Froissart,* ed. M. le baron Kervyn de Lettenhove. Brussels, 1867-77.

Fuller, Thomas. *The History of the Worthies of England,* ed. P. A. Nuttall. London, 1840.

Gairdner, J. (ed.) *Memorials of King Henry the Seventh.* (Rolls Series.) 1858.

Gates, Geoffry. *The defence of militarie. profession.* London, 1579.

Gautier, Leon. *Le Chevalerie.* Paris, 1890.

Of Gentylnes and Nobylyte, ed. K. W. Cameron, in *Authorship and Sources of "Gentleness and Nobility": A Study in Early Tudor Drama.* Raleigh, 1941.

The Geste of King Horn, in *Metrical Romances,* ed. J. Ritson. London, 1802.

A Gest of Robyn Hode, in *English and Scottish Popular Ballads,* ed. H. C. Sargent and G. L. Kittredge. Boston, 1898.

Gilbert, Alan H. *Machiavelli's Prince and its Fore-runners.* Durham, N. C., 1938.

———. "Notes on the Influence of the *Secretum Secretorum*," *Speculum,* III (January, 1928) 84-98.

Hay, Gilbert. *Gilbert of the Haye's Prose MS.,* ed. J. H. Stevenson. (Scottish Texts Society.) 2 vols. 1901-14.

Gilbert, Sir Humphrey. *Queene Elizabethes Achademy,* ed. F. J. Furnivall. (E.E.T.S., E.S., No. 8) 1869.

Gilmore, Myron P. "*Fides et Eruditio:* Erasmus and the Study of History," in *Teachers of History: Essays in honor of Lawrence Bradford Packard,* ed. H. S. Hughes. Ithaca, 1954. Pp. 9-27.

Gist, M. A. *Love and War in the Middle English Romances.* University of Pennsylvania Dissertation. Philadelphia, 1947.

The golden boke of Marcus Aurelius. London, 1535.

Gordon, I. A. *John Skelton Poet Laureate.* Melbourne, 1943.

Gower, John. *The Complete Works of John Gower,* ed. G. C. Macauley. 4 vols. Oxford, 1899-1902.

————. *Vox Clamantis,* trans. E. W. Stockton. Harvard dissertation, 1952.

Gray, H. L. "Incomes from Land in England in 1436," *English Historical Review,* XLIX (October, 1934), 607-639.

Greenlaw, E. *Studies in Spenser's Historical Allegory.* Baltimore, 1932.

Greenwood, Alice D. "English Prose in the Fifteenth Century: Caxton, Malory, Berners," in *Cambridge History of English Literature.* Cambridge, 1930. II, 332-340.

Hall, Edward. *Hall's Chronicle.* London, 1809.

Hawes, Stephen. *A Joyfull Medytacyon to All Englande.* London, 1509.

————. *The Pastime of Pleasure,* ed. W. E. Mead. (E.E.T.S., O.S., No. 173.) 1928.

Hearnshaw, F. J. C. "Chivalry and its Place in History," in E. Prestage, ed., *Chivalry.* New York, 1928. Pp. 1-36.

Hexter, J. H. "The Education of the Aristocracy in the Renaissance," *Journal of Modern History,* XXII (March, 1950), 1-20.

————. *More's "Utopia": the Biography of an Idea.* Princeton, 1952.

Hicks, E. *Sir Thomas Malory, His Turbulent Career.* Cambridge, Mass., 1928.

The Historical Collections of a Citizen of London in the Fifteenth Century, ed. J. Gairdner. (Camden Society, N.S., XVII.) 1876.

Hoccleve, Thomas. *Hoccleve's Works,* ed. F. J. Furnivall. (E.E.T.S., E.S., No. 72.) 1897.

Hoffman, F. J. *Alain Chartier, His Work and Reputation.* New York, 1942.

Holinshed, Raphael. *Chronicles of England, Scotland, and Ireland.* London, 1808.

Housman, J. E. "Higden, Trevisa, Caxton, and the Beginnings of Arthurian Criticism," *Review of English Studies,* XXIII (July, 1947), 209-217.

Hughes, E. "The Authorship of the *Discourse of the Commonweal,*" *Bulletin of the John Ryland Library,* XXI (1937), 167-175.

Huizinga, J. *The Waning of the Middle Ages.* London, 1927.

The hystory of the most noble and valyant knyght Arthur of lytell brytayne. London, 1555.

Jones, Evan. *Medieval Heraldry.* London, 1945.

Jones, G. F. "The Tournaments of Tottenham and Laffenhausen," *PMLA,* LXVI (December, 1951), 1123-1140.

Jorgenson, P. A. "Alien Military Doctrine in Renaissance England," *Modern Language Quarterly,* XVII (March, 1956), 43-49.

———. *Shakespeare's Military World.* Berkeley and Los Angles, 1956.

Jusserand, J. J. *Les sports et jeux d'exercice dans l'ancienne France.* Paris, 1901.

Keeney, B. C. "Military Service and the Development of Nationalism in England, 1272-1327," *Speculum,* XXII (October, 1947), 534-549.

Kelso, Ruth. *The Doctrine of the English Gentleman in the Sixteenth Century.* Urbana, 1929.

Kendall, P. M. *Richard III.* New York, 1955.

———. *Warwick the Kingmaker.* New York, 1957.

Kilgour, R. L. *The Decline of Chivalry as Shown in the French Literature of the Late Middle Ages.* Cambridge, Mass., 1937.

Kingsford, C. L. *English Historical Literature in the 15th Century.* Oxford, 1913.

——— (ed.). *The First English Life of Henry the Fifth.* Oxford, 1911.

Kleineke, W. *Englische Fürstenspiegel vom Policraticus Johanns von Salisbury bis zum Basilikon Doron König Jakobs I.* Halle, 1937.

Knyghthode and Bataile, ed. R. Dyboski and Z. M. Arend. (E.E.T.S., O.S., No. 201.) 1936.

Koebner, R. " 'The imperial crown of this realm': Henry VIII, Constantine the Great, and Polydore Vergil," *Bulletin of the Institute of Historical Research,* XXVI (May, 1953), 29-52.

Lees-Milne, J. *Tudor Renaissance.* London, 1951.

Lewis, C. S. *The Allegory of Love.* Oxford, 1936.

———. *English Literature in the Sixteenth Century.* Oxford, 1954.

Lewis, N. B. "The Organization of Indentured Retinues in Fourteenth-Century England," *Transactions of Royal Historical Society,* 4th Series, XXVII (1945), 29-39.

The Libelle of Englyshe Polycye, ed. G. Warner. Oxford, 1926.

Lippman, Kurt. "Das ritterliche Persönlichkeitsideal in der englischen Literatur des 13. und 14. Jahrhunderts." University of Leipzig dissertation, 1933.

Le Livre du Chevalier de la Tour-Landry, ed. M. Anatole de Montaiglon. Paris, 1854.

Loomis, R. S. "Edward I, Arthurian Enthusiast," *Speculum,* XXVIII (January, 1953), 114-127.

———. "Chivalry and Dramatic Imitations of Arthurian Romance," in *Medieval Studies in Memory of A. K. Porter.* Cambridge, Mass., 1939. I, 79-97.

London, H. S. "Some Medieval Treatises on English Heraldry," *Antiquaries Journal,* XXXIII (July-October, 1953), pp. 169-183.

Lumiansky, R. M. "The Question of Unity in Malory's *Morte Darthur*," *Tulane Studies in English*, V (1955), 29-39.

Lydgate, John. *Fall of Princes*, ed. H. Bergen. (E.E.T.S., E.S., No. 121-124.) 4 vols. 1924-27.

——. *Lydgate's Troy Book*, ed. H. Bergen. (E.E.T.S., E.S., No. 97.) 1906.

——. *The Minor Poems of John Lydgate*, ed. H. N. MacCracken. Part II, *Secular Poems*. (E.E.T.S., O.S., No. 192.) 1934.

Malory, Sir Thomas. *The Works of Sir Thomas Malory*, ed. Eugene Vinaver. Oxford, 1947.

Mann, J. G. "Instances of Antiquarian Feeling in Medieval and Renaissance Art," *Archeological Journal*, LXXXIX (1932), 254-274.

Markman, M. "The Meaning of Sir Gawain and the Green Knight," *PMLA*, LXXII (September, 1957), 574-586.

Mason, J. E. *Gentlefolk in the Making*. Philadelphia, 1935.

Mathew, G. "Ideals of Knighthood in Late Fourteenth-Century England," in *Studies in Medieval History presented to Frederick Maurice Powicke*, ed. R. W. Hunt *et al.* Oxford, 1948. Pp. 354-362.

Mattingly, G. *Renaissance Diplomacy*. London, 1955.

McCully, Bruce. "Chivalry and Romance in Fourteenth Century England." Harvard dissertation, 1910.

McFarlane, K. B. "Bastard Feudalism," *Bulletin of the Institute of Historical Research*, XX (May and November, 1945), 161-180.

——. "William Worcester: a Preliminary Survey," in *Studies Presented to Sir Hilary Jenkinson*, ed. J. C. Davies. London, 1957. Pp. 196-221.

Millican, C. B. *Spenser and the Table Round*. Cambridge, Mass., 1932.

Mitchell, R. J. *John Tiptoft*. London, 1938.

Mohl, Ruth. *The Three Estates in Medieval and Renaissance Literature*. New York, 1933.

Monstrelet. *Chroniques d'Enguerrand de Monstrelet*, ed. J. A. Buchon. Paris, 1826.

Moorman, C. "Malory's Treatment of the Sangreall," *PMLA*, LXXI (June, 1956), 496-509.

More, Sir Thomas. *Utopia*, ed. H. Osborne. London, n. d.

——. *The History of Richard III* in *The English Works of Sir Thomas More*, ed. E. W. Campbell. London, 1931.

Morison, Sir Richard. *An Exhortation to Styrre all Englysshemen to the Defence of theyr Countrye*. London, 1539.

——. Translation of Frontinus' *The Strategemes, sleyghtes and Policies of Warre*. London, 1539.

Mum and the Sothsegger, ed. M. Day and Robert Steele. (E.E.T.S., O.S., No. 199.) 1939.

Murison, William. "Stephen Hawes," in *Cambridge History of English Literature*. Cambridge, 1930. II, 223-238.

Myers, A. R. *England in the Later Middle Ages*. Harmondsworth, 1952.

Neilson, G. *Trial by Combat*. Boston, 1909.

Nelson, W. *John Skelton, Laureate*. New York, 1939.

Nicholls, F. M. "On Feudal and Obligatory Knighthood," *Archaeologia*, XXXIX (1862/63), 189-244.

Owst, G. W. *Literature and Pulpit in Medieval England*. Cambridge, 1923.

Pageant of the Birth Life and Death of Richard Beauchamp Earl of Warwick, ed. Viscount Dillon and W. H. St. John Hope. London, 1914.

Painter, S. *French Chivalry*. Baltimore, 1940.

Pauphilet, Albert. *Études sur la Queste del Saint Graal*. Paris, 1921.

Perroy, Edouard. *The Hundred Years' War*. New York, 1951.

Piers the Plowman, ed. W. W. Skeat. 2 vols. London, 1924.

Plommer, H. R. *William Caxton*. London, 1925.

Policies to reduce this Realme of Englande vnto a prosperous Wealthe and Estate, in *Tudor Economic Documents*, ed. R. H. Tawney and Eileen Power. London, 1924. III, 312-345.

Political Poems and Songs, ed. Thomas Wright. (Rolls Series.) 1861.

The porteous of noblenes. Edinburgh, 1508.

Postan, M. M. "Revisions in Economic History IX—The Fifteenth Century," *Economic History Review*, IX (May, 1939), 160-167.

———. "Some Social Consequences of the Hundred Years' War," *Economic History Review*, XII (1942), 1-12.

Powicke, M. R. "Distraint of Knighthood and Military Obligation under Henry III," *Speculum*, XXV (October, 1950), 457-470.

———. *Henry III and the Lord Edward*. Oxford, 1947.

Prestage, E. (ed.). *Chivalry*. New York, 1928.

Proctor, Thomas. *Of the knowledge and conducte of warres*. London, 1578.

A Proper Dyaloge betwene a Gentillman and a Husbandman. London, 1530.

Pugh, T. B., and Ross, C. D. "The English Baronage and the Income Tax of 1436," *Bulletin of the Institute of Historical Research*, XXVI (May, 1953), 1-28.

Putnam, B. H. *Early Treatises on the Practice of the Justices of the Peace in the Fifteenth and Sixteenth Centuries*. Oxford, 1924.

Pyers Plowman's Exhortation, unto the Lordes, Knightes and Burgoysses of the Parlyamenthouse. London, 1530.

The Record of Bluemantle Pursuivant (1471-72), in C. L. Kingsford, *English Historical Literature in the 15th Century*. Oxford, 1913. Pp. 379-388.

Reed, A. W. "Chivalry and the Idea of a Gentleman," in E. Prestage, ed., *Chivalry*. New York, 1928.

Rich, Barnaby. *Allarme to England*. London, 1578.

——. *A right exelent and pleasant dialogue, Betwene Mercury and an English souldier*. London, 1574.

Roskell, J. S. *The Commons in the Parliament of 1422*. Manchester, 1954.

——. "The Social Composition of the Commons in a Fifteenth-Century Parliament," *Bulletin of the Institute of Historical Research*, XXIV (1951), 152-172.

Rotuli Parliamentorum. 6 vols. London, 1767-1777.

Sandberger, Dietrich. *Studien über das Rittertum in England, vornemlich während des 14. Jahrhunderts*. Berlin, 1937.

Sandoz, E. "Tourneys in the Arthurian Tradition," *Speculum*, XIX (October, 1944), 389-420.

Schirmer, W. F. *Der englische Frühumanismus*. Leipzig, 1931.

——. *John Lydgate, ein Kulturbild aus dem 15. Jahrhundert*. Tübingen, 1952.

Schofield, C. L. *The Life and Reign of Edward the Fourth*. London, 1923.

Schofield, W. H. *Chivalry in English Literature*. Cambridge, Mass., 1925.

Secrees of old Philosoffres, ed. Robert Steele. (E.E.T.S., E.S., No. 66.) 1894.

Segar, Sir William. *The Boke of Honor and Armes*. London, 1590.

Sheppard, J. B. (ed.). *Literae Cantuarienses*. (Rolls Series.) 1889.

Siegel, Paul N. "English Humanism and the New Tudor Aristocracy," *Journal of the History of Ideas*, XIII (October, 1952), 450-468.

Sitwell, Sir George. "The English Gentleman," *Ancestor*, I (April, 1902). Pp. 58-103.

Skelton, John. *The Poetical Works of John Skelton*, ed. A. Dyce. London, 1843.

——. *Speculum principis* (1501), ed. F. M. Salter, *Speculum*, IX (1934), 25-37.

Smith, P. *Erasmus*. New York, 1923.

Smith, R. M. *Froissart and the English Chronicle Play*. New York, 1915.

Smith, Sir Thomas. *De Republica Anglorum*, ed. L. Alston. Cambridge, 1906.

Squibb, G. D. *The High Court of Chivalry*. New York, 1959.

Starkey, Thomas. *A Dialogue between Cardinal Pole and Thomas Lupset*, ed. J. M. Cowper. (E.E.T.S., E.S., No. 12.) 1871.

Statutes of the Realm. London, 1810-28.

Stenton, F. M. "The Changing Feudalism of the Middle Ages," *History*, XIX (March, 1935), 289-310.

Surrey, Earl of. *The Poems of Henry Howard, Earl of Surrey*, ed. F. M. Padelford. Seattle, 1928.

Three Prose Versions of the "Secreta Secretorum," ed. R. Steele. (E.E.T.S., E.S., No. 74.) 1898.

Thrupp, Sylvia. *The Merchant Class of Medieval London*. Chicago, 1948.

Tiptoft, John *The Declamation of Noblesse*, in R. J. Mitchell, *John Tiptoft* (London, 1938), Appendix I.

Tito Livio da Forli. *Vita Henrici Quinti*, ed. T. Hearne. London, 1716.

Treharne, R. F. "The Knights in the Period of Reform and Rebellion, 1258-1267; A Critical Study in the Rise of a New Class," *Bulletin of the Institute of Historical Research*, XXI (May and November, 1946), 1-12.

Tucker, P. E. "The Place of the 'Quest of the Holy Grail' in the *Morte Darthur*," *Modern Language Review*, XLVIII (1953), 391-397.

The Turnament of Tottenham, in Thomas Percy, *Reliques of Ancient English Poetry*, ed. H. B. Wheatley. London, 1927.

Twenty-six Political and other Poems, ed. J. Kail. (E.E.T.S., O.S., No. 124.) 1904.

Upton, Nicholas. *De Studio Militari*, ed. F. P. Bernard. Oxford, 1931.

Vergil, Polydore. *Polydore Vergil's English History*, ed. Sir H. Ellis. (Camden Society, XXXVI.) London, 1846.

——. *The Anglica Historia of Polydore Vergil*, ed. and trans. Denys Hay. (Camden Society, LXXIV.) London, 1950.

Vinaver, Eugene. *Études sur le "Tristan" en prose*. Paris, 1925.

——. *Le Roman de Tristan et Iseut dans l'oeuvre de Thomas Malory*. Paris, 1925.

Vogt, G. M. "Gleanings for the History of a Sentiment: *Generositas Virtus non Sanguis*," *Journal of English and German Philology*, XXIV (1925), 102-124.

Wagner, A. R. *Heralds and Heraldry in the Middle Ages*. London, 1939.

Walrond, Col. H. "Archery," in *Shakespeare's England*, ed. Sir W. Raleigh. Oxford, 1926. II, 376-388.

Watson, Sara P. "The Queen's Champion," *Western Reserve Bulletin*, N. S., XXXIV (September, 1931), 65-89.

The Weather, in *Pre-Shakespearean Dramas*, ed. J. Q. Adams. Cambridge, Mass., 1924.

Weiss, R. *Humanism in England during the Fifteenth Century*. Oxford, 1941.

Whiting, B. J. "The Vows of the Heron," *Speculum*, XX (July, 1945), 261-278.

Wyclif, John. *De Civili Dominio,* ed. I. Loserth. London, 1900.

——. *Select English Works of John Wyclif,* ed. T. Arnold. Oxford, 1869-71.

Wiley, W. L. *The Gentleman of Renaissance France.* Cambridge, Mass., 1954.

Wood-Legh, K. L. "Sheriffs, Lawyers, and Belted Knights in the Parliaments of Edward III," *English Historical Review,* XLVI (July, 1931), 372-388.

Worcester, William. *William of Worcester's Collection,* ed. J. Stevenson, in *Letters and Papers Illustrative of the Wars of the English in France during the Reign of Henry the Sixth.* (Rolls Series.) 1864.

Yates, F. A. "Elizabethan Chivalry: The Romance of the Accession Day Tilts," *Journal of Warburg and Courtauld Institutes,* XX (1957), 4-25.

Zeeveld, W. G. *Foundations of Tudor Policy.* Cambridge, Mass., 1948.

Index